HOUSE

HOW THE MISSING MIDDLE CAN SOLVE TORONTO'S AFFORDABILITY CRISIS

DIVIDED

EDITED BY ALEX BOZIKOVIC, CHERYLL CASE,
JOHN LORINC, ANNABEL VAUGHAN

COACH HOUSE BOOKS, TORONTO

First Edition

Published with the generous assistance of the Canada Council for the Arts and
the Ontario Arts Council. Coach House Books also acknowledges the support
of the Government of Canada through the Canada Book Fund and the Government of Ontario through the Ontario Book Publishing Tax Credit.

Opinions expressed in these essays do not necessarily reflect those of the editors
or the publisher.

LIBRARY AND ARCHIVES CANADA CATALOGUING IN PUBLICATION

Title: House divided : how the missing middle will solve Toronto's affordability
crisis / Alex Bozikovic, Cheryll Case, John Lorinc, Annabel Vaughan, editors.
Names: Bozikovic, Alex, editor. | Case, Cheryll, editor. | Lorinc, John, editor. |
Vaughan, Annabel, editor.
Identifiers: Canadiana (print) 20190109645 | Canadiana (ebook) 20190109939 |
ISBN 9781552453865 (softcover) | ISBN 9781770565937 (EPUB) | ISBN 9781770565944
(PDF)
Subjects: LCSH: Housing—Ontario—Toronto. | LCSH: Housing policy—Ontario—
Toronto. | LCSH: Housing—Ontario—Toronto—Finance. | LCSH: Housing—Eco-
nomic aspects—Ontario—Toronto. | LCSH: Housing—Prices—Ontario— Toronto.
Classification: LCC HD7305.T67 H68 2019 | DDC 363.509713/54—dc23

Third Floor: Housing Future

Toronto's skyline circa 2019 bears witness to the largest condo boom in the city's history – a record 100,000 units rolling out over the next few years, with almost every one sold before a shovel hits the ground, many to investors.

Yet thousands of people cannot afford a home.

Drive to the fringes of the region and low-rise construction still muscles its way over farm fields. We have not run out of land, nor are we bumping against the

Greenbelt, and we cannot seem to sprawl our way to affordability.

Scarcity in a city of abundance: affordability is not simply a supply problem. Rather, it's an issue of the right supply in the right locations – missing middle (i.e., duplexes, triplexes, fourplexes, walk-ups, etc.), purpose-built rental, mid-rise, and innovations in financing and construction that improve affordability for residents – with progressive reforms to zoning and policy that will make the type of supply we need more cost-competitive.

Removing red tape for development, as some propose, will merely result in more of the 'tall and sprawl' varieties of housing we already have. And this approach will only make the type of housing supply we really need that much scarcer and more unaffordable. Already, mid-rise has become boutique, with two-bedrooms starting in the $700,000s; townhouses are luxury properties, fetching over a million. We need to be careful about what we ask for.

Housing-affordability solutions are also marginalized by the proven model of real estate financing and development, around which policy tools merely tinker. For instance, inclusionary zoning – which requires a developer to set aside a certain share of units in a new development as affordable housing – can produce only so many units. Subsidized housing is limited by a municipal budget in a crisis of its own and can't begin to sniff at the challenge of 'attainable housing' for middle-income residents. Even some high-wage earners have found themselves on the wrong side of Toronto's timeline, the one that separates homeowners who got in before prices detached from reality and those who came up behind: house divided.

As the authors in this anthology illustrate, outdated or entrenched planning rules further divide and protect 'stable' neighbourhoods from the stratification, gentle density, and mid-rise development that yields more modest-sized, multi-unit homes in walkable and transit-connected locations. Despite the reality that an influx of new residents helps to populate neighbourhood schools and sustain the bakeries, cafés, and amenities desired by local homeowners, town-hall consultations reveal emotionally charged community opposition to height, density, increased traffic, and competition for street parking.

The housing divide is further widened and worsened by transit inequity. The residents of Toronto's low-income, high-density north-east and northwest shoulders would be riding LRTs today if it were not for political interference. Those who need transit the most stare down a mutually reinforcing housing and transit divide. Two hours of riding buses to service jobs in downtown Toronto, wages not earned, time not spent with family. Meanwhile, a visitor travelling the York subway extension to stations at Pioneer Village or Highway 407 and the adjacent hydro field would believe transit was planned by drunken sailors with money to burn.

Most transit trips are local, so I worry that not only will the priorit-ization of regional service deprive investment in local transit, perhaps unintentionally, but it also risks normalizing and codifying bizarre commute patterns and extreme distances, such as living in Oshawa and working in Mississauga. Doesn't it make better sense to double down on the right policies, planning, and investment to deliver hous-ing for a range of incomes and family sizes near employment centres? Transit-oriented development, yes, and housing-oriented planning.

At the time of this book's publication, we've seen a beachhead of new innovations in how housing is built: modular design, factory-manufactured components, the unbundling of fancy amenities and finishes, allowing DIY interiors. All hold promise for reducing home prices or rents by 20 to 40 percent. What first sold me on factory manufacturing was the speed with which homes could be assembled on the development site – in one example, a floor per day, saving a bundle of time and money, not to mention radically reducing the disruption associated with endless months of cement trucks and excavators, noise, dirt, and boarded-off sidewalks.

Many of these modular developments are predicated on no underground parking, as they are in walkable, transit-accessible locations. These innovations offer energy efficiency to further reduce costs as well as new opportunities for safer construction-related employment in controlled environments. But they also require scale to be successful.

Finally, we need to confront the reality that an entrenched, self-fortifying system of planning, development, and financing is difficult to disrupt and sidelines urgent solutions to places where affordable housing is possible, namely public land. I cringe at the practice of selling public land and air rights, both provincial and municipal, to developers, especially at below market value, for a one-time cash influx and a quantum of affordable units. It's not a sustainable approach and it squanders the opportunity for public agencies to leverage these assets for long-term revenue while developing the land for the public good.

Other cities and states have created partnerships between public agencies and developers (profit or not-for-profit) whereby both parties share in revenues from the sales, rents, and leases of mixed-use, mixed-income developments. All that revenue can be reinvested in more affordable housing, transit, or other services in perpetuity.

If we keep doing the same things, we will keep churning out the same product. *House Divided* can help us understand why and how we need to do things differently if we are to build a more equitable, less divisive city.

W*eston.* After Nina Diaz's husband left her, the fifty-eight-year-old cashier had to scramble for a place to live, and ended up renting the basement of a house in Weston owned by a family friend. She was paying $600 a month, but the landlord hiked the rent to $1,000 when one of her sons moved in. If she didn't pay, Diaz was told, the apartment would be leased to someone who wanted to run a private daycare service there. 'I wasn't feeling comfortable with that,' she says, 'but I wasn't saying anything.'

Introduction: The Stability Trap
John Lorinc

Diaz (not her real name) has worked for Metro, the supermarket chain, for twenty-five years, in Toronto and in Winnipeg. She emigrated from Guatemala to Canada in 1991, a time when it was possible to find a two-bedroom apartment on the first floor of a house in Toronto for $750, including utilities. Today, she spends 70 to 75 percent of her after-tax income, which is $32,000 a year, on housing and economizes on food. During the busy season leading up to Christmas, Diaz takes on a second full-time job, in a factory. Over the years, she has scraped together $25,000 for an eventual down payment on a condo, but no bank will extend a mortgage to a middle-aged single woman whose salary is scarcely above the poverty line.

In 2018, Diaz was finally evicted from the basement apartment. She put her name on the city's lengthy waiting list for subsidized housing, but expected nothing on that front. Eventually, Diaz found herself sharing a two-bedroom condo with another divorced woman. They each pay $800, not including hydro, but the arrangement is at best provisional. 'I don't know what to do,' she says. 'I'm very, very scared.'

Scarborough. In 2015, an investor bought a modest two-and-a-half-storey house near Kingston Road and Warden, and commissioned a fire inspection of the building. The inspectors told the investor they had to submit their report to the city. The house had been carved up for the past twenty years into three rental units, and was then occupied by an older woman on a disability pension, a single mother, and an immigrant family.

Downtown, zoning rules permit this kind of arrangement. But while secondary suites are allowed across the city, a triplex – three units in one building, as this one had – is illegal in Scarborough. The new owner had to go to the Committee of Adjustment to seek a minor variance. According to his planning consultant, Sean Galbraith, he had no trouble soliciting letters of support from numerous neighbours. 'Everybody said, "This is fine, they should be able to stay,"' Galbraith recounts, noting that several also showed up at the hearing. Even Gary Crawford, the local councillor, agreed.

Yet none of that mattered. The Committee of Adjustment blocked the minor variance. Ironically, the house – which provided affordable housing to its occupants – is located just steps from a major road with transit, amenities, and, increasingly, the sort of mid-rise condos encouraged by the Official Plan. 'The moral of the story is that restrictive zoning harms people,' Galbraith says.

Davenport. Alexander Bordokas and Kristyn Gelfand are professionally wired into Toronto's arts scene. Bordokas is a freelance music and events producer while Gelfand works as an administrator at a nightclub. The couple have three children and earned enough to rent the two lower floors of a house for $2,850. But unless an unexpected inheritance comes along, they don't expect to ever be able to buy, especially given that Bordokas is self-employed, which means he wouldn't pass the lender stress tests Canadian banks must now impose on mortgage applicants.

One day in the fall of 2018, Bordokas asked their landlord to come by and fix the stove. But when he got home, Bordokas found a so-called w12 form on the kitchen table – an eviction notice. The couple weren't in arrears on their payments and Bordokas suspects the owner, aware that rents in the area had shot up, simply wanted to find new tenants willing to pay more.

With their kids in middle and high school, the couple didn't want to leave the neighbourhood. After a scramble to find a new place, they leased a flat in another house, in somewhat better shape, but with a steeper monthly rent: $3,200. Bordokas had to borrow money for first and last. Now, monthly housing costs gobble up 35 to 40 percent of their income – which means that, according to a standard formula of the Canada Mortgage and Housing Corporation,[1] they cannot afford their home.

Do they ever think about leaving the city? 'Oh, yeah,' sighs Bordokas. The problem is that both he and Gelfand have jobs that keep them tied to a specific location. 'I don't really want to throw blame or shade,' he adds. 'Everyone I know does piecework. That's just a reality of our economic landscape.'

Mimico. A decade ago, Graeme and Jesslyn Dymond bought a cramped 1922 bungalow at the edge of a South Etobicoke neighbourhood. The selling price: $351,000. The house is located steps from a sprawling Campbell's Soup factory.

With two small children, they began thinking about expanding the house. Jesslyn's parents, as it happened, were preparing to downsize from their Swansea home, and they came up with what seemed like a win-win. On the advice of a contractor, they'd knock down the bungalow and replace it with a three-storey dwelling divided into two entirely self-contained units – the basement and first floor for Jesslyn's parents, and the upper two for Graeme and Jesslyn's young family. 'We wanted to create as much separation as possible,' Graeme says.

Even though their street has several houses subdivided into apartments, their neighbour objected at the Committee of Adjustment, and so the city appointed a mediator to work out an accommodation. Oddly, the mediator continued to press for concessions even after the committee approved their plans – 'stirring the pot,' as Graeme puts it. Then came the sticker shock. Replacing a one-and-a-half-storey home that once had an illegal basement suite with a duplex meant they had to pay a $30,000 per unit development charge, plus another $20,000 lump sum for the city's parks improvement levy – a total of $80,000. Graeme came away with the sense that the city was treating him like a developer: 'It feels a little bizarre.'

Since he and his family embarked on the project, he adds, many people have inquired about their plan, which seems like a smart way of making homeownership viable in a ruinously expensive city. Graeme advocates this approach but warns those who approach him about the 'significant' financial and regulatory hurdles. 'We were in an ideal situation,' he says, 'but it's still been a slog and a battle to get this done.'

These anecdotes only hint at the fog of dysfunction enveloping Toronto's housing sector – a dysfunction that begins with absurd real estate prices[2] and runaway rents, but really extends across much of a city where about half of all households are tenants. In the past decade, I've written stories about appallingly neglected social-housing apartments, jammed illegal rooming houses that became deadly fire-traps, families shoehorned into condos that were never intended for children, and the travails of smart, urban-minded developers fighting ridiculous legal battles with antagonistic homeowners over modest main-street projects that won't shave a dollar off their property values.

Refugees crowd emergency shelters. College students who don't make the cut for residence are shaken down for hefty rents in illegal rooming houses. Terms like *rent strike* and *renoviction* have become part of our vocabulary as rapid gentrification transforms working-class areas into conflict zones. Airbnb short-term rentals have replaced valuable apartment stock and hiked rents in tourist-track neighbour-hoods like Kensington Market. The number of people waiting for subsidized housing is almost equal to the number living in Toronto Community Housing's buildings. And for an average Toronto house-hold, it now takes about 109 months, almost nine years, to save enough just for the down payment on a typical house. A steadily growing proportion of the city's population has become permanently priced out of both the local and regional housing market.[3]

It's no coincidence that the apartment-building sector has shifted as well. A growing number of institutional investors are financing rental apartment projects, most of them upscale, because they represent safe, income-generating assets. Meanwhile, the Swedish apartment giant Akelius has been snapping up small and medium-sized apartment buildings; it owned over 3,000 units in Toronto as of 2015. The company's business model is that it pressures older tenants paying lower rents to leave, fixes up their units (a process that often involves highly disruptive renovations), and puts these apartments back on the market at higher rates.[4]

Then there are all those gleaming condo towers, which are constantly remaking the skyline and have become the object of a certain cast of civic bragging. Look inside and many have been overtaken by either short-term rentals or 'flipping frenzies.' As a *Globe and Mail* investigation discovered after examining a thousand transactions in a single forty-nine-storey tower near Yonge and Bloor, '[I]nvestors and speculators are … crowding out first-time buyers and creating unstable rental housing.'[5]

Unstable. The word is nothing if not apt. Just ask people like Nina Diaz. The rich irony is that Toronto's planning policies devote so much rhetorical and regulatory energy to the aspirational virtue of homeowner *stability*. The latest iteration of the Official Plan makes frequent references to the importance of maintaining 'physically stable' communities, and further refinements adopted in 2015 have put meat on the bones of that policy goal by codifying concepts such as a neighbourhood's 'prevailing' character, building heights, lot sizes, and so on.

In fact, as a matter of long-standing public policy, Toronto's homeowners have enjoyed a robust form of official protection that has succeeded in ratcheting up house prices while excluding an ever-expanding part of the city's population. Many neighbourhoods, ring-fenced as they are by invisible yet highly potent zoning bylaws, have seen their populations dwindle.

The result has been a kind of urban cognitive dissonance. Over the past generation, many of Toronto's residential enclaves have

Children playing in rundown rental housing, 1943.

changed little, beyond the relentless busywork of renovators or McMansion contractors. Over the same period, condo towers of ever-increasing scale have sprouted on commercial or former industrial lands, which city planners have determined can accommodate the waves of newcomers – 30,000 to 50,000 people per year – that show no sign of subsiding. Much of that growth, however, has clustered in the downtown core and a handful of other high-density hubs.

The geographical imbalance is striking: Toronto's 'stable' residential neighbourhoods occupy about one third of the city's land mass. Its commercial zones, where almost all the new mid- and high-rise buildings will go, account for about five percent of the space in the city, and only a fraction of that will be redeveloped.

Some of Toronto's older residential neighbourhoods are home to duplexes, triplexes, walk-ups, and low-rise apartment buildings, as well as single-family houses. But the zoning in the vast majority of neighbourhoods in Scarborough, North York, Etobicoke, and East York bars anything but detached dwellings. This super-stable zone, dubbed the 'Yellowbelt' by planner Gil Meslin, covers an area three times the size of Manhattan, and that's just within the 416.

Architect's Drawing of a Group of Cottage Flats Now Being Erected on Bain Avenue, Toronto, by the Toronto Housing Company. These Will Accommodate 200 Families, Who Will be Furnished With Heat and Hot Water from a Central Heating Plant. Rents Will be from $13 to $18, According to Size of Flat.

Rendering for proposed co-op at 88 Bain, Toronto Housing Company, 1913.

This bifurcated arrangement generates serious problems. The enforced stability bestowed on homeowners living in Toronto's house neighbourhoods has fuelled the mounting instability and precariousness experienced by everyone else, from social-assistance recipients to artists, newcomers, students, and all those middle-income people who didn't have timing on their side when they entered the housing market. An increasingly unhealthy symbiotic relationship connects these two Torontos, and we fail to confront it at our peril.

From the dawn of the industrial revolution, fast-growing, mercantile cities have almost always experienced problems of overcrowding. At the beginning of the twentieth century, Toronto, no exception, was in the throes of a major surge of growth. Entrepreneurs were making fortunes in retailing, manufacturing, and meat processing, and immigrants were flooding into the city, which saw its population explode from 208,000 in 1901 to over half a million by 1921.

As geographer Richard Harris shows in his book *Unplanned Sub-urbs*, the city effectively shunted working-class residential development out to the fringes to counter slumlike conditions in areas such as The Ward. At the insistence of Dr. Charles Hastings, the city's crusading medical officer of health, Toronto council also passed a bylaw in 1912 to ban apartment houses in residential neighbourhoods and limit them to main streets. (That policy foreshadows the City of Toronto's post-amalgamation goal of encouraging mid-rise mixed-use development along the so-called Avenues.) Hastings and other housing reformers feared that apartment houses, which had begun to pop up around the city over the previous decade, would degenerate into dirty, over-crowded, New York–style tenements.

Some advocates saw apartment buildings as the solution to the city's growing housing pressures, which were creating overcrowded lodging houses and rear-yard hovels. Yet other, louder voices saw them as a threat to Toronto's rigid social values. Their design undermined family privacy, encouraged women to ignore their domestic duties, and failed to meet the needs of young children. '[The city's] morals will suffer as well as its health,' opined the *Globe*.[6] 'It is a short-cut from the apartment house to the divorce court,' added another editorial cited in Richard Dennis's 1989 history of Toronto's first apartment house boom.[7] As for subsidized dwellings for the poor, there were a few experimental projects, such as Spruce Court, in Cabbagetown – one of the first developments undertaken by the Toronto Housing Company. But the city's potent social conservatism prevailed, with critics fretting that these accommodations had 'the taint of charity.' Toronto's deep-seated ambivalence toward both private rental and subsidized housing begins here.

Harris also points out in his book that early-twentieth-century Torontonians, both wealthy and working-class, and especially newcomers, strongly favoured homeownership as a domestic and financial ideal despite its cost. Indeed, in 1920, Toronto's rate of homeownership, at 60 percent, exceeded that of every other major city in North America. By 1950, after a decline during the Depression and World War II, the rate for the metropolitan Toronto area again topped 60 percent, on par with the highest-ranked American cities.

Market forces, of course, played a role in these patterns. Many lower-income families were able to buy cheap, unserviced land outside the core and housing 'kits' from building suppliers, which they used to construct their own dwellings. (Others hired contractors.) Yet all this activity took place within the framework of municipal decisions about land use, infrastructure, and, by the 1920s, rudimentary zoning. In other cities, however, prevailing political and regulatory conditions created very different housing narratives and markets, which, in some cases, persist to this day.

Two cities in particular illustrate how the evolution of twentieth-century housing followed dramatically divergent tangents.

Vienna, by the end of World War I, was a city well equipped with municipal infrastructure but desperately short of decent housing; people flowed into the city to work in its factories and found themselves trapped in derelict slums. In 1919, a municipal socialist party swept to power, fuelled in part by social unrest. Vienna's city council levied new property taxes on the wealthy and used the proceeds to create an unparalleled program of apartment construction – 64,000 subsidized units, with over 200,000 residents, completed between 1923 and 1934. Tenants paid just 3.5 percent of their monthly salaries on rent.

Red Vienna's sturdy modernist–style apartment blocks, built on city-owned land, were early examples of mixed-use development. As historian Eve Blau observes in her history of Red Vienna's architecture, 'Many of the municipality's communal facilities – the clinics, counseling centres, libraries, playgrounds, kindergartens, youth centres, gymnasiums, daycare facilities, laundries, carpentry shops, theatres, cinemas, and post offices, as well as the city-run cafes, co-operative stories, and other communal facilities and occasionally also the offices of various municipal departments – were located in the new housing blocks.'[8]

In many places, of course, idealistic social-housing programs gave way to all sorts of problems: grim, dead-end public housing complexes riddled with crime and dysfunction. But not in Vienna, where subsidized apartment living in buildings erected on public land remains a central feature of the city's housing market. Almost a century and a lot of history later, Vienna (with subsidies from the national government) continues to invest in and expand its stock of such apartments. As of 2018, almost two-thirds of Vienna's residents lived in subsidized housing, and the city topped some livability rankings of global cities.[9]

Montreal, in turn, was a city of tenants and renters even before the rise of industry in the nineteenth century; unlike Toronto, social reformers and, notably, municipal officials never set out to stigmatize this form of housing.

By the turn of the century, Montreal's working-class neighbourhoods had developed a distinctive housing form known as the 'superposed' flat. These were two- or more commonly three-storey structures, with an apartment on each floor, exterior staircases, and balconies at both the front and the back. In areas like the Plateau, the superposed flats not only created an unusually dense urban form but provided owners with an opportunity to live on one floor and generate welcome additional income by renting out the others. 'In the nineteenth century,' according to a CMHC study on Montreal's housing,

Montreal's famous external staircases, fronting 'superposed' flats, 1973.

'the appeal of real estate ownership resided in the potential rental income, rather than the propriety of one household to own its own dwelling.'[10] This model, which acknowledges the high carrying costs of urban houses, was also common in cities like Philadelphia and Glasgow, and continues to find currency in the guise of basement apartments and secondary suites.

As Richard Harris showed in *Unplanned Suburbs*, Montreal's home-ownership rates were a fraction of Toronto's – 17 percent in 1930 and just 24 percent for the whole metropolitan region in the 1950s. The CMHC study offers one explanation: in Montreal, real estate investment had long been regarded as a source of steady revenue, while in Toronto, speculative building booms ratcheted up both prices and rents as offshore investors (from Britain) sought quick returns.[11]

The postwar period did bring more detached, subdivision-style housing to Montreal's suburbs. But even these neighbourhoods had far more low-rise apartments, duplexes, and fourplexes than Toronto's postwar suburbs ever did – evidence that municipal land-use planning policies and residential building styles rooted in an earlier era continued to generate viable forms of mid-density housing. It could hardly be a coincidence that Montreal hasn't experienced the kind of real estate and rent spikes that have consumed Toronto.

There's no question that urban housing markets are substantially affected by forces well beyond the boundaries of a given city or region. International investors acquire apartments in stable areas to manage risk and generate income in diversified portfolios. Banks in Canada, keenly aware of the unhealthy amount of consumer debt that built up after the 2008 credit crisis, have become increasingly restrictive about mortgages. Housing prices are also tied to labour markets; in Toronto, which has seen its banking, technology, and professional services sectors thrive, the upward drift of salaries, often to international levels, has contributed to inflation in house prices – a phenomenon observed in other global cities with high concentrations of jobs in these high-growth fields. More locally, the city has seen a pattern of housing-cost escalation near subway and streetcar corridors as residents seek out transportation alternatives to congestion and long commutes.

Yet the stories of cities like Montreal and Vienna serve as a reminder that housing markets are shaped, often for long periods of time, by policy and political decisions made at the local level. They underscore the point that social values and biases with long roots can have either a positive or pernicious impact. Finally, the great variation in homeownership levels among OECD nations – Canada has the third-highest rate, with 68 percent, whereas the comparable figure in Germany is just 45 percent[12] – is a reminder that housing is subject to far more than just market forces.

It is also true that in the contemporary context, there are examples of cities that have confronted historic failings in their own housing markets and land-use policies, and are attempting to change course.

Two American cities, as of this writing, are doing so: Minneapolis and Seattle, both of which eliminated single-family zoning in 2018. While the U.S. Supreme Court banned race-based zoning in 1917, municipalities adopted single-family zoning bylaws to perpetuate segregation. As Henry Grabar observed in *Slate*, this kind of land-use designation 'proved as effective at segregating northern neighbourhoods (and their schools) as Jim Crow laws have in the south.'[13]

Minneapolis city council in late 2018 voted to permit three-family homes in all residential neighbourhoods and abolish parking minimums, and to encourage higher-density buildings along transit corridors. As Mayor Jacob Frey put it, 'Large swaths of our city are exclusively zoned for single-family homes so unless you have the ability to build a very large home on a very large lot, you can't live in the neighbourhood.'[14] Seattle, which has seen drastic real estate inflation due to the presence of giant tech firms like Amazon, made a similar move, up-zoning twenty-seven neighbourhoods to allow denser buildings in parts of the city that had been set aside for detached residential dwellings.

For decades, Ontario's planning laws have prevented municipalities from passing zoning bylaws regulating a building's occupants, so single-family zoning doesn't exist as a legal construct here. But the residential-detached zoning bylaws that apply across much of Toronto have created neighbourhoods filled with expensive single-family homes. Here, homeowners are likely to object to even the most modest form of residential intensification, and city policies and practices support them in doing so. Indeed, duplexes and triplexes, the least intrusive of all multi-unit housing types, are not permitted on two-thirds of the entire land mass of Toronto that is designated for residential dwellings.

Would lifting such restrictions create reforms similar to those envisioned in Minneapolis, and would these changes help bring housing costs down to earth?

A 2018 study by Ryerson's City Building Institute estimated that the City of Mississauga could add 174,000 new residential units, sufficient to house 435,000 people, if it allowed low- and medium-density infill development in established neighbourhoods. 'Even with conservative assumptions around density and land availability, there is ample space to add new missing middle family friendly housing units,' concluded the authors.[15]

Yet there is a lively and open-ended debate in the planning world about whether the sort of up-zoning approved in Seattle and Minneapolis will improve housing affordability generally.[16] According to a controversial 2019 study by Yonah Freemark, an MIT city-planning graduate student, an experiment in up-zoning in the immediate vicinity of Chicago subway stops indicated that these new transit-oriented development policies didn't produce much in the way of new supply, but they did drive up land prices – an unexpected outcome.

'The notion that increasing housing supply will magically fix our problems is one of those things that is simply too good to be true,' urban geographer Richard Florida remarked in an essay about Freemark's findings.[17] Yet, Freemark and many other commentators pointed out that the short duration of his study – five years – may have produced undercooked results.[18] And those who advocate for more housing supply as a tool to help keep rents and prices down generally advocate such policies on a city-wide or region-wide basis.

Some evidence for that viewpoint exists. There's little doubt that the abundance of apartments in Montreal has kept rents low. And in Seattle, a boom in new apartment construction from 2017 to 2019 eased that city's vacancy rate, from 7.7 percent to 10.5 percent, even though rents remained steep because of the tech sector's presence.[19]

A more nuanced assessment is that zoning reform is necessary but not sufficient. 'Advocates recognize that zoning reform on its own is not, never has been and never will be a silver bullet,' commented Alex Baca and Hannah Lebovits in *CityLab*.[20] 'The reason why up-zoning is so necessary is because other measures – such as the development of subsidized, permanently affordable buildings or the construction of market rate buildings to which rent controls should be applied – are often impossible unless zoning is loosened.'

Case in point: an historically ambitious program of affordable housing development and preservation initiated by New York City mayor Bill de Blasio in 2014. Its goal was to create 300,000 units by 2026. In the first few years of the program, the city claimed to be adding over 20,000 units per year using zoning changes and new funding to encourage private builders to participate. In particular, the plan focused on creating new affordable housing for seniors; preventing 'displacement' by helping non-profit housing agencies purchase rent-controlled apartment buildings; and mandating inclusionary housing (i.e., requiring new developments in targeted areas to include 'permanently affordable' units).[21]

The total cost has a made-in-New-York scale: $83 billion for the twelve years of the campaign's projected life. Those figures have already risen and still may not be sufficient to deliver on what de Blasio has promised to low-income families.[22]

Toronto's efforts have paled by comparison, even allowing for scale. Despite years of studies, task force reports, political pronouncements, and a handful of showcase projects involving the redevelopment of rundown social-housing projects, the city hasn't meaningfully altered our increasingly exclusionary housing narrative. Waiting lists for affordable housing are as long as they've ever been. Vacancy rates are at generationally low levels. And even a lull in the real estate market hasn't brought prices back to earth.

In the wake of a municipal election (2018) in which housing affordability figured as the dominant issue, Mayor John Tory and city council have set in motion a modest plan to spur some affordable rental development on a handful of surplus municipal properties – part of a strategy to add 10,000 new apartments over twelve years. (If one applied de Blasio's program proportionately to Toronto, it would produce 100,000 units – ten times the number proposed by Tory.) The Trudeau government's national housing strategy has generated some new investment, including measures to protect thousands of subsidized co-op housing units developed in the 1970s. Yet the city is also deferring billions in long-overdue repair costs for its social-housing stock, which will likely result in units being closed. What's more, there's no evidence that Toronto politicians are prepared to allocate substantial and sustainable financial resources to add more affordable housing, nor does there appear to be much appetite for cracking open long-standing zoning and land-use restrictions that prevent even the most modest forms of intensification in residential neighbourhoods. On that front, NIMBYism remains hard-wired into our official plan.

What's the cost of inaction, or mere tinkering?

As co-editor Cheryll Case has documented, we can already see what happens when residential neighbourhoods begin to lose population due to changes in demographics and out-of-control housing costs. Schools close. The city struggles to fund community amenities. Main-street retailers suffer. Beyond these local symptoms, people earning modest or average incomes will begin to leave the city, out of necessity. This long-term dynamic will inevitably drive up urban wages and make it increasingly difficult for some employers to hire (as cities like London and San Francisco have discovered). After all, cities will only function and produce sustainable wealth and quality of life if they are able to make space for a wide range of residents – not just those who can afford $800,000 homes.

This collection is organized into three sections: how we got here; an analysis of current impediments to change; and examples of new ideas that could alter our civic narrative.

In the first part, the book looks at the origins of made-in-Toronto NIMBYism, examples (both intentional and accidental) of an earlier generation of apartment and social-housing projects, the history of our planning orthodoxies, and the roots of Parkdale's gentrification wars.

The second section unpacks a range of the current policy issues that have impacted Toronto's halting civic conversation about affordable housing and housing affordability – everything from an examination of policy definitions of affordability and the failings of our consultation system to detailed analyses of the planning restrictions that have prevented the development of the missing middle housing that contributed to the viability of so many older neighbourhoods.

The third and most important section invites Torontonians to consider fresh and, in some cases, controversial ideas that have worked in other cities; new financial and architectural approaches to developing both social housing and affordable rental housing; and proposals for loosening the rigidity in zoning bylaws that have produced polarization and social exclusion in the service of homeowner stability.

The book also includes highly personal accounts of the past and present of housing in Toronto, on working-class enclaves, carved-up houses, multi-generational living, and homelessness.

Ultimately, *House Divided* doesn't aspire to offer a comprehensive set of solutions or a magic bullet. Rather, it should be read as a wake-up call, a provocation, and a citizen's guide for smart, as opposed to reactive, change.

❧ 200 square kilometres: The area within the City of Toronto zoned exclusively for detached single-family residential dwellings (a.k.a., the 'Yellowbelt').[1]

❧ 87 square kilometres: The area of Manhattan.

❧ All new intensification is directed toward areas that encompass about 5 percent of the city's area, while the remaining 95 percent – about 640 square kilometres – is shielded from significant development to protect green space, public spaces, employment zones, and the prevailing character of residential neighbourhoods.

❧ The Yellowbelt is 1.8 times larger than all other areas zoned for residential use.[2]

❧ From 1996 to 2011, approximately 60 percent of new housing units constructed in Toronto were in high-rise buildings, but only 3.8 percent had three bedrooms or more.[3]

❧ From 2007 to 2017, the number of purpose-built rental units in low-rise apartment buildings (i.e., under 50 units) dropped from an estimated 59,129 units to an estimated 57,664 – a loss of about 1,500 apartments.[4]

❧ Three in ten Toronto households that rent live in unsuitable housing, as defined by the Canada Mortgage and Housing Corp.[5]

❧ The City of Mississauga could add approximately 174,000 new residential units (at an average unit size of over 1,000 square feet) via low- and medium-density intensification, which translates into an additional 435,000 residents.[6]

❧ Adding just one duplex in each of the 20,000 hectares that constitutes the Yellowbelt could provide housing for approximately 45,000 people.[7]

❧ **57 days**: Amount of time required to process a residential building permit application for a missing middle housing option, compared to the twenty-day standard recommended by the Ontario government.[8]

❧ Residential units approved in buildings over five storeys since 2009: **199,211.**

❧ Number of those with three or more bedrooms: **17,271** (8.6 percent).[9]

❧ Increase in average condo rent per square foot from 2011 to 2017: **43 percent** ($2.10 to $3).

❧ Increase in average condo price per square foot from 2011 to 2017: **71 percent** ($380 to $650).[10]

❧ Average GTA non-condo dwelling selling price: **$887,025** (2018); annual income required to carry a mortgage for such a dwelling – **$160,000.**

❧ Average GTA condo selling price (2018): **$521,239**; annual income required, **$93,000**[11]

❧ Proportion of GTA households with income under $48,000 spending more than 30 percent on housing: **78 percent**; middle income ($49,000–$110,000), **33 percent**; upper income (over $120,000), **three percent.**[12]

❧ Increasing the maximum building heights in neighbourhoods from three to four storeys can increase average densities by **up to 35 percent.**[13]

❧ Airbnb units now account for more than **5 percent** of all rental apartments in ten downtown neighbourhoods.[14]

THE FIRST
FLOOR:

HOUSING PAST

Previous pages: Toronto house built in a day, early twentieth century.

Toronto, at the turn of the twentieth century, was in the midst of a housing crisis. In October 1901, the *Globe* reported that '[t]wo thousand Toronto families find themselves homeless this autumn ... or, at least, houseless.' The unprecedented demand for housing was attributed in part to an influx of new residents – immigrants, but also arrivals from rural Ontario who sought opportunity in a fast-growing, industrialized city. Toronto's housing market was in recovery from a late-nineteenth-century decline, but the emerging boom fostered residential development primarily for owners, not renters.[1] Meanwhile, urbanizing cities like New York, Chicago, and Montreal were seeing the introduction of a new building form, one that could provide the density necessary to house single workers, newly married couples, small families, and downsizing seniors: the multi-unit apartment building.

The Spadina Gardens:
A Fight over Sixteen Units in 1905
Emma Abramowicz

In 1890, the Toronto-based *Globe* profiled the twenty-suite Sherbrooke Apartments in Montreal, 'in the fashionable part of town.' The units consisted of 'a drawing room, a dining room, two bedrooms with a closet each ... maid's room, storeroom ... [and] a hoist from the kitchen below.' The building offered a co-operative kitchen plan – a private food service for all tenants, eliminating the need for full kitchens in every unit.[2] This amenity, in particular, would present a solution to a second issue oft cited by Toronto's apartment-building advocates: in the industrialized city, with independent working opportunities for single women, finding traditional domestic help was so difficult that it was becoming impossible to manage large households.[3]

The first apartment building in Toronto appeared nearly a decade later, in 1899, with the construction of the St. George Apartments at Harbord Street.[4] The King Edward Apartments, at 192 Jarvis Street, began construction in 1901,[5] and the seven-storey Alexandra Apartments, at 184 University Avenue, were built between 1902 and 1903.[6]

Construction had barely begun on the next apartment buildings when residents in established, stable neighbourhoods responded with the first of many not-in-my-backyard-style uproars. Amid the still-ongoing housing crisis in 1905, a developer proposed the four-storey, sixteen-unit Spadina Gardens. The project quickly became the centre of a battle between a group of affluent neighbours, an unscrupulous builder, and a reactionary municipal administration, resulting in a building that would fit in, both architecturally and socio-culturally, with its elite context at Toronto's north end.

The fight over the Spadina Gardens set the terms for a form of conflict that continues in Toronto to this day, one in which wealthy residents with the time and resources to devote to neighbourhood associations exert considerable political pressure in drawn-out battles against bottom-line-driven developers, as Toronto's less established residents remain without reliable sources of affordable housing.

James and Alfred Hawes arrived in Toronto in 1902 via first-class tickets aboard the SS *Dominion* from Liverpool to Montreal.[7] The brothers, in their late twenties, soon opened an investment brokerage firm in Toronto's financial district,[8] and within a year, they were invested in a five-storey residential apartment building at the south-west corner of Huron and Sussex Streets (situated today just west of Robarts Library).[9] For its design, they commissioned architect Arthur R. Denison,[10] a fourth-generation member of Toronto's colonial establishment. The building was constructed by September 1904.

The Hawes brothers moved to 27 Sussex Street to manage the property[11] but quickly set their sights on a new real estate opportunity, this time in an emerging affluent neighbourhood just north of Bloor Street.

On February 11, 1905, the *Globe*'s Real Estate Review announced that 'Messrs. Hawes & Co., who ... have now considerable interest in Toronto real estate, have purchased for $10,000 the vacant [northeast] corner of Spadina Road and Lowther Avenue. The lot is 100 feet by 130 feet, and a fine apartment house is to be erected thereon.'[12]

They chose the Spadina and Lowther corner for its elite credentials. Seventeen years earlier, Timothy Eaton, one of Toronto's foremost

Spadina Road looking south from north side, Lowther Ave., 1949.

industrialists, had built a mansion on Spadina and Lowther's northwest corner in an exclusive eighteen-unit large-lot subdivision between Bloor, Spadina, and Walmer Road. As the area's first subdivision, it drove the development of more typical, smaller-lot subdivisions to the east and north,[13] attracting buyers who aspired to the status of the original residents.

These buyers included three men who had built new homes in the Spadina-Lowther vicinity in the year prior to the Haweses' announcement: Alfred R. Williams, at 56 Madison, and Thomas Kinnear, at 20 Spadina Road, both presidents of their respective companies,[14] and Harry McGee, a rising star at the T. Eaton Co. Ltd.,[15] at 108 Lowther Avenue.[16]

The news of a multi-storey, multi-unit apartment building to be constructed in their midst was unwelcome. Joined by Robert Davidson at 36 Madison Avenue and John Craig Eaton, on behalf of his sixty-nine-year-old father, the neighbours spoke before the City of Toronto's Board of Control against the apartment-building proposal. Kinnear argued, for the group, that 'the erection of this building would destroy the value of surrounding property.'

Separately, the group of neighbours also began negotiating with the Hawes brothers to purchase the northeast corner lot from them to prevent the construction of the apartment building. They understood this move wouldn't prevent the building from going up elsewhere in the neighbourhood, but they appear to have been so opposed to it in their immediate vicinity that they were willing to pay out of pocket. The land didn't come cheap; the Hawes brothers, capitalists in their own right, offered to sell for over $50 *more* per square foot than they had spent purchasing the site.[17] The neighbours ultimately bought the northeast corner lot.[18]

But unbeknownst to them, during the month they'd been in negotiations, the Hawes brothers had managed to purchase the southeast corner at Spadina and Lowther as well. It became clear they intended to build on that corner instead.[19]

The Hawes brothers' behaviour seems unscrupulous, although they may have just been seeking insurance against a group of undeniably powerful neighbours. But based on available evidence, we can also assume they were ready for a fight. Later in 1905, when Alfred Hawes would be sued over a $229 grocery bill, he announced 'that he'd rather spend $100 to fight it than pay it.'[20] The neighbours at Spadina tried to purchase the second corner lot as well, but those negotiations broke down. By the end of March, excavation had begun, without a building permit, on the Haweses' project on the southeast corner.[21]

At this point, the City of Toronto stepped in. The City Architect was a conservatively minded civil engineer with little understanding of evolving building technologies, and he was outspoken against the emerging wave of apartment buildings, which relied on innovations like concrete construction.[22] On a concurrent apartment file in 1905, for example, he was deeply opposed to a set of overhanging bay windows that would encroach into the public realm by eighteen inches, noting that '[t]here is no telling where we will stop if we let this go.'[23]

The City Architect's office was tasked with reviewing building applications. The Board of Control – council's executive committee, comprised of many aldermen with mayoral aspirations – was responsible for awarding more contentious building permits, among other duties. The City Architect's office dragged its feet through the review of the Haweses' project. But the controllers, whose political interests depended on Toronto's powerful elite neighbourhood groups, denied Alfred Hawes a building permit in early May because 'he was alleged to have kept bad faith with the residents of the district,' even though they might be liable for damages for doing so.[24] The Board of Control recommended that a stop-work injunction be issued,[25] and, in an unusually combative move, the city disconnected the property's water to prevent any further construction.

In June 1905, Hawes petitioned Ontario's High Court of Justice to block the stop-work injunction. He found a sympathetic chief justice who seemed irritated by a conflict over what was apparently understood to be a reasonable development. When Hawes's lawyer reported that the 'building plans had lain for weeks untouched in the architect's office,' Chief Justice Meredith asked the city: '[D]o you suppose that people must await your convenience before building? … If you haven't got a large enough staff to look after the needs of the people, then you had better go out of business.'

When the judge pressed the plaintiff about the source of 'all the city's opposition to the building of this apartment house,' Hawes's lawyer offered a tart reply: did the court want 'the real reason or the ostensible one?' After the judge demanded that he explain what was really going on, Hawes's lawyer replied candidly, '[I]t is simply that there are a few people in the vicinity who object to the erection of an apartment house near them.'[26]

On June 26, 1905, the city withdrew its objections and issued a building permit for the apartment's construction.[27]

By 1908, the first residents had moved into the new apartment at Spadina Gardens. They can be said to have fit in perfectly with their well-heeled neighbours. With gentle density came gentle class diversification; many residents fell squarely into Toronto's middle class, but an equal share were listed in *The Society Blue Book*, the city's 'directory to over 4,000 of the elite families of Toronto.'[28] Late-middle-aged neighbours of Eaton's, in the exclusive subdivision across the street, moved into the building so they could age in place, as we would say today.[29] In 1911, 1924, and 1949 respectively, Spadina Gardens would become home to Mrs. Eliza Gooderham and her two adult children;[30] Sir Henry M. Pellatt, the electricity baron who built and lost Casa Loma;[31] and both of the adult sons of Governor-General Vincent Massey, heirs to the Massey manufacturing empire.[32]

The Spadina Gardens units all had three bedrooms and one bathroom, as well as an entry hall, kitchen, dining room, den, and parlour with a walkout balcony. The earliest occupants generally needed two bedrooms and kept the third for a live-in domestic.[33] The building itself complemented the streetscape, with its red-brick detailing and architectural treatments like balconies and bay windows. Several decades later, the widening of Spadina Road and the arrival of both subway lines ultimately forced the replacement of the block's nineteenth-century mansions with more mid-rise apartments and parking lots.[34]

The neighbours' failure to stop Spadina Gardens, coupled with the building's ability to blend with its surroundings, did little to stem the tide of similar NIMBY-style responses to apartment buildings as they boomed in Toronto in the years that followed. The disputants who appeared at countless Board of Control meetings rarely cited concern for apartment-dwellers' health and safety, although they often expressed concern about their property values.[35]

These campaigns didn't stop with the Board of Control. Around 1912, one Avenue Road resident named H. H. Williams paid $4,500 to a developer to prevent an apartment building's construction next door.[36] A few years earlier, in 1909, Toronto barrister Lindley Bowerman had built an eight-metre soundproof fence on the edge of his Rosedale property to block views and noise from the Nanton Apartments next door. He couldn't simply lodge noise complaints because the offending sounds weren't unduly disruptive. They included evening piano-playing and people talking near open windows at night. When the city asked that he remove the fence, Bowerman expressed his sense of entitlement: '[W]e were there first, and I don't want to be driven out.'[37]

Despite these conflicts, apartment buildings proliferated across the city centre. By 1912, there were just under one hundred listed in *The Toronto City Directory.* Struggling to ensure a level of safety and to address the objections of powerful neighbours, the city implemented eight-metre setbacks on a street-by-street basis, often as reactionary responses to specific proposals. These requirements were ostensibly designed to bring apartment buildings in line with the existing street line, but the rule had the effect of reducing the available floor area sufficiently that some projects would become financially infeasible and would not be built.[38]

In May 1912, the city declared a full-scale ban on apartment buildings in residential neighbourhoods, listing boundaries that included today's Riverdale, Beaches, the 'Avenue Road hill area,' Rosedale, Summerhill, Roncesvalles, Parkdale, High Park, the Junction, Dufferin

Spadina Gardens, 1974.

Grove, the Annex, the Village, downtown north of College, and the Garden District, among other streets and pockets.

As the *Toronto Star* noted, 'It is frankly admitted by members of the Council that even if yesterday's by-law stands the test of the courts, it will repeatedly be broken by Council itself. At every meeting, by-laws will be passed repealing it with regard to some special instance. Whoever has pull enough to get plans through Council will be able to erect an apartment house in residential areas. There will be endless deputations pro and con in each case, and the time of committees and Council itself will thus be burdened with apartment house decisions …'[39] In other words, a blanket neighbourhoods-wide ban on what was seen as reasonable density would just foster constant appeals for variances and exceptions. This would mean more paperwork, more appeals, more taxpayer dollars, and more antagonism between the municipality, developers, and neighbourhood associations.

The apartment-building restrictions remained in place until after World War I, when council began relaxing the regulations by permitting three-unit apartment houses, but only in downtown neighbourhoods.[40]

Toronto's experience with the distinct typology of larger medium-density apartment buildings, however, would be limited to developments like the Gloucester Mansions, between Yonge and Church; the Palmerston Apartments at Herrick Street; and the Hampton Apartments at Metcalfe and Winchester. All share several notable qualities: they are located on residential streets; are wider than houses but employ architectural features to break up their masses; rise to no more than three-and-a-half storeys; and come equipped with multiple bedrooms, separate living spaces, and character features like fireplaces. It's a typology not found among the city's new builds today.

Toronto's earliest apartment buildings remain predominantly rental in tenure. They offer a spectrum of quality, upkeep, and architectural integrity, and their affordability reflects this spectrum. They are also extremely limited in number, largely due to a conservative municipal administration's blanket ban designed to preserve single and semi-detached residential neighbourhoods at all costs.

As today's neighbourhood residents and municipal administrators, we might consider the wealth of attractive, medium-density character apartments that Toronto could have had. We can take the time to imagine the contemporary versions of such a typology: what are the crown mouldings, grand fireplaces, leaded windows of today? We can ask ourselves why, amid a housing crisis comparable to that of October 1901, there shouldn't be room down the street for a building that could blend in through high-quality compatible design while providing young couples and families, seniors, students, new arrivals, and others with an opportunity to share in our quiet, tree-lined, neighbourly residential communities.

Toronto homeowners have been trying to keep apartment buildings out of their neighbourhoods for about as long as Toronto builders have wanted to build them. With its growing population, increasing white-collar employment, and rising property values, Toronto experienced a boom in apartment construction in the Edwardian years. The city issued its first building permit for an apartment building in 1899, and by 1914 had issued 249 such permits. British geographer Richard Dennis, who has studied early Toronto apartments carefully, found 290 'apartment houses' in the 1918 city directory.[1]

The Genesis of the Yellowbelt

Richard White

City council, presumably reflecting the wishes of the property owners who elected it, did what it could to resist. It had had the authority to prohibit 'laundries, butcher shops, stores, and manufactories' on private property since 1904. In response to the apartment boom, it sought to expand this list to include apartment buildings, and the province acceded, amending the Municipal Act in 1912 to permit municipal prohibition of 'apartment or tenement houses and garages used for hire or gain' – revealing that automobiles were invading cities at the same time as apartments.[2] The city promptly enacted a bylaw putting this restriction into effect, which affected nearly all residential streets. It excluded commercial streets, on which many apartment buildings would be built.

However, this prohibition seems not to have been strictly applied. In the Beaches neighbourhood, dozens of apartment houses were added to the residential fabric in the two decades after the bylaw was enacted.[3] Some were just alterations to existing homes, but others were entirely new buildings, built on sites cleared of older houses, and these ranged from fourplexes (which mimicked houses) to substantial four-storey structures with as many as twenty suites. Property owners wishing to erect them applied to the city for permission to deviate from the bylaw, and the City Property Department, after inspecting the site and soliciting the opinions of nearby owners, nearly always granted that permission, in this one neighbourhood at

Low- and mid-rise apartments proliferated after World War II.

least. The message is twofold: homeowners were not all dogmatically opposed, and city authorities had the power to do what they thought was right.

Little housing of any sort was built in Toronto in the 1930s and 1940s, but after World War II, with the economy expanding and the population growing, new apartment buildings began cropping up again. These early postwar buildings encountered little opposition. Many were built at the edge of the city, where there was minimal urban fabric to disturb, and those built within the city were mostly on major commercial streets, where the existing bylaw permitted them. Most were still low-rise walk-ups, though taller buildings with elevators did begin to appear in the early 1950s.

For several decades, Toronto resisted the international trend toward planning, but finally took the plunge in 1955, setting up a substantial planning apparatus that included an accomplished Chief Planner and several experienced professional planners for his staff. After a few years of study, these new planners released a booklet spelling out what Toron-

'Areas of stability': models pitching the suburban dream, later the Yellowbelt, 1956.

tonians should expect in the years ahead. Toronto, they believed, would be a 'Changing City' – as the title of their booklet had it – for it was on the verge of becoming a true metropolis.[4] They projected that the entire expanse of Metropolitan Toronto, much of it farms and market gardens in the mid-1950s, would be urbanized within twenty-five years, making central Toronto into 'downtown' for a million more people. Downtown would need more of everything, from office buildings to hospitals to streetcars. And with the number of automobiles increasing even faster than the number of people, the city also needed roads and expressways to protect its older residential streets from becoming nothing more than routes for getting to and from downtown.

The planners also drew attention to the new phenomenon of the 'non-family household' – unmarried adults living alone or with roommates rather than family – and the unprecedented demand for apartment living it created. Projections showed the number of apartment suites in the city tripling over the next twenty years, which meant numerous new buildings, many of them high-rises.

Where to put these buildings posed a challenge. The planners anticipated that some old housing would be demolished by its owners,

Real estate sales models, 1956.

yielding potential sites, and that commercial streets still provided options. But this would not be enough to meet the demand: Toronto needed more sites for apartment buildings. The planners were also predicting a slight increase in population, meaning more people on less residential land. That is to say, Toronto was about to experience a surge in residential density – a 17 percent increase in the next twenty years, the planners projected.

The planners' approach to all this was to devise plans for growth one neighbourhood at a time, and then, at some point in the future, knit their neighbourhood plans together into an overall city plan. They began with the older residential neighbourhoods around the city centre – the Annex, Deer Park, and Rosedale – which the planners believed were urban gems that Toronto should act immediately to preserve as best it could. Of course, these neighbourhoods would have to change, like everywhere else, and the neighbourhood plans reflected this, with certain areas designated for new apartment buildings.

When the planners presented these draft plans to the local public, they encountered stiff opposition. Nevertheless, the planners pressed on, preparing draft plans for a few more neighbourhoods. But the process was not working. Opponents stood firm at public meetings, demanding time-consuming changes to the plans. The planners were not sure what to do, and for a time made little progress on the overall city plan. But they returned to it in 1965, and after requesting and receiving submissions, they released a new comprehensive report, 'Proposals for a New Plan for Toronto.'

Their report is a valuable piece of the city's planning history, reflecting several mid-1960s priorities, but its vision for Toronto's residential areas is perhaps its most striking element. It proposed three classifications: 'improvement areas' (inner-city areas slated for publicly funded urban renewal), 'areas of stability' (most of the low-density residential city), and 'areas of private redevelopment' (where high-density apartment buildings would be permitted). The areas of stability, it states, 'should be regarded as inviolate, and a firm commitment made that no basic changes through zoning or other public action which is not in keeping with the character of the area will be allowed for a period of ten years.'[5] This unequivocal statement is the first of its kind to appear in any formal city document. Here is the genesis of the Yellowbelt.

The report was discussed, modified, and distilled to its essence, in which form it was approved by council in 1968 and by the Province of Ontario in 1969. The plan retained the threefold classification of residential areas, though it gave them new names, and the city's areas of stability – now labelled 'low density residential' areas – thus became 'inviolate' by provincial law. The earlier planners' effort to renew residential areas and increase residential density by adding new apartment buildings to the urban fabric had been stymied, their vision of Toronto as a 'changing city' rejected. A new protectionist mindset had replaced it, among both planners and councillors.

What had brought this on? Why had the acquiescence of the 1950s – or, for that matter, the flexibility of the pre-war years – given way to such staunch opposition in the 1960s? This is the key historical question, and its answer is complex and elusive.

First, the inner-city residential neighbourhoods where apartments were envisioned, such as the Annex, were increasingly occupied in these years by upper-middle-class gentrifiers who lived in them through choice, and who liked the neighbourhoods' historical character and wanted to protect it. A 1969 plan for Cabbagetown devised by its residents – not by city planners – declared one of its fundamental objectives would be retaining 'the present low-density character of the area.'[6] Moreover, many of these well-educated gentrifiers were steeped in the 1960s ideology of citizen empowerment and had adopted the New Leftish notion that developers were exploitative capitalists. Their resistance was ideological.

In their defence, one must note that these early gentrifiers chose to live in the city's older urban neighbourhoods – they were the advance guard of the 'rediscovery of the city' movement, as urban historians now often label it. Moreover, they challenged the modernist orthodoxy in which older, congested urban areas were viewed as a problem to solve rather than an urban form to enjoy. Their stance, and their conviction they were on the right side of history, is thus understandable. It is also true that many of the apartment buildings proposed in the late 1960s were bigger and taller than those built a decade earlier.

The planners and councillors who made Toronto's low-density residential areas inviolate no doubt believed they were acting in the public interest. And the act of institutionalizing that belief in formal plans and bylaws is considered a major accomplishment of the 1970s reformers. Perhaps they were, and perhaps it was.

But the circumstances that prompted their actions no longer prevail. Far more people want to live in truly urban environments now. Mixed-age streetscapes are proving to be attractive; mixed-income populations and increased residential densities are accepted planning goals; urban designers and architects have new and better ideas about how cities can grow. That is to say, policies that were in the public interest fifty years ago are not necessarily in the public interest today. And the old frontier notion that the first to arrive can build a fence to keep everyone else out might not be the soundest principle for a growing, twenty-first-century metropolitan city.

Redevelopment of existing residential areas was once permitted in Toronto, and in fact it created desirable, mixed-income neighbourhoods. The idea that it should not be permitted – an idea that emerged only in the 1960s but is now dogma in Toronto planning and politics – is the product of an historical moment that has passed. Like the prohibitions once imposed on Sunday tobogganing and sidewalk cafés, perhaps the prohibition on residential redevelopment should be allowed to pass as well.

For an architecture buff, there may be no better place to live in Toronto than the Garden Court Apartments. Nestled in Leaside, facing Bayview Avenue, Garden Court was built in the early 1940s and has staying power to this day. When I've taken architects visiting Toronto on tours of the city and we arrive at the Garden Court, the sentiment is almost always the same: 'Wow – this is amazing! What's it doing in Toronto?'

The Lesson of Garden Court

Michael McClelland

What is so unexpected is the huge expanse of a formal interior courtyard within the block, surrounded symmetrically by elegant buff brick buildings. In Toronto, a city that has long been parsimonious with open space, this complex is *sui generis*, not only without precedent, but also with no real successors.

The plan is simple: ten buildings organized around a central courtyard, with smaller, more private courts in the corners of the roughly square 2.4-hectare site. Garages are neatly arranged along the north and south property lines.

The question is, what inspired the developer, Blake Jackson, and his architects, Page + Steele, to take on this flight of fancy in Toronto? And what can we learn from their story that could be applied to residential development in a city that appears to crave low-rise apartments but tends not to build them?

With Garden Court, many elements make it specific to its time and place. First, there is the French background. One of the architects, Harland Steele, had finished his education by attending a brief course at the École des Beaux-Arts at Fontainebleau. The school, also called the Écoles d'Art Americaines, had a mission to export the best of its classical beaux-arts training to the English-speaking world – an ambassador, of sorts, for French taste.

The architecture program was started in 1921, with Jacques Carlu among its first directors. A French architect born in 1890 and known for his art deco style, Carlu had designed the interiors of ocean liners and, locally, the stylish seventh-floor auditorium/banquet hall atop the former Eaton's store at College Park in Toronto.

A basic principle of the *école des beaux-arts* training was that a project had to be understood as a sequence of spaces or thresholds in which the urban context, the building itself, and all its details could be experienced and appreciated together. When one enters and walks through the courtyard at the Garden Court, the strong axial layout of the plan, the simple massing of the buildings, and the streamlined horizontal banding in the brickwork all operate in harmony. The repetition, clarity, and restraint all contribute to the experience of moving through these spaces.

While the exterior is the showstopper, the interiors are also of interest. With over one hundred units, most are planned to have cross-ventilation and direct access to the courtyards. Unlike most apartment buildings, there are no interior corridors and no elevators. And while most of the units are not large, they are carefully designed to be as efficient as possible. They are very livable.

The landscaping was the work of Howard and Lorrie Dunington-Grubb and Sven Herman Stensson, the leading landscape architects of the day. The conservative formal garden they developed here, with their trademark of shallow stone retaining walls around sunken garden lawns, fits neatly with Page + Steele's beaux-arts plan. The landscape and the buildings also work together to create pleasing entry sequences. Usually, the Dunington-Grubbs (a husband-and-wife team) used sculpture to accent their garden designs. In this case, the modest sculptural piece that originally sat on the central axis of the plan was replaced by an unfortunately tall evergreen, which now blocks views.

This landscape design also responds to the larger context of Leaside, a Garden City suburb planned in 1912 on the idealistic premise of being a new town complete with employment, shops, and residences. At the time, the city was experimenting with similar imported ideas about housing and landscape design. The newly formed Toronto Housing Company in 1913 announced it was developing a pair of

An aerial view of Garden Court, looking east from Bayview.

subsidized workers' housing co-ops – Spruce Court, in Cabbagetown, and 88 Bain Avenue, near Withrow Park south of the Danforth. Influenced by Letchworth Garden City, in England, both were designed by the architect Eden Smith. These apartment complexes were built as a series of two-storey arts-and-crafts-style 'cottage flats' enclosing landscaped central courtyards.

At 400 hectares, Leaside was one of the largest and riskiest real estate ventures in Toronto at that time. Leaside's designer was landscape architect Frederick Todd, an American who had initially worked for Frederick Law Olmsted, the visionary credited with conceiving Central Park in Manhattan.

When Todd, considered Canada's first professional landscape architect, moved to Canada, he worked for the Canadian Northern Railway, laying out parks and communities from the high-end neighbourhoods of Shaughnessy and Point Grey in Vancouver to public spaces in Regina, Winnipeg, and St. John's. Leaside was one of his

Entry threshold into Garden Court.

CNR projects. City planning, at the time, was deeply influenced by the Garden City movement, and particularly the work of Americans like Clarence Stein, a contemporary of Todd's.

Much of Todd's work was inspired by the Garden City movement's central idea that cities could be improved with an enhanced connection between the natural landscape and newly designed communities. Leaside remains an anomaly in Toronto, and it now appears much like many of Toronto's other early-twentieth-century suburbs. The reality is that Todd's vision for Leaside lay dormant for almost two decades before it could find investors. In the end, the development of the Garden Court Apartments was an innovative response to the concept of this new community.

It is unclear how Blake Jackson selected this site, but his vision of garden apartments echoed nicely with Todd's progressive suburban ideals. Jackson was a successful entrepreneur, and his company, Jackson-Lewis Construction, which built the Garden Court, went on to become one of the largest general contractors in Toronto. (The firm still operates, as the Aecon Group.) Deep in the provincial archives lie Page + Steele's drawings for the Garden Court Shopping Centre, proposed for the north east corner of the site facing Bayview, complete with shops and a well-designed bowling alley on the second floor. This would have completed Jackson's vision for modern living in Leaside.

The low density of the Garden Court makes it difficult to replicate this kind of housing project now in a city with soaring real estate prices. It is part of our recent history, but the value of history is that we can see other options outside the current constraints of today. Those are constraints of our own making. We tend to see landscape in housing as 'defensible space,' not as pleasing views and vistas. We see apartments simply as a unit count, not as unique, habitable spaces. We lack romance and imagination in building new housing. It was the quality of the design of Garden Court that drew many of Toronto's first modern architects, like John B. Parkin and Gordon Adamson, to become early tenants here. Frederick Todd, Blake Jackson, the Dunington-Grubbs, and Harland Steele all played a part in creating this joyful bit of Fountainebleau-inspired modernism in Toronto.

Its lesson is simple: to build good architecture, you have to start with the beautiful.

D otted throughout the leafy streets of South Rosedale, nineteen modestly scaled apartment buildings contribute unobtrusively to the architectural stability of this tony enclave. Plain and square in comparison to the fancy arches, dormers, and columns of the neighbourhood's stately homes, these brick structures are now considered sturdy examples of Toronto's brief fling with mid-century modernist apartment architecture.

The War of the Rosedales:
How Low-Rise Apartments Came to 1950s Rosedale
Ed Jackson

I moved into one of these Rosedale apartments in 2013, attracted by its green courtyard and bubbling fountain. Relieved to find rental accommodation in such pleasant surroundings, I fell in love with these buildings and soon became curious about their history.

How did such homely, low-slung structures end up in a place like Rosedale?

It came as no surprise to discover they had faced considerable opposition from residents when they were built. Historically, the name Rosedale has served as a metaphor for privilege. It signifies a place where the rich and powerful of early modern Toronto came to build their mansions, on winding streets safely separated from the congestion of downtown. Partially moated by ravines, Rosedale's exclusive terraces were intended to be difficult to access unless you owned a private vehicle.

But the extraordinary spurt of growth in postwar Toronto changed all that. By 1950, Rosedale was no longer a remote enclave, and it found itself encircled by burgeoning new suburbs. Two new bridges spanning the Rosedale Valley ravine – one that opened in 1950 as part of the Mount Pleasant Road extension north of Jarvis Street, and the other extending Sherbourne Street north in 1953 – provided easy links for middle-class workers who wanted to live closer to downtown.

Housing was in critically short supply in Toronto after World War II. A federal wartime order had overridden local zoning restrictions, allowing the establishment of rooming houses to meet the need for

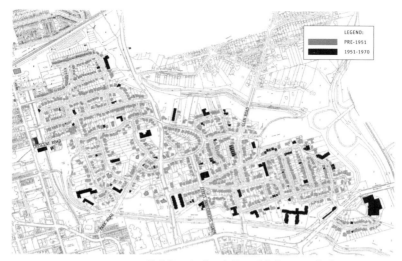

Buildings in South Rosedale by period of construction.

low-cost rental accommodation. Rosedale's rambling mansions, already becoming too unwieldy and expensive to maintain without servants, offered convenient opportunities for conversion to rooming houses. The area's elite burghers soon grew alarmed at the intrusion of what they perceived to be too many undesirable neighbours living in rented rooms.

In 1952, Toronto's City Planning Board produced a comprehensive zoning bylaw to support an official city-wide plan adopted two years earlier. The bylaw represented the city's first attempt to create a blueprint for future land use, replacing a hodgepodge of local spot zoning that had evolved over time.

The new bylaw established South Rosedale as a so-called 'RIA district.' This designation permitted detached private dwellings as well as duplexes and garden court apartments restricted to a height of nine metres (or three storeys). This bylaw set off a decade of furious public debate – and subsequent amendments – that linked and ultimately limited the existence of both rooming houses and apartment buildings in the district. A *Globe and Mail* headline wryly described the battle as the 'War of the Rosedales.'

One planning consultant told Rosedale residents the only way to solve the boarding-house problem was to tear down large old homes and replace them with luxury apartments. Meanwhile, an association of guest houses claimed the existence of rooming houses had been crucial to ensuring that the area's housing stock didn't deteriorate. An English planner also weighed in, characterizing the proposed apartment buildings as 'a decorated form of packing crates.'

The spectre of invading apartment buildings – 'tenements' to many Rosedale homeowners – became suddenly real with a developer's 1951 proposal to ignore the three-storey height limit by constructing a ten-storey, 380-suite apartment building at the corner of Mount Pleasant and Elm Avenue, next to Branksome Hall, the elite girls' school. Roused to action, the South Rosedale Ratepayers Association, one of the oldest such groups in Canada, advertised an emergency meeting to oppose the massive plan. The meeting, held in October 1952, in Branksome Hall's gymnasium, was packed. With its articulate and professional membership, the association soon became a powerful player in many subsequent city debates about residential zoning.

The proposed Elm Avenue apartment required the demolition of Guiseley Hall, a sprawling Victorian mansion built by Joseph Cawthra, a wealthy nineteenth-century Toronto merchant. After the last surviving member of the Cawthra family died in 1951, the future of the property, now a deteriorating white elephant, was up for grabs. Reuben Dennis, an enterprising developer who later came to be known as the city's largest landlord, immediately swept in to option it.

Responding to ratepayer ire, city council's property committee eventually refused to issue a building permit for the eight-storey edifice, and Dennis was sent back to the drawing boards. A new and more compact design produced by well-known architect Edward I. Richmond passed the zoning guidelines, and in 1955 the city finally issued a permit for the Clifton Manor complex that now survives at 5–11 Elm Avenue. But this was only one of many zoning challenges to follow.

Rendering: 16 Rosedale Road, Bregman and Hamann Architects, 1958.

Beset by conflicting pressures, city council committees dithered about whether rooming houses should remain and if they should allow more apartment buildings to be constructed, not just in Rosedale but across the city. A letter to the editor in the *Globe and Mail* at the time captured the level of burgeoning hysteria: 'Building permits are being applied for daily in droves, soon to be transformed into dozens of yellow brick intrusions.'

In 1955, after many contradictory decisions, council amended the residential bylaw governing apartments for South Rosedale, adding requirements specifying more regulated lot coverage, brick construction, architect-designed plans, and increased off-street parking. Council also decreed that only existing rooming houses meeting so-called Class A standards – which included owner occupation, proper sanitary facilities, and a minimum sleeping space for each occupant – would be allowed to remain.

Meanwhile, developers took full advantage of the extended political delays, hurrying to option properties and request building permits for new apartment construction. The builders then later made the case that it was not fair to impose bylaw restrictions retroactively, and they would go bankrupt if forced to cancel their plans. The city's aldermen agreed, exempting sixty apartment buildings already in process across the city, including several in South Rosedale.

Developers were also enterprising in finding ways to evade Rosedale's nine-metre height zoning restriction. One tactic was to create an additional floor of half-basement apartments. A further bylaw amendment eventually restricted this workaround, but the tactic proved successful, at least initially. Half of Rosedale's apartment buildings have a fourth floor of semi-basement apartments.

Another tactic involved circumventing the interpretation of a building's height above 'grade level,' defined in the zoning language as being level with the street on which the building fronted. Some builders dodged that nine-metre restriction by embedding several floors of their buildings into neighbouring ravine slopes *below* grade level.

In response, the residents' battle for neighbourhood preservation expanded to head off the assault on these slopes. This new clash focused on a 1955 request for permission to build a seven-storey apartment complex on a five-acre lot at McKenzie and Dale Avenues, just steps from the Castle Frank subway station. That building would descend three storeys into the Rosedale Valley ravine. The newly formed Save Our Ravines Committee called on the city to stop this development by expropriating the Dale Avenue ravine plot to save shrinking parkland. The city considered the petition, but eventually decided the cost of this piecemeal action was too high.

Frustrated by delays, the Dale Avenue developer sought relief in the courts. In 1956, an Ontario Supreme Court judge granted an order requiring the city to issue a permit to construct the Dale Avenue complex, including its ravine-slope floors. It remains the largest apartment building in South Rosedale. Other developers with outstanding building permits also won court orders allowing them to proceed with construction.

In the midst of all this legal jousting, the Ontario Municipal Board (OMB), in August 1955, mandated a one-year halt on all new apartment construction in Toronto to give the City Planning Board time to clarify zoning restrictions. Surveying months of municipal indecision, the *Globe and Mail* at the end of 1955 handed down its own verdict: 'a year of floundering and near chaos in the field of zoning.'

The Planning Board and the city's new chief planner took several years to complete their new Toronto-wide review of zoning, including restrictions on density in residential areas like South Rosedale. A policy document released in 1958 divided the city into twenty-five planning districts, including Rosedale. The board then fast-tracked Rosedale as one of the first to receive an in-depth planning appraisal (as it happened, three members of the Planning Board lived in Rosedale). As part of the board's new community consultation approach, a smartly designed, 104-page report was circulated to all the residents, who turned out in the hundreds at public meetings.

The 1960 report conceded that 'over the past several years there has arisen what can only be described as a deep-seated fear of apartment buildings, especially among those who live or want to live in the more desirable residential districts.' However, the authors found that while 40 percent of the residents in South Rosedale already lived in apartments, apartment buildings took up only 5 percent of the land area in the district. Growth was possible but it had to be carefully controlled. 'The primary objectives in Rosedale should be the protection, preservation and enhancement of the planning district as a first-class residential area' for residents 'of high financial, social and professional standing,' the report concluded.

No further apartment development would be permitted and any future construction would be awarded to a new category of residences: townhouses, duplexes, and semi-detached dwellings. In addition, all further development into ravine slopes would be prohibited to preserve a continuous ravine park system. When this zoning plan for South Riverdale was finally approved by the OMB in 1962, homeowners heaved a sigh of relief. South Rosedale ratepayers had finally nixed the construction of any more low-rise apartment buildings, apart from the nineteen already built or approved.

Crescent Avenue, Rosedale, 1957.

Over the intervening years, several of these apartment houses have been converted to luxury co-ops or condos, but some, including the one where I live, remain as well-tended rentals. Their continued existence demonstrates how successfully such multi-unit buildings can be integrated into a low-density residential neighbourhood. With the long passage of time, it seems a workable truce has developed between single-family homeowners and their apartment-dwelling neighbours.

Or has it?

The latest battle in Rosedale is over a proposal for a four-storey luxury apartment complex on Dale Avenue, right next door to the notorious ravine-hugging project that caused such a stir back in the 1950s. Construction would require the demolition of three attractive mid-century-modern bungalows on the south side of Dale. Nearby neighbours oppose the project, and the proposal has exposed rancorous divisions within the residents' association.

The conflict has raised questions about whether South Rosedale's fifteen-year-old Heritage Conservation District evaluation had simply failed to recognize the value of heritage architecture of a more recent vintage (1950s). The city opposed the demolition of the modern bungalows. As of early 2019, the development was stalled, pending an appeal to the Local Planning Appeal Tribunal, the replacement for the OMB.

The response to the most recent Dale Avenue project can't quite be called a simple case of déjà vu, although the usual anxieties about density and property values probably lurk in the background. In the 1950s, homeowners objected to the construction of apartment buildings that opened the door to middle-class rental accommodation in a once-exclusive area. In 2019, Rosedale's current residents seem equally reluctant to accept a high-end project catering to a luxury clientele, even though architecturally it matches the low scale of the 1950s-era apartment buildings. When it comes to change in Rosedale, even sixty years on, it seems no still means no.

My elderly neighbour was visiting with an old friend, and the friend pointed to a small dwelling across the street in our East End neighbourhood. We were sitting on our front porches, as we had over the decades, within a companionable distance. So I listened, too, as her guest explained to us how she had lived there many years before.

One Neighbourhood Shifts
Diane Dyson

It was more than forty years ago, the guest explained, when she had just arrived in Canada with her daughter. Her cousins had taken them into this home – a two-storey house that measures 3.6 metres across. 'We were three families there, living together,' she explained.

The street had teemed with people then. House by house, this same neighbour's son, who had grown up on the street, could enumerate the families of five, seven, and even nine people who lived under one roof. Children were stacked into bunk beds and basements. Extended family or, sometimes for the sake of a few dollars, lodgers and boarders, all squeezed into back bedrooms.

Today, fewer people live in our neighbourhood. According to the most recent censuses, from 2006 to 2016, the population in the neighbourhood dropped 20 percent. Where once five thousand people lived, there were now four thousand, and this hollowing-out has occurred in a neighbourhood within easy walking and biking distance of both the subway and downtown core.

Our neighbourhood's family homes have gradually been acquired by single adults, or couples who sometimes had a single child and sometimes didn't. New homeowners told us our area was a bargain! A dinner club for 'single ladies' met monthly. When these smaller families grew, they usually moved away to other neighbourhoods, ones with homes that had more bedrooms and bathrooms, often one for each child, and perhaps a guest room/office.

More recently, as housing prices have climbed to more unattainable levels, double-income families with multiple children are settling in and staying on the street, having grabbed a rung on the real estate ladder. The dinner club gave way to a mothers' (and occasional fathers') morning hangout.

Through all these years, neighbours still gather regularly to visit on sidewalks and porches, to enjoy the night air and a chat.

Still, these demographic changes have very real, ground-level effects. As the higher-income earners who can afford to buy into our neighbourhood are almost always white, we have lost the ethnocultural diversity of our enclave. Neighbours are no longer likely to grow vegetables in their front yards; $17 personal pizza has replaced $1.50 slices; and art stores are elbowing aside the older dry-goods shops. The local playground has been landscaped, with several more pieces of equipment added, trees planted, and the first covered outdoor hockey rink. Basement apartments have disappeared.

Some tensions among the newcomers and long-timers have played out at the micro level. One neighbour scolded another for her sagging, crowded porch, suggesting she tidy it. Loud teenagers who roll by from nearby public housing cause twitters of alarm among other neighbours. The restaurant at the corner (long ago nicknamed the Kick 'n' Stab) and the alleyways that knit our streets together are now the regular targets of 311 calls and the subject of occasional community safety meetings.

A strange outcome as we have become a gentrified neighbourhood is the rise in crime. My ex, who grew up in the area, says, 'No one ever knocked over an old lady, because she was probably somebody's grandmother.' Those involved in petty crime were more likely to go where the pickings were better.

On the whole, though, most residents appreciate the social mix. New neighbours describe the neighbourhood's 'grittiness' as part of its appeal. Theirs is a romantic ideal, this attachment to the idea of mixed neighbourhoods. Indeed, researchers like the late Clyde Hertzman, a University of British Columbia population health and early learning expert, have argued that a mixed neighbourhood is good for poor folks. Hertzman argued that local services were better when the 'sharp elbows of the middle class' were there to protect them.

Other academics caution, however, that when resources are scarce, higher-income neighbours tend to squeeze out lower-income people. We see it in Regent Park already, where local swimming lessons and specialized school programs get snapped up. One only has to look at the family income levels of children in alternative schools to see this divide in the education system. At the same time, in neighbourhoods with more mixed incomes, services such as food banks, which serve poor folks, tend to be pushed out when the area becomes upscale. The new science/math and International Baccalaureate specializations in our local high school have grown as the technical shop classes have faded, victim to lowered popularity and slashed funding.

If we are all to live together with our disparate social identities, it's worth heeding a few other warnings on how mixed neighbourhoods are fundamentally idealistic. Recent American neuroscience research has found that living in a mixed-income neighbourhood places a double burden on children who grow up poor, especially boys, because they face the disadvantages of poverty (relating to lack of resources), as well as the stigma of inequality (relating more to social status).

It's a learning we should heed as decision-makers tout the virtues of mixed neighbourhoods and these divisions are inscribed into our communities. Within sight of Lake Ontario, a new housing development was approved by our city council with a 'poor door' – a separate entrance for residents ostensibly living together, which shuts off parts of the building to all residents.

Another caution comes from research on the newly rebuilt Regent Park that finds that people segregate themselves by their social identity, living parallel lives in the same geography. I see it where I live, too. Another neighbour once commented to me, as we stood together watching the local children play, that he thought our neighbourhood works because 'we are all the same.' What did he mean? I believe it was a comment and reflection on both our class and our life stage, that if we needed to borrow a keyhole saw, some diapers, or a Bundt pan, we could find it among our neighbours.

Sign announcing the arrival of a new east end community centre, 1946.

Still, the comment set me back, and not only because of our apparent differences. I was a single mother of grown children, and he was a gay man with no children and a long-time partner. But much of my professional life has been about building strong communities, and in Toronto, that's meant bridging differences.

The question boils down to this: how do we live in a community with those who are not like us?

An understanding of how to live in a mixed neighbourhood is becoming moot in my corner of Toronto. The challenge of figuring out how different income classes can coexist is dissolving before we have had a chance to address it. The last people I know with low incomes in the community are ensconced in nearby co-op housing, hanging on in social housing, or bouncing between basement apartments – tenures that often end in eviction when the homeowner decides to renovate. Most of the street's older, long-time residents have either died or moved away, cashing in on their equity, to be closer to grown children. After a nearby house sold, June, who had moved onto the street in 1973, cooed about being a 'quarter-millionaire!'

The occupations of our new neighbours expose the extremity of these demographic changes. The taxi drivers, waiters, and secretaries who lived here when we first arrived, almost thirty years ago, are now mostly gone, and people who hold those jobs these days live in farther-flung places. Nowadays, our weekly neighbourhood hangouts include surgeons, ad executives, chefs, civil servants, and web developers.

Yet, to be fair, long-time or new, neighbours feel the tension and the worry.

I once conducted a focus group with parents from the Beach because of my work at a local non-profit. They feared their children wouldn't be able to negotiate Toronto's ethno-racial diversity because the neighbourhood was so predominately white. David Hulchanski's Three Cities research reported that some census tracts in 2006 in that community were 98 percent white.

On the doorsteps, I hear east-end neighbours worry about housing affordability, asking how kids raised in our neighbourhoods will live in the places they grew up. Over beer at the local pub, some of my more precarious (read: younger) neighbours fret about their rent rising or 'renovictions.' I also wonder how the education assistants at the local school or the woman who hands us our dry cleaning can afford to live in our community.

There are visible harms from these growing divides. In our neighbourhood, the grade school has become an easy target for closure because the student population dropped by half since my children attended, despite the creation of a new alternative school inside its walls. Heated debates abound on Facebook about each new restaurant opening (or closing: goodbye, Coffee Time) or other evidence of gentrification. My elderly neighbour who lives next door lost most of her peer group and has to settle for me, a well-intentioned do-gooder who cannot speak Greek. (We rely on sign language or bilingual interveners to share more than the basic hellos.) Her son tells me she wishes she had had the chance to learn English so she wouldn't feel so alone now.

Our street and the wider community are evolving into the homogenized upper-class neighbourhoods that can be found across the city. Individually, we are left to balance our own personal monetary gains against the wider losses of others who once lived among us or who want to now. I can't help regularly reminding my own children that we will reap hundreds of thousands of dollars of *unearned* profit when I decide to sell. Left to the market, these divisions will only amplify, despite a common longing for community, for a chat across a front porch, for a place where we each belong.

Who lives in that small house across the street from us now? Two men who are busy renovating it. I don't know their names. They moved in a few years ago, but they don't talk to us. The neighbourhood is shifting.

Louis' Confectionery once stood on Christie Street. In a city photograph from 1949 it looks to be going strong, its Coca-Cola sign freshly painted, next to Papsin's Dry Goods and the barbershop of Mr. Thomas McAllister. Seventy years later, the building remains: home to the office of some inscrutable company, the windows frosted, hemmed in by a narrow sidewalk and roaring traffic.

Why Density Makes Great Places

Alex Bozikovic

I live down the block from here. As I walk by, I sometimes reflect on this image and wonder at what's been lost. No doubt neighbourhood kids would skip into the candy store, operated by Mr. Papoff, with their nickels – maybe the same floppy-haired, suspendered kids who wander the area in other archival photographs, chasing a ball or mugging for the man with the camera. They're gone now.

The black-and-white city of seventy years ago is not really that distant. And yet those vanished shops, for me, symbolize a great gulf between the city of the early twentieth century and our own. That distance is measured in density.

Density – a term that has become a dirty word in our discussions about urban growth. It's the unwelcome commodity that the condo towers will bring, that will creep onto the block if that triplex goes ahead, something whose 'impacts' must be 'mitigated.' It is, in our civic conversation, almost always a bad word.

And yet it simply means people, and there once were more of them in this part of the city – a lot more – than there are of us today. The city in 1949 was exploding with births and new arrivals, approaching a million people, and the low neighbourhoods that held them were jammed. Eighteen-foot houses divided into apartments took in two or three families. Families took in boarders.

And the cramming would continue. By 1971, the population of Seaton Village – Bathurst to Christie, Bloor to Dupont – was 9,200. In an area of about 1,000 metres by 600 metres, and with fewer than a thousand low buildings, it's hard to imagine them all; today that same area, still cozy, is home to about 5,600 of us.

These numbers are abstract, but I wonder what it felt like in 1949, or 1969, to walk these same streets. The numbers must have created a kind of civic intimacy. Who would you see on the sidewalks on a Saturday in July? What was it like, for a twelve-year-old, to march with the army of children tobogganing at Willowvale Park on a snowy day?

The scattered anecdotes I've heard from veteran neighbours confirm it: this truly was a place where everyone knew everyone. By the 1960s, the 'Canadians' and the Jews and the Italians and the Greeks did really mix at the public school and parks and local swimming pools.

It would be too easy to cast this as a utopia, to imagine a Toronto version of Jane Jacobs's idealized sidewalk ballet. In the old, Anglo Toronto, the tightness of the neighbourhood was oppressive to many cultural insiders and exclusive to outsiders. In August 1933, a pro-Nazi mob battled neighbourhood Jews and Italians in what became

Christie St. looking north from Yarmouth Rd., 1949.

known as the Christie Pits Riot. Such overt racism and xenophobia faded only incrementally. West Indian residents who arrived in large numbers starting in the 1950s found a home here, but not always a friendly one.

Still, Toronto's embrace of diversity, while imperfect, is real – as real as anywhere in the world. And that civility was born in places like this, in neighbourhoods where people of all stripes spent time together. The 'casual, public contact' that Jacobs loved so much in New York's West Village, she also found near Seaton Village in the late 1960s. The public life of the city was incredibly rich.

And, to some degree, it still is. Those of us who are lucky enough to live in a place like this *do* know our neighbours. We do know each other's kids and dogs. We have playground friendships and school pickups and shared swim lessons and encounters at the grocery store. Once or twice a year at street parties, a larger group comes together for a potluck of samosas and lasagna. At moments like this, Toronto lives up to its epithet as the 'City of Neighbourhoods.'

But community – even here – is something a bit forced, something that needs to be bred and tended. The fact is that we are not as bound to the neighbourhood as our forebears would have been. Many of us drive cars daily. It's hard to say hello to your neighbours from the driver's seat. Many of us work far away. The factories and works on Dupont Street are gone.

Yet this is about as good as it gets in North America. It exemplifies what planners call walkable urbanism.

There are, however, two problems with this picture. First, what is good about this place is coming apart. And second, we, as a society, resist making more places that have these fine, humane qualities.

When I say 'coming apart,' I mean in a literal sense. Today's Torontonians are likely to have smaller families than their parents did and are more likely to live single. The average household size has fallen from 2.8 people in 1986 to 2.4 in 2016. And yet we each expect more space to live in. The two-and-a-half-storey houses that have been so flexible for a hundred years now – shifting as they do from one-family to two or three and then back – are generally shedding people. The neighbourhood is full of what planning jargon calls 'house-form buildings,' and these have been housing progressively fewer people. I can think of two dozen examples of these being renovated from multiple apartments to single-family. Very few go the other way.

The census figures bear out my observations: the area's population has been roughly static over the past decade, even through a visible influx of younger people like my family.

These shifts are relatively typical for Toronto, and we collectively fail to understand what they mean. The density math is relentless: in order to simply house the same number of people, we need to add more homes. Yet we are, for the most part, doing the opposite.

And on a larger scale, we are failing in a larger way. While city planners and leaders pay lip service to the virtues of growth, roughly half of today's Toronto is shrinking. Much of the postwar city never had a chance to be as dense as my home neighbourhood; most of Metro Toronto was built at the scale of the automobile, for people who would travel by car. It was born sparse. But now, those postwar neighbourhoods are losing people. Big families have become empty-nester couples, and they are selling their houses to affluent and small new families. A new generation of buildings is going up in the Yellowbelt. It should be, and could be, the missing middle; instead, the new stock is comprised of predominantly large buildings that shelter roughly the same number of people. These blocks should be filling up with people of all ages, people who can build a new community infused with the real diversity that the old Toronto didn't have. Instead, planning allows big buildings and low density. This kind of 'stability' is a missed opportunity.

But this is no surprise. The city is led by people who see density as a bad thing, people who have grown up largely in suburbs and have adopted a politics of division and the imperative of more elbow room.

I live with the legacy of people who thought another way. My neighbours and I enjoy a remarkable array of public assets. Within ten minutes' walk of my home are four publicly funded schools, two sizable parks, two public swimming pools, and a public ice rink. Essentially all of these amenities were created during the period from 1945 to 1970. The Toronto of that era, a smaller and poorer city, was also a more crowded city: people needed, and demanded, public amenities.

In 1952, a *Toronto Star* editorial bemoaned the deaths of two children killed by trucks. The children 'lived in densely crowded areas and they had nowhere else to play but on streets teeming with trucks and motor cars,' the editorial complained. 'The parks department operates over 50 children's playgrounds, 20 wading pools for small tots, and 13 swimming pools for older children. But in many areas, and particularly in densely populated sections, there are not enough.'[1]

The paper was reflecting the loud advocacy of people across the old city, which prompted a massive program of public works. It was in this period that the city bought and expropriated – and tore down! – a dozen houses to expand my local neighbourhood park. It also added a wading pool.

Today we tend to look back on this big-government, bulldozer-happy era with a profound skepticism. And yet in Toronto, the products of this period are still with us. Public pools and rinks and playgrounds have enriched my life and the lives of those in my family. We like to share.

And there remains lots of room at the pool, lots of space in the park, even a bit of room on the Christie 126 bus. The massive 1960s high school that sits nearby has plenty of capacity. The city is nowhere near as full as it used to be.

And neighbourhoods like Seaton Village would be better if they were more full. Density is, simply, the source of everything that is great in a city: good conversation, good art, good food, a good afternoon at the pool with your kids and their friends. Good public places. 'Casual, public contact.'

And the virtues of density are reflected in the shop fronts that I see daily. The confectioner Louis Papoff is long gone. I often pass one corner store that's closed and another more ancient one, which is owned by my neighbour and remains open. His shop is where my still-young kids go for their candy, crossing the road with care and finding the treats, and an adult who knows their name and helps them make change. Along with all the big projects, this is what we need: more people, more sweetness.

The commonly told history of Parkdale is a narrative riddled with myths. In 2006, Carolyn Whitzman and Tom Slater characterized the neighbourhood's transition from the past of a 'well-to-do suburb' turned 'declining slum' to a future of a 'resurgent village' as a myth of stability in the form of single-family homeownership that never fully existed in the social conditions of the neighbourhood.

The Urban Legend:
Parkdale, Gentrification, and Collective Resistance
Ana Teresa Portillo and
Mercedes Sharpe Zayas

By uncovering the smoke and mirrors of planning, marketing, and social policies aimed at justifying the racialized class project of gentrification, we hope to reveal how the flaws of neighbourhood planning based on the false dichotomy of stability and instability have normalized the displacement of working-class communities of colour, psychiatric survivors, and the poor. We also recognize the creative potential that arises at critical junctures, in this case when the unsustainability of 'stability' reveals itself and makes possible democratic and decommodified claims to space led by the struggles of the working poor.

This reading of the neighbourhood emerges through the historical articulations of the single-family home as a site of contestation: first as a colonial formation in the settlement of Parkdale; then as a relic aimed to preserve and strengthen segregation along racial, gender, and class lines; and finally as a space for capital accumulation that depends on residential displacement. While the stability of the single-family housing form never existed here, Parkdale has emerged as a significant site for working-class organizing and radical relationships of care. By drawing from the erased histories of collective action in the neighbourhood, we can begin to justify planning practices that support the diversity of housing and equitable futures.

The single-family home in Parkdale traces its roots to a colonial formation designed to produce private property through the subversion of Indigenous forms of sovereignty and land stewardship. The land known as Parkdale is encompassed within the traditional meeting place of the Huron Wendat and Petun First Nations, the Seneca, and the Mississaugas of the Credit First Nation. The land is subject to the Dish with One Spoon Wampum Belt Covenant, a peace treaty between the Anishinaabe, Mississaugas, and Haudenosaunee to share the land's resources – as long as the dish never runs dry.

The treaty was not recognized under *terra nullius*, a legal principle the English Puritan colonizers of North America used to argue that Indigenous nations didn't have rightful ownership of their territory because 'they enclose no land, neither do they have any settled habitation,' according to University of Essex sociologist Colin Samson. These false premises were used to negotiate the Toronto Purchase in 1787, an agreement understood by the Mississaugas of the Credit First Nation as a form of rent rather than an agreement to cede their rights and claim to the land. Following a revision of the Toronto Purchase in 1805, the land now known as Parkdale was gifted and sold to military personnel and corporate entities whose names and legacies are embedded throughout the neighbourhood. In 1812, the British Crown gifted 97 hectares to Captain James Brock for settlement. Between 1831 and 1840, Irish-born Colonel Walter O'Hara accumulated over 160 hectares to develop a Georgian-style family mansion named the West Lodge, and later subdivided his property to create streets such as Roncesvalles and Sorauren, to be sold for development.

In 1875, the Toronto House Building Association purchased an additional twelve hectares with the express purpose of building elegant single-family mansions to sell to wealthy Anglo-Saxon families. The neighbourhood became known as one of Toronto's first commuter suburbs and a space of leisure along the waterfront. The expansive homes, enclosed from the outside and lined with servant quarters, represented colonial imaginations of luxury and superiority. The single-family home became significant because of how it was used to construct whiteness as an ideal where settlers, military leaders, corporations, and landowners were centred as the subject of land-use planning, meaning, and the law.

Parkdale's transition from a wealthy commuter suburb into a working-class neighbourhood was the by-product of municipal, provincial, and federal policies and global economic shifts that created an opportunity to disrupt the logic of the traditional single-family home. Following the Great Depression, over half of South Parkdale's single-family dwellings were subdivided into multi-tenant housing, leading to a significant increase in working-class tenants. The rise of day labourers and lone individuals created a moral panic that upset middle-class values and postwar nuclear-family ideals, and led to the neighbourhood being labelled as a 'slum' by both the media and the government.

As mid-twentieth-century planners embraced modernist ideologies of automobility, efficiency, and progress, Parkdale became a prospective site for a new state-of-the-art public infrastructure project: the Gardiner Expressway, one of the newly created Metro government's earliest transportation schemes. The proposal to demolish hundreds of homes along the waterfront was justified under the label of 'slum clearance,' based on the aging conditions of the housing and the perceived disinvestment and shifting demographics of the neighbourhood.

The municipally imposed residential demolition prompted the construction of several high-rise apartment towers in an attempt to offset middle-class displacement. This resulted instead in white flight, as many homeowners relocated to Toronto's new suburbs while their homes were either left vacant or subdivided into smaller single-room-occupancy units, now known as rooming houses. The area's single-family housing stock fell prey to its own regulating power, whereby the changes happening in Parkdale took on forms that could no longer support the valorization of the desire of property owners.

While the post-demolition 1960s are often referred to as a period of 'disinvestment,' this era also saw the transformation of single-family housing to the affordable-housing stock that would become the site of neighbourhood-wide organizing for tenants' rights, workers' rights, and social justice.

A Victorian rooming house, seen in the 1980s.

By the late 1970s and early 1980s, a series of provincial and federal reforms deeply impacted the economic and social livelihood of the neighbourhood. Federal immigration changes in the mid-1970s led to the settlement of racialized immigrants, temporary foreign workers, and political refugees, mostly from the Caribbean, East and South Asia, and Latin America. During the late 1970s, two nearby residential psychiatric centres closed in favour of 'community-based care.' By the early 1980s, over one thousand patients were discharged into the neighbourhood without any clear pathway toward housing or aftercare support due to the neo-liberal retraction of the welfare state and the government's attempt to absolve itself of responsibility for the livelihood of psychiatric survivors.

The physical, social, and economic revision of the neighbourhood allowed for the contestation of the single-family home as an ideal form. Rooming houses, boarding homes, halfway houses, subdivided rentals, apartment towers, and the expansion of the social housing sector provided refuge for day labourers, psychiatric survivors, lone women, urban Indigenous populations, formerly incarcerated community members, and newcomers. During this period, racialized and working-poor tenants began to transform the neighbourhood by engaging in radical home-making practices and relationships of care.

The result of these transformations led to an emergent social infrastructure in the neighbourhood, including the formation of organizations like the Parkdale Activity-Recreation Centre, created by a collective of psychiatric survivors to provide a communal space similar to a living room for deinstitutionalized patients who had nowhere to go but their rooms or the streets. The creation of community spaces reflected a shift away from private regulated spaces, like the single-family home, toward relational emerging spaces that made room for alterity, learning, and collective struggle.

Although the traditional single-family home became transformed into a space for gentle density and affordability, it continued to suffer under the weight of its historical status as a site of capital accumulation. Artificial affordability was created in Parkdale through intentional disinvestment in housing by the private and public sectors. While affordability allowed for survival for many residents, it often came at the cost of adequacy and dignity, with many units run by negligent landlords who perpetuated a culture of harassment and systemic disrepair. The neglect of affordable units was often blamed on tenants rather than on the predatory practices and mismanagement of landlords. These landlords – or slum landlords – built their profit by failing to invest in and maintain their properties, but also underservicing residents. Prolonged decay and attacks on working-poor tenants are the struggles from which a rich and complex organizing landscape has emerged in Parkdale. Tenants' associations, building occupations, and eviction-prevention efforts are just some examples of organizing endeavours that have grown in mode and practice over the years to demand decency and assert collective power.

Yet, following the waves of municipally led gentrification that made Parkdale a more 'desirable' neighbourhood for investment throughout the 1990s and early 2000s, slum landlords paved the way for the current and ongoing 'renoviction' and 'repositioning' projects of corporate landlords such as MetCap, Akelius, and Timbercreek. These corporate landlords indirectly pressure tenants out of their units in order to enable vacancy decontrol, conduct cosmetic renovations, and raise the cost of units through inflation and above-guideline rent increases. In addition to the wide-scale corporate upscaling of units, affluent single families have also been reconverting rooming houses into single-family homes by taking advantage of rent gaps and 'disinvested' properties for capital accumulation. As these predatory practices continue, the dwindling stock of affordable housing in the neighbourhood faces the threat of disappearance while tenants are at increasing risk of displacement and homelessness.

A common phrase used by these agents of displacement is that the neighbourhood is *being cleaned up*. We hear the phrase used by real estate brokers who seek to blame residents for systemic forms of discrimination, like poverty; by commercial landlords to justify higher prices and increased revenues; and by corporate landlords to advance an international investment strategy predicated on mass evictions. In fact, the persistent repetition of this phrase in recent years calls into question how neighbourhood change is being represented, and who controls the narrative of a gentrifying community.

The notion of 'cleansing' a neighbourhood speaks to a white spatial imagination that dreams of a fictional space where stability, stratified wealth, and modern aesthetics coalesce and become understood as a beautification project. This dream is staged through intensified exploitation of service workers, a pronounced investment in security technologies, mass displacement of local communities, and moral panics that criminalize the poor and equity-seeking community members. It is this white spatial imagination that is central to the neo-colonial project of gentrification, which aims to reconfigure racial and class formations and local economies in order to create and profit from a widening gap between deeply affordable and market-rent units.

In the process of 'cleaning up' Parkdale, the area's housing has increasingly become a contested space featuring speculative battles fought between the forces of market-led development and organized opposition to residential displacement. It cannot be stated more strongly that displacement-based development is a strategic response to the growing strength of tenants, workers, and community members.

The Parkdale Rent Strike of 2017 was not only successful in decreasing above-guideline rent increases across a series of buildings owned by property management firm MetCap Living; it also represented a popular mass movement led by working-class tenants. The radical organizing we see in Parkdale today is based on the acknowledgement that Indigenous, racialized, differently abled, and lower-income residents are integral to the vision of a healthy and just community. The centring of equity-seeking community members shifts the locus of meaning away from whiteness and capital accumulation as ideals, and instead articulates a radical spatial imagination that (re)values difference and relationships of care. It is within this shift that we hold the most promise for planning the future of the residential street.

Consider the collective land ownership model known as the Parkdale Neighbourhood Land Trust, a radical stewardship approach built on the basis of permanent affordability and development without displacement. The land-trust model effectively transitions land from public or private ownership, so property is permanently held in trust by and for the community. The PNLT's first piece of land is a community garden that has been the site of land stewardship for over a decade by a collective of Tibetan and newcomer seniors. The Milky Way Garden has allowed community members to cultivate a collective vision for food security, urban agriculture, and shared learning borne of multiple and overlapping histories and experiences of struggle.

More recently, the PNLT's core focus has been to prevent the loss of deeply affordable units in rooming houses spurred by upscaling and deconversion through a two-pronged strategy aimed at acquiring and preserving rooming house properties, while simultaneously advancing eviction prevention through tenant organizing. Rooming house tenants have been particularly vulnerable to illegal and informal evictions through aggressive and abusive landlord practices. Because of the high level of isolation faced by these tenants, the fight to stay in their homes has created the need to foster and deepen new and existing social ties by confronting the predatory actions of their landlords through resilient forms of community leadership, such as tenant-led building committees. This reshifting of influence and care among tenants questions the more institutionalized forms of support that often alienate service users. The significance of caring relationships in working-poor mobilization is central to the land trust's organizing model for housing justice. As of May 2019, the PNLT successfully acquired its first rooming house, allowing the collective to permanently protect fifteen units of deeply affordable housing under community control.

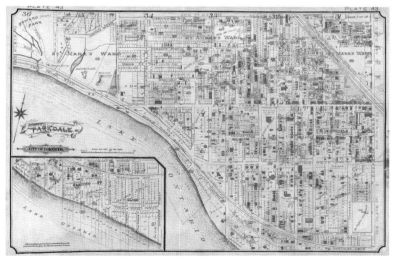

Parkdale, 1893.

The shifting forms of single-family homes have allowed for the emergence of a plethora of local and grassroots practices of social justice and socio-spatial redistributions of wealth and social capital. It has also given space to dynamic debates and elaborations of community principles that land and housing should be collectively owned, decommodified, and democratically governed by communities. Government policy, international real estate markets, and a culture of white supremacy can be dismantled through collective organizing that champions the ideas and livelihoods of those experiencing precarity in housing. By building stronger networks of support through collective struggle, we can establish the groundwork to envision holistic housing models that foster a continuum of care under the premise of dignified and healthy housing for all.

When the streetcar deposits us at the usual intersection, my wife and I walk past the shops and markets and brimming restaurants, then turn the corner to our block. Behind a line of old trees, our gabled brick house stands where it has for well over a century. Of course, it's not our house, exactly. The owners inhabit the first two levels, their friend lives in a basement suite, and my wife and I are on the third floor. These days, we don't aspire to own a house in Toronto; we prefer to keep our goals within the realm of possibility. We

Our Own Front Door

Tatum Taylor Chaubal

are, unabashedly, millennials; for better or worse, our generation's economic plight is well-documented. But in some ways, our scenario is already ideal. We live on a quiet residential street in an animated urban neighbourhood – the best of both worlds. We get to say 'our house' when we're inviting people over. And we have the benefits of living in a former Toronto estate, without the mortgage or the yardwork. We even have our own front door, at least for now.

Inside the vestibule, six built-in mailboxes line a wall. None of them is ours. Faded stickers against the steel memorialize apartments 7 through 12; 1 to 6 seem lost to history. Usually, these details settle into the backdrop of our mundane comings and goings. But when I think to notice them, this little entry space transforms into a mausoleum: the words on a wall are the only remnant of the building's former life as a rooming house. Who anxiously checked for deliveries here? When was the last time these boxes were opened? For all I know, the keys to their locks could lie on the ocean floor by now.

A few inches to the right of the mailboxes, one inner door, which almost never opens, leads to the landlords' ground-floor inner sanctum; they have their own entrance through a side addition. The other door leads to our staircase. Two flights turn tightly upward; negotiating for passage through the hallway, where our bicycles are parked, is like solving riddles for the Sphinx. We remember the acrobatics of our movers, who ultimately chose the outdoor fire escape to deliver our bookcases.

Mailboxes, 2019.

The constraints of the staircase open up to the airiness of our living room, where the walls angle up and up to a vaulted ceiling that, at some point, acquired a skylight. Our parents joke that we're the madwomen in someone else's attic. But when light sprawls through the space from every side, we think of it more as a low-slung penthouse.

This housing typology – slicing a floor from someone else's house – was new to me when I moved to Toronto. I grew up in Houston, where single-family houses swimming in deep yards are a norm that extends beyond the upper crust. More recently, I had lived in a tiny pre-war studio in New York. I knew a few peers who rented in subdivided row houses, but living in even part of a semi-detached or detached house was unheard of.

After I joined my wife in Toronto in 2012, our first home together was on the ground floor of the old Sheldrake Hotel, a four-storey apartment building on the edge of Allan Gardens. We loved the hardwood floors, and the view right onto the park. At the time, we didn't realize how uncommon this scale of housing was in Toronto. When we eventually caught the urge to explore a new neighbourhood, our options were limited. Purchasing our own home was out of the question due to an overhang of student debt. The vacancy rate was low – then, as now – and most of the apartments we could somewhat afford were in towers no older than me, with sharp-cornered, spartan white walls, clean chrome faucets, and windows to the sky. I'd been spoiled, indulging my penchant for living with quirky room configurations, the ghosts of past tenants, and proximity to the earth.

Consummate urbanites, we both thrive on the energy of Toronto's geographic core, with its density and cultural complexity. Our jobs are downtown. My wife usually cycles to work, and I depend on public transit. Access to our professional and creative communities is important to us. We don't lack affection for the suburbs and, in fact, often find ourselves in the 905, visiting our family. But our hearts and livelihoods belong to a downtown that is increasingly driving away people of our age.

We ended up inheriting our sliced-house apartment from friends, which, we've since learned, is a frequent means of transcending the lottery of the Toronto rental market. They had lived there for several years but were graduating into the world of condo ownership. Back when they had moved in, the floor below had been its own separate rental apartment, but the owners had since reincorporated it into the main living quarters.

As a heritage planner, I spend my days studying old buildings, relying on a belief that the archives are a kind of oracle – research is just a matter of asking the right questions. But I know this assumption is flawed. I've dated our house to the late 1870s, and city directories show that, beginning in the 1930s, the number of listed units fluctuated between one and six, with frequent turnover of occupants. This pattern has continued over the decades, through to our tenancy. (The directories can't seem to account for the twelve apartments suggested by the mailboxes.)

Beyond this skeletal chronology, I know that nailing down the details of the house's evolution would be an imposing challenge.

Alterations in vernacular interiors and the shifting of partitions between apartments are changes that don't necessarily find their way into the building records. And, of course, the history of rooming houses in Toronto is often tied to the histories of marginalized and transient communities, whose members are generally underrepresented in archival documentation.

Indeed, the story of our house stokes my imagination through its very incompleteness. Naturally, our mental map of the house brings our door, our stairs, and our floor to the forefront. But if we mentally reconfigure the spaces, peering down halls to add new rooms or squinting at walls just hard enough to erase them, we can conjure the house's past and future lives. We know that our period of residence, our iteration of the house, and our mostly artificial sense of ownership constitute a very small portion of the story. For now, we're happily ensconced in our palace of rafters.

There are names for units like ours: mother-in-law apartments, granny suites – terms that allude to arrangements with adult children who carve spaces from, or add annexes to, their own houses to accommodate elderly parents. But my wife and I are neither mothers-in-law nor grannies. We're just urban-minded millennials. The flexibility of old houses like ours goes beyond serving the needs of a multi-generational household – it helps address a widening gap in Toronto's housing market.

While millennials in Toronto are grappling with a dearth of housing that's affordable, ours is not the only gap, nor is it necessarily the most urgent. In a city with a growing homeless population, severe shelter crowding, and an affordable-housing crisis, diversifying rental housing types for young professionals doesn't seem to be the direst priority. However, the challenges of broader housing affordability affect a significant percentage of the population in Toronto and other urban centres. Toronto must make space for people who range in socio-economic status, profession, cultural background, and age, and that means encouraging flexibility in meeting their housing needs.

Our house has expanded and contracted throughout its history to accommodate different configurations of tenants, and it will surely continue to do so. In the not-distant future, it is likely that my wife and I will be nudged out so the landlords can reincorporate the floor into their home. They told us as much when we first moved in, but we thought it was worth the risk. Every now and then, this looming prospect drives us to check apartment websites and imagine ourselves into a new space. This exercise is cold comfort. The house next door has a granny suite that just went on the market, a one-bedroom, but at nearly triple the monthly rent. Our reaction to reading this number started at bemusement and quickly plummeted to anxiety.

At this rate, it's difficult to plan our next move. We've spent years trying to establish ourselves in a city that seems to have less and less room for us and our generation. There is so much talk in Toronto about our diverse population, and that certainly counts among the characteristics we most value here. But when will the housing market reflect that diversity? I hope we'll be around to find out.

Previous pages: Ryding Avenue trailer eviction, 1948.

It's easy to believe that our cities operate within a framework of plans and policies, attuned to address the issues of the day. In reality, the plans that govern our urban environment are often products of inertia. They carry forward the unintended consequences of yesterday's good intentions and the long shadow of past prejudices.

A City of Houses
Gil Meslin

Take the two words – *stability* and *character* – that have shaped the planning of Toronto's residential neighbourhoods for the past half century. Those terms became established as part of the city's guidance for low-rise residential areas in the late 1960s, encompassing even older ideas about how Torontonians should live. These layered views and regulations from earlier eras strongly inform today's policies.

Toronto has a long history of antipathy toward apartments. In the years around 1900, when Toronto prided itself on being a 'City of Houses,' the arrival of apartments prompted serious pushback from local leaders. This form of housing was seen as unhealthy, immoral, and corrosive to the ideal home and household structure. Apartment living was blamed for everything from idle housewives ('and we know who provides mischief for idle hands'[1]) to marital discord. 'If there is anything destructive of morality and home life it is the herding together of many families under one roof,' Alderman A. J. Keeler said in 1907. 'We have the best citizenship where one family is under one roof.'[2] Ultimately, in 1912, the city banned apartments from residential streets.

Half a century later, in the 1960s, Toronto was experiencing dramatic change: suburbs were rapidly expanding outward, and some leaders feared a hollowing out of the central city. In central neighbourhoods, blockbusting in the name of urban renewal was paving the way for high-rise apartment developments. Planned subway expansion and expressways had introduced uncertainty about the future shape of the city. And gentrification was beginning in neighbourhoods such as the Annex and Cabbagetown.

In response to these dynamics, planners in effect carried the 1912 ban forward: they decided that most low-density residential areas should be regarded as 'stable' and protected from intrusions that would 'detract from their character or reduce their stability.' As a 1966 draft of the Official Plan put it: 'When specific areas of stability have been established, the area should be regarded as inviolate, and a firm commitment made that no basic change in zoning in character will be allowed for a period of ten years.'[3]

Ten years became twenty, twenty became thirty, and, by 1999, the newly amalgamated City of Toronto was preparing a new Official Plan. The notion of protecting the stable character of low-rise residential areas remained a central element of planners' vision for the city, and the new OP extended it across the new city's larger geographic area. In the new plan, low-rise residential areas became designated as Neighbourhoods. In these areas, the plan stated, the first goal should be 'reinforcing and enhancing the established physical character.'

Today, another twenty years later, the city's current Official Plan retains almost the exact same language. 'Neighbourhoods are considered physically stable areas,' it states. '[D]evelopment in established Neighbourhoods will respect and reinforce the existing physical character of the neighbourhood.'

What does 'physical character' mean? While the Official Plan recognizes walk-up apartments as being part of the housing mix in Neighbourhoods, in practice none have been allowed to be built on residential side streets, even where other such buildings exist.

Over time, a deference to 'stability' and 'character' has shown that what is really being protected, and encouraged, is owner-occupied, single-family housing. When the OP states that Toronto is 'a city of Neighbourhoods,' this is a euphemism for 'a city of houses.'

A City of Homes. A City of Neighbourhoods. A City of Houses. All one and the same.

A CITY OF PEOPLE

Toronto, today, is a place of all-or-nothing urbanism. Residential growth is directed toward a relatively small portion of the city – the

Centres, Downtown, the Avenues – while most residential areas are insulated from any meaningful intensification. The language of 'stability' and 'character' has been used to exclude walk-up apartments and other forms of neighbourhood-scale multi-residential housing from low-rise residential areas for nearly five decades, illustrating how the 1912 prohibition of walk-up apartments on established residential streets has carried over to the present day.

While planning policy ostensibly supports small apartment buildings, other regulations ensure this form can almost never be realized. Restrictions on the size and proportions of buildings make walk-up apartment buildings effectively impossible to reproduce today. In this way, the city is speaking out of both sides of its mouth. It permits walk-up apartments in some areas, but not the physical form that has historically made them possible.

Why, other than policy inertia, do we persist with the application – and fortification – of land-use policies that were designed to address yesterday's challenges, and also embed the prejudices of the past? We no longer conflate apartment-style housing with the conditions once found in late nineteenth- and early-twentieth-century tenements. We no longer wonder about the 'morality' of apartment living. We no longer fear urban flight and blight. We are no longer a city of Anglo-Canadian homeowners. We are a diverse city of immigrants, and close to half of all Toronto households rent. So why?

The central rationale, flowing through the history of policies that have restricted walk-up apartments in proximity to single-family homes, would seem to be the threat these dwellings are perceived to pose to nearby property values.

The first question: does a negative impact on property values even exist, and if so, to what degree? The Toronto neighbourhoods where historic walk-up apartments can be found are today among the most desirable – Forest Hill, Cedarvale, Hillcrest, the Annex, Roncesvalles, Deer Park. Based on what we know about property values in these areas – even in proximity to existing walk-up apartments – any effect, if it exists at all, would seem very small and very local.

The second question: is it the city's responsibility to protect every last increment of capital gain that a homeowner may have accrued? Does it serve the greater good to protect the assets of those who own by preventing the construction of housing that might serve those who rent – and, in doing so, rendering huge swaths of the city increasingly inaccessible to renters?

There are, of course, other concerns regarding the introduction of walk-up apartments in low-rise neighbourhoods, such as access to light and preservation of privacy. How dire, however, is a little more shadow on one's backyard, if one is fortunate enough to have a backyard? How serious is the 'impact' on one's life of a few more windows, with a few more people living behind them, and who look outside once in a while? These are not 'noxious uses,' the kinds of problems zoning was ostensibly tasked with banishing from residential neighbourhoods. Rather, these nuisances are the price of living among other people in a city that must grow through infill and intensification.

And Toronto is growing. By most measures, it is booming. It has grown by 230,000 people over the past decade, while also adding close to 70,000 dwelling units. The question, however, isn't whether the city is growing, but *how* it's growing, and where current trends will lead in the long run. The current highly concentrated growth masks the fact that the interiors of many low-rise residential areas have, over a period of decades, lost population, as well as housing units. These areas are today home to tens of thousands fewer people than in the 1970s. As gentrification has progressed, rooming houses have been converted back to single-family homes, apartments have been consolidated, and the prevalence of renters and lodgers living alongside families has decreased.

To be sure, zoning and Neighbourhood designations have not been the only forces affecting the population in Toronto's central residential areas. Broad economic forces, an extended period of historically low interest rates, and global capital flows have pushed centrally located single-family housing stock beyond the economic reach of most households. There has been the impact of long-term demographic

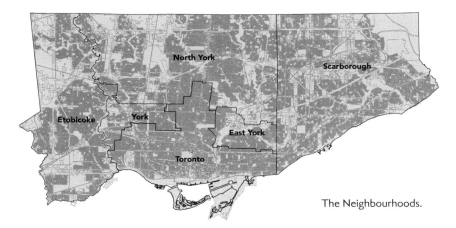

The Neighbourhoods.

cycles – booms, busts, echoes, and onward. Older adults are staying in their homes longer, rather than downsizing, meaning many houses have fewer people living in them today than once was the case. Families are also having fewer children, as increasing costs of living and later-in-life household formation contribute to smaller household sizes.

However, policy matters. And instead of finding ways to counter these pressures, we have held on to – and even reinforced – policies that exacerbate exclusion.

The formally designated Neighbourhoods in Toronto's Official Plan represent close to half of the city's area and the majority of those lands zoned for residential uses. If the current approach continues, Toronto's neighbourhoods will become the exclusive preserve of those who can afford to own single-family houses. These domains will also include the streets closest to schools and parks and farthest from the clamour of heavy traffic, with all the associated impacts on safety and air quality.

So when we talk about the missing middle – neighbourhood-scale duplexes, triplexes, and walk-up apartments – we are talking about forms of housing with the potential to make wide areas of the city more accessible to a broader range of households, owners, and renters, at various stages of life, across the income spectrum. This conversation is fundamentally about inclusivity and affordability. It's about an urban structure that first and foremost addresses the needs of people, not of property.

I would like to focus on one particular missing middle form: the neighbourhood-scale walk-up apartment. More than other types of missing middle housing, the walk-up has characteristics that uniquely position it to meaningfully counter the growing exclusivity of Toronto's neighbourhoods:

- They are permanent. Purpose-built walk-up apartments make a lasting contribution to the diversity of a neighbourhood's housing. As we have seen across the city's central neighbourhoods, rooming houses or houses-turned-apartments may proliferate for a time, but when house prices reach a certain point, those units are often converted back to single-family use. Duplexes and triplexes – purpose-built for multi-residential use – may be more durable, but they do not fall under the city's regulation of rental demolition or conversion, which applies only to buildings of six or more units. Laneway and secondary suites exist at the whim of the owner and can easily be removed from the market for personal use. Walk-up apartments, however, endure, and they fall within the purview of regulations enacted to protect and preserve rental stock.

- They can help preserve affordability. While Toronto's inventory of century-old walk-up apartments is durable, these buildings are not immune to upward pressure on rents. They are cherished – those who have lived in them tend to speak highly of the experience – and are also in great demand. Building new walk-up apartments on residential streets could relieve the upward pressure on the existing stock. Building them at scale could potentially produce a new generation of apartments that allow others to filter down, becoming more affordable.

- They are efficient. The city has begun to take incremental steps toward introducing certain types of new units in neighbourhoods, developing frameworks to facilitate the creation of secondary suites and laneway housing. On many blocks, however, it is possible to build only a handful of laneway housing units – a single walk-up building could provide more units on a single site. Given the scale and urgency of the housing-affordability crisis, their potential cannot be ignored.

• They fit in. A neighbourhood-scale walk-up provides a relatively high number of dwelling units while maintaining a street presence compatible with the scale and rhythm of surrounding houses. This efficiency of land use is not achieved through height but through building depth and lot coverage.

• They represent evolution. Toronto is a young city. Because so much of it has been built out relatively recently through postwar suburban expansion, the prevalent land use is low-rise, single-family residential. A time will come – perhaps sooner than many of us think – when it will become necessary to rethink that land use, particularly in those areas that are centrally located or near transit infrastructure. Reintroducing walk-up apartments on residential side streets, even in a controlled manner, establishes the precedent of changing single-family residential to purpose-built multiple residential, even while maintaining a low-rise residential character.

• A moment in time: If we do hope to see neighbourhoods evolve, we need to begin this process now, while it still makes economic sense. Land use is shaped in part by economics: a permitted form of development won't be realized if it doesn't make financial sense. The presence of homeowners who bought when house prices were still relatively modest provides a window of opportunity. If we wait, as houses continue to be improved, rebuilt, and expensively resold, those long-time owners who purchased their homes at far lower prices will move on, and the window will close. At that point, we may find single-family homes locked in by land economics.

• Changing attitudes: To win broader support for making neighbourhoods more accessible, it will be necessary to challenge the belief that more units, more people, and more renters pose a threat to a residential street's property values. This concern underlies our planning frameworks and is at the heart of much of the opposition to change. It stands in the way of tackling inequality; indeed, as the city's socio-economic divides widen, we need to actively challenge this fear. Tangible examples are more powerful than words, and a new walk-up apartment on a residential side street would provide an opportunity to dispel myths, address concerns, and change minds.

• A range of options: Policies at the provincial and municipal level encourage building complete communities – compact, transit-supportive neighbourhoods where services and amenities are easily accessible. But we provide few pathways to allow more people to find homes on streets in communities that are already complete. Apartment units – rental or ownership – make such neighbourhoods more accessible and more inclusive. They expand economic access, providing more affordable points of entry in Neighbourhoods where house ownership has become prohibitively expensive. They also provide options for living in Neighbourhoods at various stages of life, including making aging in place possible by allowing residents to downsize and find alternate accommodations nearby.

There is no silver bullet that will solve all the challenges of housing affordability and spatial exclusion. A complete solution to the growing inequality of access to housing in Toronto's designated Neighbourhoods includes rooming houses, secondary suites, laneway homes, and a range of purpose-built rental housing. Tackling the broader issue of affordability will also require that senior levels of government invest in social housing.

These goals, however, are not mutually exclusive. If we are to plan for a city of people, we must be able to talk about all of these objectives at the same time.

A CITY OF CHANGE

The reintroduction of walk-up apartments on residential streets would directly respond to many of the issues facing Toronto today: socio-economic segregation, growing inequality, declining economic access to neighbourhoods, long commute times, the importance of building complete communities.

Some modest but thoughtful changes to land-use policy would enable the development of more such apartments. We would need to update building and lot requirements in the zoning bylaw and revisit the Official Plan's interpretation and application of 'physical character.' With such changes, it would be possible to respect the scale of Toronto's neighbourhoods while enabling more people to live in them.

Yes, this kind of reform trades stability for change, but it would be considered, intentional, and incremental change. And in truth, there is only ever change. Cities are never-ending works-in-progress. They are built and rebuilt, layer upon layer. They adapt to meet the needs of new populations, technologies, and uses. Or at least they should.

Stability, in fact, is a myth that has come to be embedded in our land-use policies. If you look at Toronto's neighbourhoods, the cost of housing has changed. Demographics and household characteristics have changed. Local populations have changed. The tenure mix of housing has changed. Even the houses themselves – the very essence of that notion of physical character – have changed, one by one, through renovation and redevelopment.

This river I step in is not the river I stand in. If we fail to shape the city we want, we may one day, with regret, survey what the city has become. The reintroduction of walk-up apartments on residential streets would be change with purpose, change toward creating a more inclusive city.

We need to choose: the stability myth or the reality of change? A city of homes or a city of people?

On my sketching trips through Toronto, I often come upon unexpected clusters of mid-rise urbanity far from the downtown core. While Toronto's inner suburbs evoke images of polarized housing types – single-family homes over here, towers in a park over there – the built form on the ground is more complicated. In fact, there are areas throughout the city with zones of 'gentle density,' all those forms of housing between detached houses and high-rises.

The Mid-Rises of Metropolitan Toronto
Daniel Rotsztain

The illustrations included in this chapter offer up examples of the 'missing middle' from each of Toronto's six former municipalities. They reflect various periods in the city's development and different circumstances in which this neglected housing type overcame Metropolitan Toronto's anti-apartment bias. The examples I chose represent mid-rise apartments far from the noisy arterials where Toronto usually situates its high-density housing. Rather, these elegant apartment buildings are nestled between detached and semi-detached houses, demonstrating how these two forms can comfortably co-exist within the city's neighbourhood fabric.

TORONTO

68 KENDAL AVE

OLD CITY OF TORONTO

68 Kendal Avenue (1912)

While the Annex is the poster child for housing variety, recent efforts to add density have met with resistance from local homeowners. Proponents of the missing middle can point to Audley Court, a walk-up in the Annex on Kendal Avenue, just south of Dupont Street. Here, among the pointy roofs lining this typical Annex street, an elegant mid-rise apartment built in 1912 accommodates eight apartments in the space of two lots.

Audley Court's neoclassical balconies soften its proportions while complementing its neighbours' decorative bargeboards and ornamental trim. Used for a period of its history as a hotel, its units are now owned separately as condominiums.

ETOBICOKE

58 EMERALD CRESCENT

ETOBICOKE
58 Emerald Crescent (1938)
At the turn of the twentieth century in the formerly independent towns of Mimico and New Toronto, contractors built multiple housing types to accommodate growing populations of workers employed in the nearby rail yards and factories. To continue to attract immigrants and workers to the area in the 1950s, the Town of Mimico began demolishing older homes on large lots and replacing them with apartment buildings.

Today, between the lake and the Gardiner Expressway in south Etobicoke, there is a pleasant mix of housing types. On Emerald Crescent, near Cliff Lumsdon Park, three modest apartment buildings fit well with their neighbouring bungalows and small houses. Though all are well proportioned, 58 Emerald Crescent stands out for the Italianate moulding surrounding its windows and entranceway.

EAST YORK

135 SAMMON AVE

EAST YORK

135 Sammon Avenue (c. 1957)

Characterized by mid-century high-rises, East York doesn't otherwise deviate much from the familiar postwar suburban template of streets lined with bungalows. Yet, through the middle of old East York, parts of Cosburn Avenue achieve a 'mid-rise row' feel – a transition from single-family homes that began in the 1950s and was never quite completed.

A peculiar example of East York's gentle density can be found on Sammon Avenue, a tertiary street that runs parallel to Danforth and links several of the borough's main arteries. The three-storey apartment is unlike anything else nearby, standing out from the street's bungalows without dominating them. A few storefronts converted to residences farther east indicate that Sammon was once more commercial than it is today, which may explain how an apartment was approved here by East York council.

NORTH YORK

112 RAJAH ST

NORTH YORK

112 Rajah Street (1958)

While detached homes dominate North York's residential streets, the city also created the conditions for more mid-rises than you would expect from a suburban municipality. One cluster can be found south of Highway 401 and west of Bathurst, in Lawrence Manor. Surrounded by swaths of detached houses and a few high-rises, several streets between the 401 and the Baycrest Health Centre, including Wasdale Crescent and Neptune Drive, are lined exclusively with two- and three-storey apartments.

On Rajah Street, number 112 is a simple, rectangular eight-unit structure whose cheap corrugated exterior detracts from its otherwise understated charm. This district would benefit from more shops, but the neighbourhood is well connected to the city by the 109 Ranee bus.

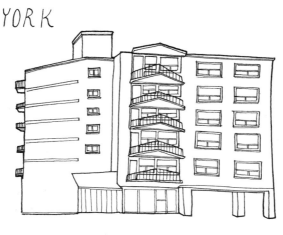

YORK

36 CHURCH ST

YORK

36 Church Street (1963)

York's streets are scattered with a more eclectic mix of housing types than other parts of Metropolitan Toronto that had stricter zoning codes. A smattering of mid-rises can be found in most of the former city's neighbourhoods, including along streets such as Wychwood Avenue, north of St. Clair West; in Rockcliffe-Smythe, near Black Creek; and in Mount Dennis.

Weston, one of York's historic centres, is surprisingly urbane for a neighbourhood so close to the 401. While its main drag is chock-a-block with small shops and high-rise apartments, a few mid-rises can be found among the mansards and decorative bargeboards of its less dense side streets. One example is the Churchill Towers, a six-storey apartment distinguished by its decorative yellow brickwork and chevron balconies.

SCARBOROUGH

138 BELLAMY RD NORTH

SCARBOROUGH

138 Bellamy Road North (2005)

The middle is truly missing in Scarborough. Other than a few early-twentieth-century mid-rises lining Kingston Avenue near the Toronto border (Victoria Park Avenue), Scarborough is defined by detached houses and high-rises, with little in between.

The Ujamaa Housing Co-op, on Bellamy Road North, is one exception. Fifty-six affordable units are provided within this gently curving, five-storey structure, built in 2005. A short distance from the Eglinton GO station, this recently built mid-rise co-op should be seen as a model for the ongoing densification of Scarborough.

Toronto is a city of many neighbourhoods developed over many decades before amalgamation.

The city's residential neighbourhoods dominate its geography. Of 641.45 square kilometres of land within the City of Toronto's borders, 50 percent (321.43 square kilometres) is zoned for residential uses. On these lands, development activity is restricted to those uses permitted under the appropriate section of Chapter 10 or 15 of City of Toronto Zoning By-law 569-2013, or the active bylaws of the pre-amalgamation municipalities (Toronto, North York, York, East York, Scarborough, and Etobicoke).

Toronto's Residential Zones:
A Field Guide
Cheryll Case

There are six different types of residential zoning. The 'R' category, mostly found in the old City of Toronto, is the most permissive – here, all housing types are permitted – while the 'RD' and 'RA' designations are the most restrictive (only detached dwellings and apartment buildings, respectively). Areas with RD zoning, which have been dubbed the Yellowbelt, are the most extensive, covering over 200 square kilometres, an area larger than Richmond Hill, Aurora, and Newmarket combined. With RD zoning, the greatest share of land has been restricted to the lowest-density, costliest, and most exclusionary form of housing. In Scarborough, East York, North York, and Etobicoke, between 68 and 76 percent of all residential land has been designated RD, exclusively for detached homes.

These zoning differences across the city directly affect the nature of Toronto's neighbourhoods – their density, their diversity, and their

Zone Category		House Type						
		Detached	Semi	Town	Duplex	Triplex	Fourplex	Apartment
	Residential (R)	✓	✓	✓	✓	✓	✓	✓
	Residential Multiple Dwelling (RM)	✓	✓		✓	✓	✓	✓
	Residential Townhouse (RT)	✓	✓	✓				
	Residential Semi-Detached (RS)	✓	✓					
	Residential Detached (RD)	✓						
	Residential Apartment (RA)							✓

relative wealth. Apartments have the most capacity to house multiple families within a single structure whereas residential detached properties have the least. Traditionally, detached homes were designed to accommodate single families, although in many older parts of Toronto, such as the Annex, houses have often been carved up into apartments.

At the same time, the zoning within a given neighbourhood doesn't necessarily predict the type of housing that can be found there. Much of the former City of York is zoned 'RM,' which allows every type of dwelling except townhouses. Yet most neighbourhoods are dominated by detached houses. Similarly, in the former City of Toronto, many neighbourhoods are zoned R, but are mostly made up of single-family dwellings. In these areas, and others zoned R, RM, RT, or RS, Official Plan policies prevent detached houses from being converted into semis, towns, duplexes, or any other housing type with increased capacity to house families. As a result, the total area restricting housing to low-capacity detached houses extends well beyond the 200-square-kilometre Yellowbelt. Through these policies, the tradition of adding housing capacity to detached houses is being erased.

Toronto has struggled to increase housing capacity within RD neighbourhood areas. In 1999, in response to low vacancy rates, city council ended the ban on basement apartments, allowing secondary suites in single and semi-detached houses throughout the city. Some residents groups criticized this move, warning that the proliferation of secondary suites would cause house prices to decline (they didn't).

The secondary-suites policy was a tentative first step toward improving access and the supply of housing options within neighbourhoods. Almost twenty years later, council approved a policy allowing homeowners with rear laneway access to develop rental dwellings at the backs of their properties. But council has rejected calls to allow rooming houses – currently allowed in only a handful of downtown wards – to be permitted across the city, even though many illegal and frequently unsafe rooming houses operate in parts of Scarborough and near community colleges.

The terms housing affordability crisis and condominium boom have defined the last decade of headlines about Toronto's real estate trends. Despite the introduction of corrective measures, such as a foreign buyers' tax, concerns regarding the existence and potential scale of a housing bubble persist. At the same time, we are constantly reminded about the sheer number of cranes that dot Toronto's skyline and mark the city as an economic success story. As of early 2019, the number exceeded one hundred – equivalent to the number operating in New York, Los Angeles, and Chicago combined.

Supply, Demand, and Demographics

Sean Hertel and Blair Scorgie

The result is staggering. Toronto's multiple skylines are rapidly evolving and expanding. This phenomenon raises the question: in a city that is expanding so swiftly, with a steady supply of new condominium units coming on the market, how can Toronto be experiencing a housing affordability crisis? Why don't the laws of supply and demand seem to be working?

To unpack this riddle, we need to begin by asking the right questions. In this case: What are we building? Where are we building? And for whom are we building?

Thanks to the work of researchers and advocacy groups, it's become increasingly clear that, in Toronto, there is a mismatch between the forms of housing that are being supplied and those in demand. Many macro-economic factors influence the housing market, including interest rates, mortgage regulations, development charges, land transfer and property taxes, immigration policy, and global trade. Yet the municipality does influence this sector with a set of land-use planning policies, which encompass the Official Plan, Zoning By-law, and other performance standards. If we want to understand the failings of the local housing market, we need to figure out what's not working in our land-use planning policies.

The City of Toronto contains approximately 850,000 detached single-family dwellings, roughly 40 percent of its total housing inventory. The city also contains about 320,000 semi-detached and row-house dwellings, and about 308,000 townhouse, multiplex, and low-rise apartment units – 14 and 15 percent of its total housing inventory, respectively.

Put another way, there are more detached single-family dwellings in Toronto than all other forms of low-rise residential housing combined. The majority of the city's semi-detached, duplex, triplex, four-plex, and walk-up apartment buildings – a.k.a. the 'missing middle' – predate modern zoning regulations. Most are found in the older parts of the city (including the former City of Toronto and portions of the boroughs of York and East York), where they are permitted under zoning bylaws. Yet the zoning regulations in the postwar suburban boroughs (North York, Scarborough, and Etobicoke) don't allow these very same residential building types. Not surprisingly, this kind of housing is effectively missing from many of amalgamated Toronto's newer neighbourhoods, most of them developed from the 1950s through the 1980s.

In other words, the city's overly stringent zoning regulations both prevent the diversification of the low-rise housing stock and constrain its supply. Given that the city has developed all the way to its borders, Toronto's neighbourhoods can be considered, from a policy perspective, physically built-out to their desired and intended density. The only way most of Toronto's neighbourhoods can intensify is through the addition of basement suites, which are now permitted across the city, and laneway suites, which are permitted in certain zones throughout the former City of Toronto and East York.

So what about the demand side?

Tens of thousands of newcomers settle in Toronto and region each year. Based on the number of cranes dotting our skyline, you could be forgiven for thinking this growth was significant and potentially even unprecedented.

From 2006 to 2011, Toronto grew by an average 30,000 people annually. This figure climbed to 33,000 from 2011 to 2016, a modest increase. But these increases aren't distributed evenly across the city's geography. According to a 2017 City Planning report, 'about half of the population growth in the City of Toronto from 2011 to 2016 was south of Bloor Street, between Victoria Park Avenue in the east and the Humber River in the west.'

However, if we consider the last twenty years, the growth story begins to look a bit different. From 1996 to 2016, Toronto's population rose by approximately 15 percent, which averages about 0.75 percent per year – a relatively low and stable rate. In fact, across the Greater Toronto and Hamilton Area (GTHA), the City of Toronto has the second lowest percentage-based rate of population growth during this period. So, while Toronto is growing, the growth rate does not entirely explain the rapidly increasing demand for ground-related housing.

The overall growth numbers, moreover, tell only part of the story; demographics explain the rest. As in many large cities in the developed world, Toronto's households are shrinking. In 1996, the average household consisted of 2.65 people. By 2016, that number has decreased to 2.45 – a decline of 7 percent. As household size falls, we require an increasing number of separate housing units to accommodate the same number of people (at the peak of the baby boom, seven or eight people may have lived together in a three-bedroom home; today it will be five people, perhaps just four).

The composition of those households has also evolved. Couples are still getting married and having children, of course, but they are marrying later in life and having fewer children. On the flip side, seniors are living longer, healthier lives. They also remain independent for longer and are less likely to be living with adult children in a multi-generational home.

As for housing expectations, many young families still want ground-related housing in neighbourhoods outside the downtown or away from major centres. For these couples, such housing decisions may be made years prior to parenthood – the result of a deep-seated system of values that are inherently part of North American living and ingrained for the majority of the population.

Toronto's housing stock doesn't exactly suit this demographic picture. From 1996 to 2016, the number of units in Toronto increased by over 23 percent, or about 1.15 percent per year. In other words, we have built new housing one-and-a-half times faster than the rate of population growth.

Yet over the past two decades, the total population of Toronto's residential neighbourhoods has declined by approximately 200,000, even as the city's total population grew by about half a million.

What accounts for this gap?

By constraining the supply of new ground-related housing in Toronto and directing development to a relatively small area (the downtown, major centres, and the Avenues), we are effectively doubling down on these demographic trends.

The result is twofold. Intensifying areas (think of King and Spadina, for example, or Yonge and Eglinton) are experiencing sharply increased strains on the carrying capacity of infrastructure and local services (e.g., crowded subway platforms). By contrast, low-rise residential neighbourhoods that have endured population loss are seeing the closure of schools and child-care facilities, a decline in main-street retail, and an increased per capita tax burden pertaining to the maintenance of parks, roads, sewers, watermains, and waste-removal services.

The combination of soaring residential real estate prices and stringent zoning regulations in 'stable' neighhourhoods has prevented either of these building pressures from easing. While many young couples, families, and empty nesters don't necessarily require a detached single-family dwelling, they may still aspire to have a few bedrooms, some outdoor space, a bit of privacy, some peace and quiet, and, possibly, accessible features. Duplexes, triplexes, fourplexes, row houses, townhouses, and walk-up apartment buildings can fulfill the full range of these needs. However, such forms of ground-related housing comprise a relatively small portion of the city's housing mix, and we simply are not building more of them.

This dual dynamic poses a complicated political problem with potentially long-lasting social and economic impacts. As University of Toronto housing expert David Hulchanski has documented in his Three Cities studies, the contrast between 'have' and 'have-not' neighbourhoods is becoming increasingly stark.

'While Toronto has a wealth of opportunity,' the Toronto Community Foundation's 2017 Vital Signs report added, 'increasingly, neighbourhoods are divided into rich and poor, with fewer mixed communities.'

As a result of the widening mismatch between supply, demand, and the city's demographics, Toronto's low-rise neighbourhoods have become exclusive bastions for a minority of wealthy, established, largely older, and Caucasian residents. We ignore this spatial and socio-economic asymmetry at our collective peril.

The issue of affordable housing was front and centre in Toronto's 2018 municipal election. The city has seen skyrocketing home prices and rents for well over a decade, and now ranks as one of the world's most expensive regions when it comes to housing costs.

Defining 'Affordable'

Katrya Bolger

Against the backdrop of these wider trends, nearly half of all renters in Toronto now spend more than 30 percent of their income on rent, according to the 2018 Canadian Rental Housing Index. Moreover, a 2018 City of Toronto report indicated that rents in purpose-built units have risen to a fifteen-year high, while vacancy rates are the lowest they've been in sixteen years. Meanwhile, tens of thousands of city residents remain on waiting lists for social housing, underlining the severity of the crisis.

All this means housing has become essentially 'unaffordable' for nearly half of the city's tenants, according to the Canada Mortgage and Housing Corporation's (CMHC) long-standing definition of affordability.

Statistics like these have led residents and politicians to characterize the situation as a crisis. Yet, despite all the urgent debate, scant attention has been paid to what 'affordability' really means, and how shifting official definitions of this term have affected the provision of new housing in the city.

The City of Toronto currently defines affordable rental housing as units priced at or below the average market rent (AMR), by unit type. But advocacy groups have criticized this definition. The Association for Community Organizations for Reform Now (ACORN Canada) argues that any measure of housing affordability should be based on a clear understanding of what affordability actually means for individuals and families in a given market, rather than being based solely on prevailing prices for rental units in that area.

The national definition of affordable housing has been revised over time. CMHC's threshold (i.e., housing that costs less than 30 percent of pre-tax household income) has been in use since the 1980s.

In fact, the expenditure-to-income metric can be traced back to nineteenth-century studies of household budgets, and was reflected in the common turn-of-the-century saying, 'one week's pay for one month's rent,' according to University of Toronto housing expert David Hulchanski. The 20 percent rule of thumb was used until the 1950s, but rose to 25 percent during the 1960s, before eventually settling at the current standard. Most social-housing providers, including Toronto Community Housing and many co-ops, still use a rent-geared-to-income formula for determining rates for their tenants.

The city's benchmark, by contrast, is a market-based definition of affordability, not a measure of a household's ability to pay. When average market prices rise faster than average household incomes, the city's working definition of affordability actually becomes increasingly unattainable.

The decision to rely on market averages reflects our society's increased reliance in recent decades on the private sector to provide most housing. In Canada, the average market rent is determined based on an annual CMHC survey that looks at all occupied units in the country. In 2018, the average market rent for a one-bedroom apartment in Toronto was $1,202 a month, with $1,426 for a two-bedroom unit.

Yet the cost of market housing (including for rental units) has risen far faster than incomes, making the average-rent benchmark meaningless when it comes to defining affordability. In a recent study, ACORN argued that truly 'affordable' would be around $930 a month for a one-bedroom unit. According to the CMHC benchmark for affordability, the pre-tax household income required to afford an average Toronto rental ($1,200–$1,400/month) is $52,000.

But is $52,000 an average income? While the 2016 census showed that median household income in the city is almost $66,000, the survey also found that 56 percent of Torontonians – over 1.3 million people – earned less than $40,000 before taxes.[1]

The lack of a shared definition of affordability among the different levels of government suggests a problematic disconnect, leading some critics to say that aligning definitions may go some way toward ensuring that, moving ahead, governments take a more consistent or coordinated approach to affordable housing.

In refining its approach to affordability, Toronto may look to other major Western cities to benefit from their experiences. In Vienna, for example, 60 percent of residents live in social housing and rent is controlled so people do not pay more than 30 percent of their income. The city's long-standing investment in social housing and large housing subsidies from the national government means there have been no shortages in recent times, and social housing wait-lists are virtually non-existent.

The perceived success of Vienna's approach to affordable housing gives credence to the income-based approach. The city's track record, however, cannot be explained solely by how Vienna defines affordable housing; it depends heavily on a long history of social-housing construction, financial commitments from government, and a political culture that accepts a substantial role for the state in the provision of housing for its citizens.

Vienna receives €450 million (C$676.7 million) a year from its national government for housing, supplemented by the special housing taxes administered by the city itself (cities in Austria have more wide-ranging taxation powers than the average Canadian city). Vienna's annual housing budget amounts to about $900 million a year. In comparison, Canada spends roughly $2 billion a year on social housing for the entire country.

As Austrian architect Gabu Heindl noted in a 2017 interview with *The Tyee*: 'There's a big tradition based on the time of Red Vienna, which was between the two world wars when Vienna had a socialist government. Vienna has been famous for municipal housing that was built then and after 1945 in quite extensive numbers. So, when it comes to Vienna … there's absolutely an understanding that it's a municipal task to provide affordable housing and to subsidize housing.'

Montreal offers another example of a city with more affordable housing, much of it in the form of privately owned apartments. While

First tenants of a house built in a day, 1911.

Montreal has a relatively stable and diversified economy, it hasn't experienced the sort of extensive real estate speculation that afflicts Toronto and Vancouver. Besides an abundance of low-rise and relatively affordable private rental stock, Montreal has promoted market-based housing policies and programs for low-income groups, including an October 2018 plan to develop 12,000 social and affordable housing units on the island by 2021 using rent supplements, the purchase of lands by the municipality, and funding support for specific housing projects. Some of the financing to support these initiatives comes from the provincial government.

What the Montreal experience highlights is the importance of built form (e.g., an abundance of modestly priced rental apartments in low-rise buildings in areas like the Plateau), combined with the commitment of governments (municipal and provincial) to investing in affordable housing (e.g., the city's 'inclusive strategy' calls for 15 percent of new housing units to be 'affordable'). With these components, Montreal's housing market has remained more affordable, even though its housing policies aren't guided by a specific definition of affordability.

Housing experts and advocates alike suggest that any plausible definition of affordable housing should be based on a clear understanding of what affordability actually means for individuals and families. For many housing activists, this goal means the definition should be linked to an objective measure of household income, since that figure most clearly reflects what low-income and moderate-income residents can afford.

The benchmark of affordability has real implications for what ultimately gets built because this metric is used to guide planning policies and individual development applications.

In New York City, for example, Mayor Bill de Blasio's ambitious 2014 housing strategy calls for the construction or renovation of 300,000 units by 2026, many of which are targeted at residents with an income below $46,000 per year. In the program's first four years, a remarkable 120,000 affordable units have been built. This reveals the need to focus on a range of income brackets, and not just average prices, when developing an affordability plan. De Blasio's plan reflects a household's actual ability to cover the rent – not only what is minimally affordable.

Canada is one among few Western countries to depend nearly entirely on market mechanisms for its housing stock. About 95 percent of Canadian households currently obtain their housing through the open market. However, households living in poverty with poor social safety nets don't have enough spending power to influence private housing developers, which means the housing markets tend not to respond to their needs.

While governments have introduced tax breaks for developers, waived development charges or provided direct funding for building projects, such decisions need be driven by a clear sense of who is going to benefit, and how those most vulnerable will be protected. In this respect, the current definition of housing affordability in Toronto has not helped produce units that low-income to moderate-income households can actually afford.

What follows are my experiences as a low-income and recently homeless Torontonian struggling to secure and maintain stable and affordable housing.

To that end, I'll be mostly critical of the policies of the following agencies and programs: Toronto Employment and Social Services (TESS), which administers the Transitional Housing Assistance Program and the Housing Stabilization Fund (HSF); Ontario Works/Ontario Disability Support Program, which provides a maximum accommodation allowance of $495 per month; the Personal Needs Allowance, a former OW-related program that provided $27 per week to shelter clients; and the Community Start-Up Program (C-SUP), a former housing support program administered directly by OW/ODSP.

The Four Catch-22s of Housing Insecurity for Low-Income Torontonians

John Clapp

Before becoming homeless in June 2018, I rented sublet accommodations for about a decade and always paid my rent on time. As most rooms for rent are sublets, and as that was all I could afford, I had little choice but to rent as a sub-tenant.

As a result, I've had virtually no tenant rights. However, my lack of tenant rights did not prove to be the primary cause of my housing insecurity and recent homelessness – at least, not directly.

In February 2017, after moving into a new sublet, I applied to the City of Toronto for $600 to cover only my last month's rent, rather than the full HSF stipend of $1,700. But TESS denied my request because I was subletting a room rather than renting a room directly from the property owner.

According to provincial rules, OW/ODSP recipients don't qualify for the HSF grant when they are in sublet market rental arrangements, even though such arrangements make up the greater portion of the housing opportunities they can afford.

This is the first Catch-22.

Interior of Yonge Street Mission, 1915.

Not paying last month's rent was also a crucial factor in my recent homelessness. That meant I was not entitled to two months' notice to vacate, which, in turn, gave me insufficient time to find a new place to live. Similarly, ow/odsp recipients are also ineligible for most rent subsidies if they sublet.

This is the second Catch-22.

Even when approved, the rent subsidy payments aren't issued until the third week of the month, rather than the first week, when rent is generally due.

This is the third Catch-22.

That lag time makes it more difficult for homeless applicants to get housed, especially if they're also not eligible for the HSF. After all, what landlord will accept partial rent payments on the first and third weeks of the month?

Let's assume that a homeless applicant does fulfill all the eligibility requirements for the HSF and Transitional Housing Assistance Program. To add insult to injury, the approvals process for obtaining a grant from the HSF can take up to three weeks, so the cheque could end up being issued too late for a homeless individual to secure an arranged housing opportunity.

This is the fourth Catch-22.

It wasn't always this difficult getting housed on social assistance.

The last time I was homeless was from June 2004 to June 2005, at which point my only income was the Personal Needs Allowance, a provincial grant. When I found housing, I applied and was approved for both OW and C-SUP.

The entire process took about *five days*, not three weeks.

In 2009, however, the provincial government downloaded C-SUP to the municipalities, whereupon it evolved into the HSF. And that's when the four Catch-22s came into effect.

Homeless shelters are at maximum capacity.

As of the third quarter of 2018, there were 97,744 people on Toronto's social housing waiting lists. Applicants are told to expect to wait up to eight to ten years for placements.

At the same time, many rooming houses are being replaced by Airbnbs. The average one-bedroom apartment costs $2,400 per month or more, and the city's primary rental vacancy rate for 2019 is 1.1 percent.

Given the scarcity of affordable housing, does it not make sense to extend housing supports to include sublet market rental arrangements, issue rent subsidy payments by the first of the month, and expedite the HSF approval process?

I would argue that it does. But what do I know?

I'm just a homeless person on the receiving end of these policies.

W hen one drives through the quiet neighbourhoods of Scarborough, Etobicoke, or North York, all those winding residential streets lined with detached homes look much as they have for the past few decades. But if you could peer behind the walls, you wouldn't

Two Million Empty Bedrooms
Joy Connelly

find homes filled with children. Rather, you would see empty-nesters who have raised their families and may no longer need a three- or four-bedroom house plus finished basement. But this is the neighbourhood they've known for years, and they're not yet prepared to downsize. As for the families these homes were designed for? Priced out, many are moving to St. Catharines, Oshawa, or anywhere they can afford.

The result: though Toronto is rapidly growing – the city added over 230,000 residents from 2006 to 2016 – over half of Toronto neighbourhoods became less dense, losing about 210,000 people from 2001 to 2016. And despite an acute affordable housing shortage, Toronto now has over two million spare bedrooms – a vast but utterly underutilized resource.[1]

HOW DID THIS HAPPEN?

From the architecture of the homes to the way neighbourhoods were laid out, Toronto's postwar suburbs reflect the needs of the baby-boomer families of the 1960s, when over 30 percent of Canadian households had five or more people.[2] Two generations later, that figure had fallen to less than 10 percent. By 2011, the average Canadian household size was 2.4 people,[3] the fertility rate was 1.6 children per woman (down from a peak in the 1960s of 3.9),[4] and more people have no children at all.

While the demographics of these neighbourhoods have shifted dramatically, their built form has remained frozen in time. Across most of Toronto's suburban residential areas, the city does not permit duplexes, triplexes, laneway houses, townhouses, small apartment buildings, shared houses – in fact, any of the categories of homes that reflect Toronto's shift to smaller families.

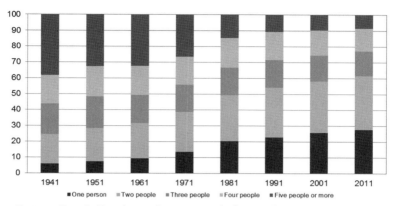

Statistics Canada, Distribution (in percentage) of private households by number of people, Canada, 1941 to 2011, Canadian Megatrends, last updated May 17, 2018.

PRESERVING A WAY OF LIFE?

Why hasn't Toronto's Official Plan kept up with changing demographics? One obvious answer is that the people who live and vote in the Yellowbelt like their neighbourhoods the way they are. In both the U.S. and Canada, the creation of the suburbs was rooted in the nuclear family and all that supports it: domesticity, home ownership, stability, and order.[5] For many who settled in Scarborough, Etobicoke, East York, and North Toronto, the detached home was a symbol of family life at its best – a reward for prudence and hard work, and an oasis from the messiness of urban living. These homeowners enjoyed the privacy and independence that a detached house on a spacious lot offered: a quiet environment defined by little-used roads and backyards.

These are not simply white-bread values held over from the 1950s – they are a very real part of the Canadian dream for many immigrant families. A 2012 federal government study showed that newcomers 'overwhelmingly' said they planned to buy a home and, despite many obstacles, achieved 'higher than expected home ownership levels.'[6]

Writing about the wave of Chinese-speaking immigrants who moved to northeast Scarborough in the 1980s and 1990s, historian Arlene Chan observed, 'It was a dream of theirs to move into the suburbs, where they could have a bigger property and a better life … a big house with a two-car garage.'[7]

SACRIFICING OUR CHILDREN TO THE 'SINGLE-DETACHED LIFESTYLE'

Until recently, many have been willing to make sacrifices to preserve this way of life: working two jobs, living in debt, foregoing holidays, and so on. But because the run-up in housing and rental costs has outpaced the growth of real household incomes, this formula has become less and less sustainable. We may have reached the point where we are in danger of sacrificing the next generation, and the very family values that inspired the suburbs in the first place. Let's start by looking at the prospects for young people in the inner suburbs:

• *School closures.* According to Cheryll Case's report, 'Protecting the Vibrancy of Residential Neighbourhoods,' 105 of the Toronto District School Board's schools are under review because of low enrolment. Should they close, 48 percent of Toronto neighbourhoods would be less family-friendly than they were before.[8]

• *Cost of Living for Post-Secondary Education Students.* Sharing a big house with other students has long made going to the University of Toronto's downtown campus affordable. But how do students at U of T's Scarborough campus, or York, or Humber, or Seneca find an affordable home near campus when shared living is illegal in nearby neighbourhoods?

• *Family Formation.* Are housing costs forcing the next generation to defer starting a family? Many young couples simply cannot afford a new baby when child-care costs would eat up the earnings they need for mortgage or rent payments. As for the 47 percent of Toronto adults aged twenty to thirty-four[9] who live with their parents, how does one settle down with a partner, let alone start a family, when you don't have a place of your own?

• *Fleeing Toronto.* An August 2018 Angus Reid poll reported that 59 percent of renters between the ages of eighteen and thirty-four are 'seriously considering' leaving the Greater Toronto Area because of the high cost of housing. According to Generation Squeeze, an advocacy group for millennials founded by University of British Columbia population-health expert Paul Kershaw, it would take fifteen years for young Canadians to save for a 20 percent down payment in Metropolitan Toronto. In 1976, families required only six years to achieve the same goal. Are the parents of adult children willing to forego watching their grandchildren grow up simply because there is nowhere for our children to live?

MORE CHOICES FOR THE INNER SUBURBS

There are many reasons to support the gentle intensification of the Yellowbelt: to take the pressure off the agricultural lands surrounding our city, to reduce sprawl, to provide effective public services, and to increase our tax base.

But for the people who live in Scarborough, Etobicoke, and North York, the most important reason may be to preserve the very values that drew them to suburban living. In her 1995 study, sociologist Laura J. Miller said the suburban ideal was 'an environment in which family ties can be strengthened.'[10] So let's embrace that goal.

Let's permit small ownership and rental apartment buildings for seniors who want to stay in the neighbourhood but are through with clearing eavestroughs. We need more two-bedroom apartments to accommodate a home office, a spare bedroom, or simply a lifetime's accumulation of lovely things, as well as more one-bedroom apartments for seniors who will need the proceeds of their house sale to finance their long-term care.

Let's facilitate new models, such as co-housing for seniors who want to keep their independence but don't want to become isolated as they grow older, or backyard second suites to enable seniors and their adult children to stay together while enjoying their own privacy. These models have not yet been recognized in current Yellowbelt zoning. They should be actively encouraged.

Let's increase affordable opportunities for young families: duplexes and triplexes to allow young couples to buy while they rent other parts of their house; townhouses that offer children a backyard at a price their parents can afford; and rental homes of all sizes.

Let's allow young singles to stay in the neighbourhoods in which they grew up. Anyone earning less than Toronto's $30,089 median income for an individual[11] has been entirely shut out of the condo market and cannot afford the average $1,098 for a one-bedroom in the inner suburbs.[12] As for a more affordable bachelor apartment? In east Scarborough, for example, there were only ninety-eight bachelor apartments available in the private rental market in 2017. In north Etobicoke, there were only thirty. In all of North York, with a population of 656,000, the housing stock contains only 1,332 bachelor units.[13]

Let's legalize shared houses for students, newcomers, and other singles seeking a family atmosphere at a price they can afford. In her 2014 study of Toronto's suburban rooming houses for the Wellesley Institute, analyst Lisa Freeman noted that rooming houses in Toronto's inner suburbs are home to immigrant seniors nudged out of their children's homes, lifelong suburbanites who didn't want to leave the area, and former downtowners looking for a quieter alternative to downtown living.[14] These tenants are not interlopers. They are suburbanites living in the postwar parts of Toronto who happen to have low incomes.

Every one of these initiatives would allow the inner suburbs to sustain family values into the twenty-first century. The picket fences will stay. And families will be able to stay together.

In the opening of her 2014 novel, *Love Enough*, Dionne Brand paints an uninviting picture of Dupont Street: 'It is perhaps because this street is so ugly; car-wrecking shops, taxi dispatch sheds, rooming houses, hardware stores, desolate all-night diners and front yards eaten up by a hundred winters' salt.' Despite its industrial grit, the six-kilometre stretch from Avenue Road to Annette Street has not been immune to Toronto's real estate boom. Subject to thirteen rezoning applications and a recent city-led regeneration study, Dupont, like many other arterials, is undergoing a transformation.

Why the Middle Is Missing:
A Developer's View
Andrea Oppedisano

By the late 2020s, many of its factories and autobody shops will have been replaced by sleek mixed-use condos backing onto the railway corridor that swoops through midtown.

Part of these looming changes can be attributed to Adam Sheffer. With a background in finance and new to the development world, he is the keen young principal at Originate Developments Inc., the firm behind a small infill project at the corner of Dupont and Brunswick. In 2017, he sought approval from the Committee of Adjustment to replace two single-family detached homes with six town homes that will likely sell for $2 million each.

The process, which he describes as 'pretty positive,' ran into a hiccup with only days left to the hearing date – a disagreement between city divisions about the width of a proposed driveway. The urban designers supported a narrower lane while the engineers wanted it wider. 'We got caught in the crosshairs,' remarks Sheffer. 'There is a reason why engineers don't plan cities – we would all have the exact same house.'

Lane widths aside, Sheffer's project raises tough questions: given that a subway stop is only metres away, should this type of housing be built in such a location? And if it's not, what prevents forms that are both denser but still in keeping with their urban surroundings?

'If I'm being totally honest,' muses Sheffer, 'I don't think we are doing the best thing for the community. I think we are building beautiful homes, but to build six $2 million townhouses is probably not what the city needs.'

Like many other successful, fast-growing cities, Toronto needs more affordable places to live, including the sort of low-rise apartments and walk-ups found in many older neighbourhoods such as the Annex, where Sheffer's luxury project is located.

If you want to identify one reason for this absence, read Chapter 4 in Toronto's Official Plan, and the Neighbourhoods policies. Residential Neighbourhoods make up approximately 60 percent of residential land in the city, and the OP requires that any new development respect and reinforce their existing physical character, which is determined by the size and configuration of lots, heights, massing, scale, and building types. The net effect of these policies means a developer or property owner can only build what already exists. That's why builders like Sheffer are far more likely to develop luxury townhouses than low-rise apartments. This allows the zoning to be tweaked through the Committee of Adjustment process instead of requiring a full rezoning or an amendment to the Official Plan.

Yet, unlike most builders, Sheffer is pursuing a missing-middle-type project. His next project proposes replacing two existing detached homes with a four-storey rental apartment building on Huron Street, just south of Dupont Street, about 250 metres from the subway entrances. Given that the two buildings currently contain nineteen affordable rental units, the project is subject to Toronto's rental replacement policies, which restrict their demolition outright. Complying with the policies, Sheffer's project will replace the existing nineteen rental units at similar rents while adding thirty-three new market-rate apartments.

This modest project, in theory, should be a slam dunk. It appears to fit into the Annex by continuing one of the prevailing built forms in the area. Sheffer's design would not tower over or crowd neighbouring homes.

Yet the plan has met significant resistance on multiple fronts. City planners told Sheffer's team to reduce the density, provide more parking, and make the units bigger. The Annex Residents' Association, the community's powerful ratepayers group, also raised red flags. 'The area is supposed to be stable and you are adding density,' Sheffer was told.

Such objections, rooted in a narrow reading of the Official Plan's Neighbourhoods policy, reveal the confusion over what we mean when we talk about density.

In land-use planning, density is a measure of how intensely the land is used. Toronto's zoning bylaws express density in terms of floor space and, in particular, the ratio of the gross floor area (that is, habitable area) to the size of the lot (a.k.a. Floor Space Index, or FSI). In many older Toronto neighbourhoods, property owners are allowed up to what's often called 'one times coverage,' which means the floor area in their dwellings should be no more than the area of the lot itself. There are, however, many variations on how to apply this limit: a one-storey building that covers the entire lot has the same density as a four-storey building that takes up only a quarter of the property.

But as Jane Jacobs warned decades ago, many people misconstrue density and overcrowding. Sheffer is keenly aware of a rich irony with his proposed rental project: its FSI is actually *lower* than the density for the six luxury townhouses he's building a few blocks away. 'When a site can support something in every way other than the prescribed density, for there to be opposition using the Neighbourhoods argument seems odd,' he says. 'Toronto is in dire need of purpose-built rental. Our FSI here is lower than the six town homes at Brunswick. I don't get it.'

A 2008 Neptis Foundation report notes that while density can usefully describe urban form in *quantitative* terms, its ability to capture *qualitative* characteristics is limited. Density is a regulatory concept expressed by the physical parameters of a building. But the regulation of density is a poor way of achieving larger city-building outcomes, such as providing housing choices like affordable rental.

Builders, for their part, evaluate a potential project using four main components: the price of land, soft costs (architectural, engineering, financing, legal and development fees), hard costs (construction), and expected profits.

As in most industries, time is money. The longer it takes to get a proposal approved, the more money will be spent on soft costs. If it takes the same amount of time and resources to obtain an approval to build a tower or a mid-rise, there is little incentive to develop the lower option, despite consumer demand.

From a financing perspective, Sheffer explains that rental buildings are valued differently: they are always going to be worth less per square foot than a condo or town home, which means builders have to work harder to secure the funds needed to carry out construction. Development charges imposed on new housing don't help, either. These levies, meant to pay for the additional infrastructure required by new development, are the same across the city, regardless of land-use designation or tenure – charges imposed on a condo are the same as those of a rental building. Even though the city needs more mid-rise rental housing, the obstacles to building such stock pile up.

The bottom line is that the odds seem to be stacked against the missing middle projects like the one Sheffer wants to construct on Huron Street. While some planners insist policies are doing what they were intended to do – protect stable residential neighbourhoods – perhaps it's time to ask difficult questions: by continuing to protect residential areas with elaborate land-use rules, whom are we excluding?

Lower-income tenants and families, certainly, but also those builders who would create low-rise rental projects but for all the bureaucratic impediment and homeowner resistance they encounter along the way. In fact, Sheffer has heard the message loud and clear: *Stay out of the Neighbourhoods.*

'There are similar projects that look viable on paper,' he observes, 'but the opposition from the residents' associations and the planning department led me to pass.'

His next development will be a high-rise condo on Sheppard Avenue.

In December 2015, Toronto city council quietly adopted a complex land-use planning regulation known as Official Plan Amendment 320 – a set of policies governing the city's neighbourhoods and apartment neighbourhoods. As it moved through the approvals process, OPA 320 generated almost no public scrutiny. Only thirty-five people attended the statutory public meeting held to solicit input. The council debate, in turn, attracted virtually no media coverage or debate among pundits.

Dissecting Official Plan Amendment 320

Blair Scorgie

But this bylaw wasn't just one of the many minor technical decisions council routinely makes. Though approved by Ontario's minister of municipal affairs in July 2016, the policy generated plenty of pushback, with fifty-seven appeals launched by neighbourhood and ratepayer groups as well as various landowners. The majority were resolved, and in December 2018, the Local Planning Appeal Tribunal (LPAT – the successor to the Ontario Municipal Board) signed off on a final version of the bylaw. It now constitutes the city's formal land-use policy governing the evolution of Toronto's neighbourhoods.

OPA 320 is arguably one of the most consequential planning policies ever approved by the post-amalgamation Toronto council. This ambiguously worded document will dictate what can and cannot be developed in Toronto's residential neighbourhoods for decades to come. As such, it may play a critical role in determining everything from real estate values to the built form of Toronto's neighbourhoods, which account for about two-thirds of the city's land mass. But OPA 320 will also regulate who gets to live where, because it has imposed subtle restrictions on the physical changes that may occur in neighbourhoods.

In a city that adds tens of thousands of people each year and struggles to provide affordable housing to many, the impact of OPA 320 raises difficult and important questions about how Toronto intensifies. Beyond its ambiguity, the general direction of OPA 320's policies is also counterproductive. Instead of maintaining their stability, the regulations will directly contribute to the creation of neighbourhoods that are static, inflexible, and in decline. The cumulative effect will be to drive up the cost of housing at unprecedented and unsustainable rates while creating a mismatch between the forms of housing that are being supplied and those that are in demand, among them low-rise missing middle forms, such as duplexes, triplexes, and walk-up apartments.

These trends will exacerbate wealth polarization and socio-economic segregation throughout Toronto, and especially in the Yellowbelt. The land-use restrictions will also accelerate the population loss already taking place in many residential enclaves, which will in turn render communities less vibrant and resilient. Those neighbourhoods will see the closure of school and child-care facilities, the decline of main-street retail, and an increased per-person tax burden relating to the maintenance of municipal infrastructure.

Herewith, a semantic guide through a policy that aspires to freeze Toronto's neighbourhoods.

'PREVAILING CHARACTER'

Most of us have a sense of what makes our neighbourhoods distinct: the mix of architecture, the trees, the width of the side streets, and so on. What's more, a neighbourhood's character evolves over time, reflecting countless decisions by the people who've lived there over an extended period.

The Official Plan, however, seeks to define, at a theoretical level, precisely what we mean when we talk about a neighbourhood's 'prevailing physical character.' The definition includes a range of criteria:
- patterns of streets, blocks, and lanes, parks, and public building sites;
- size and configuration of lots;
- heights, massing, scale, and dwelling type(s) of nearby residential properties;
- prevailing building type(s);

- setbacks of the building from the street or streets;
- prevailing patterns of rear and side-yard setbacks and landscaped open spaces;
- continuation of special landscape or built-form features that contribute to the unique physical character of a neighbourhood; and
- conservation of heritage buildings, structures, and landscapes.

While some degree of change is anticipated to occur through renovations, additions, and infill development, neighbourhoods are meant, as a matter of policy, to remain physically stable, and therefore protected from intensification.

OPA 320, however, introduced an additional condition: that new development should respect and reinforce a neighbourhood's 'prevailing' physical character (as well as 'prevailing' densities, dwelling types, setbacks, and the location, design, and elevation relative to the grade of driveways and garages).

But what does 'prevailing' really mean when we talk about a neighbourhood's physical character? There are many ways to interpret this word: 'frequent,' 'occurring on many occasions,' or 'in quick succession.' Does it mean 'the majority'? Likely not. While revised language[1] approved by the LPAT in December 2018 provided a bit more clarity, the term remains inherently ambiguous. How do we define some of the phrases in that ruling – for example, 'most frequently occurring'? How do we determine a 'mix of characters'? And what constitutes a 'significant presence'? To layer onto the confusion, the policies direct us to consider nearby residential properties when determining what 'prevailing' means with respect to height, massing, scale, and dwelling type, but they don't define how to determine where those nearby residential properties are.

To secure a building permit, homeowners, planners, and developers must now grapple with OPA 320's definitional complexity. For instance, if someone wants to build a project in the middle of a residential block, how should they calculate what constitutes the prevailing character of that particular place? Is the frame of reference limited to the eight dwellings immediately surrounding that property, or does it extend farther, to the entire block? If, for example, there are a few houses that are taller, wider, or deeper, or that contain secondary suites nearby, is that a prevailing form? Even though these buildings may contain multiple units, their ground-floor entrances and appearances at street level could be consistent with the look and feel of a single dwelling unit. Under such circumstances, is it appropriate to renovate detached single-family dwellings to include one or more secondary suites?

Or let's suppose the property's owners are empty-nesters with grown children starting their own families. Mobility is becoming an issue and there are few accessible-housing options within the neighbourhood. Rather than selling and moving away, they decide to leverage the equity in their home to renovate it into three separate units, two of which will be rented out to cover the cost of their mortgage and renovations. To these owners, this change would seem both reasonable and practical. However, there is a risk that their neighbours, the residents' association, and potentially even the city will oppose these changes, arguing that such renovations don't respect the area's prevailing character.

'PREVAILING BUILDING TYPE(S)'

Toronto's Official Plan identifies a range of residential building types that are generally considered appropriate throughout the city's neighbourhoods. These include detached houses, semi-detached houses, duplexes, triplexes, townhouses, and walk-up apartment buildings. The city's land-use policies envision that all neighbourhoods will remain four storeys or less in height, with relatively low densities.

But OPA 320 adds a crucial condition. It states that new development should respect 'prevailing' building type(s). What do we do when neighbourhoods have more than one prevailing building type? Or when they have several? Again, the city's neighbourhoods policy provides no direction on how to determine which is which.

Take the case of a proposed three-storey apartment building on a lot surrounded by single-family homes. The design calls for ground-

Aerial view of a Toronto subdivision, 1950s.

floor entrances, and the building will look, from the sidewalk, like a three-storey house. Under these circumstances, is this modest apartment building appropriate? The owners may be small-scale developers who specialize in building and maintaining purpose-built rental housing. They believe there is a shortage of rental housing and feel the site poses a great opportunity to diversify the existing housing stock. Their project has been designed to fit in harmoniously with the neighbourhood.

Yet there will be a risk that neighbours, the residents' association, and potentially even the city will try to block this modest venture, arguing it runs afoul of the policies that protect the area's character. Indeed, the city's planning department has already sought to block such projects, citing precisely these provisions in OPA 320.[2]

'GEOGRAPHIC NEIGHBOURHOOD'

Besides the language regulating the prevailing physical character of neighbourhoods, OPA 320 for the first time introduced criteria to define the geographic boundaries – major roads, ravines, etc. – of neighbourhoods as they relate to individual development sites. It's one more layer developers, contractors, and homeowners now need to account for when they propose missing-middle-type projects.

With our geographic neighbourhood boundaries in place, we must now evaluate development proposals against the prevailing physical character of the entire area. Where the city's previous land-use policies allowed for some degree of interpretation, OPA 320 layers on additional criteria – more conditions that builders will need to satisfy in order to secure a building permit.

• *Block Scale* – This includes adjacent and surrounding properties, which front onto either side of the same street within the same block; and

• *Neighbourhood Scale* – This includes properties on adjacent and surrounding blocks, within the previously determined boundaries of the geographic neighbourhood.

The policy goes on to state that future development will be 'materially consistent' with the prevailing character of the geographic neighbourhood, at both scales. 'In instances of significant difference between these two contexts,' according to the LPAT's December 2018 ruling about OPA 320, 'the immediate context will be considered to be of greater relevance. The determination of material consistency will be limited to consideration of the physical characteristics of properties within the geographic neighbourhood. Any impacts of adjacent, more intensive development in another land use designation may also be considered when assessing the appropriateness of a development.'

These words seem to mean that new developments are compatible or can co-exist harmoniously with what already exists in a geographic neighbourhood in terms of design or materials. But where do we draw the line between flexibility and rigidity? And are we meant to assess the compatibility of a proposed project according to what else exists within the block, or does OPA 320 cast the net even wider? We are meant to consider both scales, with priority given to the immediate context when there are significant differences. Yet even the LPAT's additional interpretation doesn't completely clear up the confusion.

Think about the case of that proposed three-storey apartment building cited above. How does it compare to all properties that front onto the same street within the same block, as well as the properties that encompass the broader geographic neighbourhood? And what becomes of this project if it sits on a property that happens to be located near the edge of the neighbourhood – for example, adjacent to a major street that is served by public transit and has a few other three-storey apartments? Given these factors, is this three-storey apartment building appropriate for that community? To the property's owners, who see it as a unique opportunity to put up some modest purpose-built rental housing, the context seems both reasonable and practical. Yet the language in OPA 320 allows the neighbours, the residents' association, and potentially even the city to argue that it doesn't fit.

INSIDE OR OUT?

To protect Toronto's residential stability, the Official Plan states that higher-density forms of development along major streets should not be taken into account when assessing a neighbourhood's prevailing building type(s) or its physical character. It is as if the policy implies that such dwellings, and their residents, aren't a legitimate part of the neighbourhood, and may actually form part of a separate geographic neighbourhood condition.

Consider the example of a property that fronts onto a major street traversing a geographic neighbourhood. It may contain a low or mid-rise apartment building whose residents shop in the same places as the homeowners living in the interior of the adjoining neighbourhood. They may send their children to the same schools and walk their dogs in the same parks. Yet, for the purposes of the city's new neighourhood planning policies, these dwellings are actually 'distinguishable from those located in the interior of the neighbourhood' due to the differences in lot configuration, access to transit, exposure to traffic, and proximity to developments of even greater height, mass, or scale.

We can find this kind of form along many corridors, including Bayview, Mount Pleasant, Eglinton, Lawrence, Kingston Road, Woodbine, York Mills, Finch, Jane, Islington, Kipling, and many others corridors, most served by transit and, in some cases, bike lanes.

What is the Official Plan saying here? Is the intent to prevent these higher-density forms – older apartments, mostly – from infiltrating the low-rise neighbourhoods behind them? Or is the policy suggesting that these apartments are, in fact, not part of the neighbourhood? It is unclear, and the policies are open to a significant degree of interpretation.

To further complicate matters, the Official Plan also distinguishes properties internal to a geographic neighbourhood from those situated on a major street that passes through that neighbourhood – in other words, properties that form the community's outer edge. Prior to modern zoning regulations, low and mid-rise apartment buildings were constructed on streets like Mount Pleasant, St. Clair West, and Lawrence West. Today, these older buildings – officially known as 'legal non-conforming' uses – continue to operate, but they cannot be replicated, even though the zones at the edges of neighbourhoods remain ideal places for higher-density forms, such as townhouses and walk-up apartments.

For the purposes of assessing a new project, the planning rules effectively treat these older non-conforming buildings as if they didn't exist – that is, they can't be seen as creating any kind of precedent. Yet does it make sense to ignore them entirely? Can't we see them as providing a form of development that creates a transition between busier traversing major streets and the residential ones internal to neighbourhoods?

Not according to the pre-OPA 320 version of Toronto's Official Plan, which not only discouraged low-rise intensification on major streets; it stated that exceptions within low-rise areas – i.e., the mid-rise apartments that can be found on side streets in many older areas – don't count when reviewing a neighbourhood's prevailing physical character.

Corners, where side streets intersect with main streets, provide yet another source of ambiguity. There are many examples in the older part of the city of corner buildings that face onto a main street but extend back into the neighbourhood. Some have apartments with side entrances facing onto the residential street. Are these part of the residential neighbourhood or not? It could be appropriate to see such corner properties (also known as 'edge conditions') as having the potential to establish a transitional zone between a major street and a neighbourhood. But as with so much else in the new neighbourhood's policies, OPA 320 isn't especially clear about the degree to which this kind of development would be appropriate.

There are several issues with this kind of thinking, not least of which is that the policy contradicts other crucial land-use planning objectives, such as provincial growth-plan targets that call for intensification capable of supporting higher-order transit.

PLANNING FOR CHANGE

Grounded as it is in the rhetoric of stability, Toronto's Official Plan has sought for decades to inoculate the city's residential neighbourhoods from certain types of change that once occurred organically. The policy, far more rigid than anything found in the Official Plans of other Ontario municipalities, states that no changes will be made through rezoning, minor variance, consent, or other public action that is out of keeping with the physical character of a neighbourhood. Given the potential interpretation of these regulations, and the antiquated state of existing zoning bylaws, it stands to reason that modest, compatible, and sensitive low-rise intensification may not be considered an appropriate form of development anywhere within the city's established neighbourhoods.

Despite its seemingly prescriptive nature, this policy language is open to a significant degree of interpretation and debate, much of which has played out at the OMB and its successor, the LPAT. Even professional planners find the language hard to interpret. But beyond their semantic ambiguity, the general direction of these policies is counterproductive. Instead of maintaining the stability of neighbour-hoods, OPA 320 will directly render many Toronto neighbourhoods static, inflexible, and vulnerable to decline.

The scale is important to note here. Established neighbourhoods occupy over half of the city's physical land mass. What's more, a 20,000-hectare swath of Toronto's neighbourhoods – equivalent to about one third of the city's size – is designated solely for detached single-family dwellings.

The city's annual growth rate has been increasing steadily over the last several years. From 2006 to 2011, Toronto grew by an average of 30,000 people per year, and that pace increased to 33,000 annually from 2011 to 2016. Since the last census period, Toronto's population further jumped by about 45,000 people from 2015 to 2016, and 58,000 people from 2016 to 2017.

All this growth – as well as future population increases – is now targeted for a relatively small part of the city, which encompasses the downtown, urban centres like Yonge and Eglinton, and a select number of major arterial corridors, many of them lined with large, underutilized properties such as car dealerships, malls, or former industrial sites. These areas are subject to specific urban structure and land-use policies that direct development (and therefore invest-ment) toward high-rise point tower and linear mid-rise buildings. In the aggregate, these land-use policies serve to preclude missing middle forms of ground-related housing, even though so many Toronto neighbourhoods have been well served by precisely this type of gentle density for decades.

If the city were to simply permit the construction of one duplex per hectare in all the neighbourhoods zoned exclusively for detached single-family dwellings (a 200-square-kilometre area), we could add housing for 45,000 people. As outlined above, this is consistent with Toronto's annual rate of population growth. Instead, the city has approved stringent regulations that prevent the diversification of our low-rise housing stock and constrain Toronto's housing supply.

These restrictions block young couples and families from entering the housing market, and prevent empty nesters and seniors from finding smaller, more accessible forms of housing within their neighbourhoods. Ultimately, these rules create a mismatch between the forms of housing that are being supplied and those that are in demand.

Toronto's housing crunch has reached crisis levels, thanks in large measure to the arcane language embedded in our Official Plan. If we don't change course, and soon, the city will run a very real risk of alienating and pricing out an entire generation of young people – a development that will have significant negative implications. We have an opportunity to forestall decline. But to shift courses, we'll need to update our land-use planning frameworks so they align with the realities of a fast-growing city.

'A community is defined not only by who resides within it but also by those who do not.'

– Osita Nwanevu, *The New Yorker*, November 2018

Inside and Outside:
A Meditation on the Yellowbelt
Anna Kramer

The basement-dwelling tenant whose rent helps pay the mortgage on the house upstairs. The high-rise apartment building standing between a fast-moving traffic arterial and a neighbourhood of houses. The Torontonians buying houses in Hamilton to escape Toronto prices. These divisions operate on multiple scales, from the building to the neighbourhood to the city. What do they have in common? I will argue that they are all, in part, shaped by planning policy.

To see this process, we need to look beyond policy statements and examine their effects. Current planning wisdom enshrines the values of sustainability, public participation, and community benefits. Toronto's Official Plan calls for a denser, lower-carbon city, where people can walk, bike, and use transit instead of driving, while taking advantage of existing infrastructure and amenities. Provincial legislation calls for protecting the surrounding rural greenbelt. Planning processes require community consultation and community benefits. All this is to the public good.

If you ask the development industry, it is time to cut these regulations to pieces. Planning, to a developer's eye, is basically red tape. Loosening rules on development would result in more housing and more affordability. Yet the assumptions about deregulation do not offer an adequate view of the situation. There are competing theories on the consequences. Real estate economists model whether and how adding supply would lower costs, while critical geographers and activists point to examples of redevelopment as gentrification and displacement.

While supply-side arguments are often simplistic, it is worth examining the system by which the city is currently being planned – a system that espouses progressive ideals yet shapes housing in a manner that is extractive, exclusionary, and unsustainable. Land-use planning has exacerbated inequality between the landowner and the renter; between the person who lives in a neighbourhood and the person who lives outside it; between those whose quality of life is protected and those whose day-to-day existence is not valued; and, ultimately, between individuals who can afford to live in the city and individuals who can't.

STABLE NEIGHBOURHOODS

Existing low-density neighbourhoods cover the majority of Toronto. The built fabric of neighbourhoods varies from stately Victorian brick homes to eclectic self-built houses, single-detached to row houses. The zoning also varies within neighbourhoods. The older parts of Toronto have a greater mixture of types, from single detached to low-rise multi-units. The inner suburbs are mostly limited to single-detached. What they do have in common is that they are well-served by social infrastructure like schools, parks, and libraries, mostly within walking distance of transit and main streets with shops. And most homes are separated from major flows of traffic, which pose a danger to human health through exposure to noise and air pollution. Even a few hundred metres of distance can make a measurable difference in particulates and decibels.

What they also all have in common is that Toronto's 'Neighbour-hoods' policy effectively prevents any significant number of new homes from being added. The Official Plan and zoning rules restrict redevelopment to renovations and rebuilds that conform to the existing form and character – streets lined with low density and low-rise houses.

Meanwhile, many such areas have lost population density over time. For reference, the newest regional Growth Plan calls for four hundred people and jobs (combined) per hectare in the densest urban growth centres and two hundred people and jobs per hectare around subway stations. In this context, the fact that some Toronto neighbourhoods have lost fifty to two hundred people per hectare in the past two generations, despite being clustered near subways and proximate to downtown, is notable. This population loss in 'stable' neighbourhoods works against all the intensification occurring in growth centres.

Population density lost between 1971 and 2016

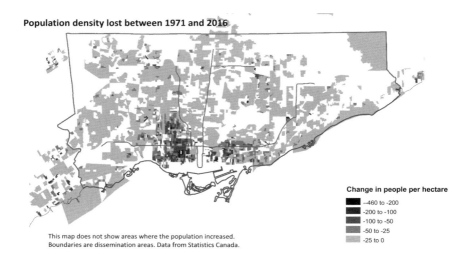

This map does not show areas where the population increased.
Boundaries are dissemination areas. Data from Statistics Canada.

Change in people per hectare
- -460 to -200
- -200 to -100
- -100 to -50
- -50 to -25
- -25 to 0

At the same time, the cost of housing in these neighbourhoods has diverged significantly from median incomes. There are ways for the less affluent to live here, but they come with real caveats. In areas zoned for low-rise housing, owners rent out entire houses, suites within houses, or rooms within houses. Some of this hidden rental may be affordable, especially for longer-term tenants protected by rent control. But some may be unsuitable, especially basement apartments that were never designed or intended for habitation. Such housing is often insecure, as the owner can remove tenants if they want to move in or sell the property.

It's remarkable how many homeowners in Greater Toronto own their homes outright, without a mortgage – 36.8 percent, according to the 2016 census. For these people, the housing crisis doesn't exist, and rising prices are a bonus. We don't know enough about the partially hidden and insecure-rental landscapes in neighbour-hoods, or about the diverging situations of homeowners based on time of purchase. But we do know that prices for incoming renters or buyers are very high, and, as a result, these neighbourhoods are becoming more exclusive.

Would allowing denser development help? That is difficult to predict precisely. And yet homeowners are already pouring massive amounts of money into renovating their houses in neighbourhoods. If so much investment is going into essentially rebuilding neighbour-hoods within the limitations of the existing building envelopes and footprints, why not add some more units while we're at it?

GROWTH CENTRES AND AVENUES

While excluding new housing from neighbourhoods, the city's land-use plans direct development to 'Growth Centres' and major corridors in mid-rise and high-rise form. Almost all the new homes meant to accommodate Toronto's population growth are planned for these areas. In districts designated for intensification, there are often layers of ever more detailed plans. These include high-level policy (such as the province's Growth Plan and the city's Official Plan, which calls for mixed-use mid-rise along avenues); detailed area plans that set out appropriate heights; and urban design guidelines that ensure that new buildings' volumes won't overshadow adjacent neighbourhoods while leaving enough space for the public realm along the street.

Despite these multiple layers of planning policies, which have involved community consultation, the development process is neither smooth nor predictable. In almost all cases, the zoning for particular sites has not been updated to match current policy vision. When zoning does not match plans on a development site, the city must enact a rezoning or an official plan amendment. This rezoning process is a negotiation that can take more than a year. It may involve multiple city departments with sometimes conflicting requirements (heritage, transportation, urban design), the city councillor, local residents, and the developer.

The rezoning process captures some of the value of new development through fees to pay for planners' time and 'voluntary' contributions to pay for public amenities. Such payments come in addition to development charges, which amount to tens of thousands of dollars per unit. The value extracted from new development, along with the land transfer tax, contributes significant revenues to the city budget and enables city council to keep property taxes relatively low. In fact, the city relies on the development of new housing, and the buying and selling of existing housing, to cover a growing share of city costs. In other words, rather than being seen as a public good or a community benefit in itself, new housing can be regarded as a zone of extraction.

The requirement to rezone also makes the development process less predictable than it would otherwise be. It adds uncertainty in time, cost, and built form. An applicant does not know how long a planning approval will take, how much they must pay for community benefits charges, and what density the city will ultimately permit. Developers must build this uncertainty into their business model when contemplating projects, and the additional risk makes development more expensive.

There is an economic debate about whether these additional costs are passed on to buyers of market units or absorbed into land costs. But there is little discussion about how the high cost of development discourages more modest projects on smaller and less profitable sites. By making these projects less financially viable, the cost of regulatory uncertainty cuts out a group of smaller-equity and non-profit developers that could otherwise add housing.

Purpose-built rental housing already faces challenges to compete with condo projects for development feasibility. Condos are largely financed by pre-sales while rental projects tend to take longer to recoup initial capital costs. If a developer is going to go through the long and uncertain development approval process, they might as well build the tallest luxury condo tower possible in a high-profile area, preferably one with little neighbourhood opposition.

The knock-on effects of these policies reach across the city. The way development actually works in Toronto effectively limits housing development to larger projects by experienced and well-capitalized real estate firms. The economic and planning system, moreover, incentivizes an abundance of small condo units, pre-sold to investors, in high-rise buildings outside existing residential neighbourhoods. We can speculate about whether or not the current system also discourages the kind of housing we need – family-size, purpose-built rental, in or near residential neighbourhoods with community amenities and social infrastructure.

These layers of policies, plans, and development processes enable a transfer of wealth from young to old and from renter to landowner. In any case, landowners gain the most from rising prices, whether the land is a development site within the small area available for intensification, or property beneath one of those low-density homes. Those who already own property, win.

PLANNING RATIONALE?

There are reasons for underzoning.

Restrictive underzoning in the context of stable neighbourhoods is meant to protect the good and desirable features of livable neighbourhoods: light, air, quiet, and trees. But is it possible to protect these qualities while allowing for more affordable housing units to be added?

Extractive underzoning in growth centres and along avenues is meant to allow the city to both control new development and capture value from new development for investment in community benefits. Section 37 contributions – payments made by the developer in exchange for additional density – have underwritten new libraries. Parks levies have funded new green spaces. And the city uses development charges to pay for infrastructure like sewers, transit, and roads.

But who ought to pay for these city-building investments? Should the burden fall on all city residents according to their ability, or does it rest on the shoulders of newcomers through high housing costs, with the greatest burden falling on those with lowest incomes?

The patterns and processes of housing systems in the city, which are shaped by planning, ultimately extract time and resources from the everyday lives of people in the city, particularly renters and newcomers, both in cost of housing and in quality of life. In the current practice of adding density-on-density in growth centres and along corridors while keeping affordable housing out of neighbourhoods, the quality of life of existing and future residents in high-density areas is overlooked. The impacts of the uneven development on people's lived experiences are stark.

Most high-growth areas are not designated as 'Neighbourhoods' in city plans, and it follows that they are not afforded the same consideration, protection, and amenities as traditional low-rise residential enclaves. Although the downtown has been designated as a Growth Centre since 2006, it wasn't until recently that the city enacted a land-use plan, known as TOCORE, acknowledging that residential intensification has taken place throughout the formerly commercial downtown. TOCORE's objective is to play catch-up, finding ways to add social infrastructure like parks, libraries, schools, and community amenities to what amounts to a giant new neighbourhood.

New condo clusters in Liberty Village, the South Core, and lower Yonge Street have been added along transit corridors that are already overcrowded and do not have significant capacity for new passengers. Plans for transit-oriented development tend to focus on 'higher order transit' like rail, ignoring the more extensive and frequent transit network of buses and streetcars that are within walking distance of most Toronto neighbourhoods.

The siting of higher-density buildings is also often problematic. Because homeowners see condo towers as undesirable neighbours, the city has directed them to land parcels along major corridors and highways, or packed onto former industrial lands.

The city's lack of consideration for the residents of higher-density and more affordable areas has a long tradition in Toronto. Although most people wouldn't draw a comparison between high-rise condos downtown and inner-suburban apartment towers, there is continuity in these development patterns. The wave of modern high-rise apartment buildings constructed between the 1960s and the 1980s, and which now form the bulk of (relatively) affordable purpose-built rental in the city, were erected around the intersections of major arterial roads and along highways, mostly in the inner suburbs. In Scarborough, main streets like Lawrence and Eglinton are lined with apartment buildings and commercial strips, which together form a protective wall around low-density single-family neighbourhoods. Contemporary large-scale redevelopment plans for commercial strips like Scarborough's Golden Mile repeat the pattern. Similar patterns of density-on-density can be seen in the plans to 'revitalize' multi-unit social-housing neighbourhoods by adding market condos, and in Official Plan amendments to consider intensification in apartment neighbourhoods.

THE COSTS OF EXCLUSION AND EXTRACTION

The costs of these patterns of development are steep, both on a personal and collective level. What's more, they are felt unevenly. Household formation rates among young people in Toronto and Vancouver are lower than in other Canadian cities, and can be attributed directly to higher rents and low vacancy rates. The most recent census (2016) showed that almost half of young adults in the Toronto region live with their parents. Renters are much more likely to be paying more than half their income in housing costs. Debt for newer homeowning households is increasingly burdensome, even as many more established homeowners have paid off their mortgages. Many people are spending so much of their time and savings on housing in one way or another: long commutes, crowding, high rents, large debts. High housing costs also push young people to forgo or delay creating families, to live in unsuitable or unaffordable housing, to spend too much of their incomes on rent or mortgages. What is a city that keeps people out or clinging to the margins of neighbourhoods, squeezed into peripheries, edges, and basements?

Of course, some residents have been dealing with the housing crisis for much longer than others. The newly house-insecure could choose to forge a politics of solidarity with those for whom housing insecurity is not a novelty. Yet such an alliance would require those with moderate or middle incomes to abandon the notion of housing as a wealth-generating extractive investment and reframe it as a movement that regards housing as a social good. Addressing these housing inequalities asks us to rethink planning policy and processes.

WHAT IS WORKING AND WHAT MIGHT WORK

Some of the City of Toronto's and Ontario's land-use planning regulations do work to protect affordability. The city's rental replacement policy, for example, prevents the redevelopment of existing apartment buildings, although it does not incentivize new affordable rental. Partial rent control prevents rent hikes above the rate of inflation for existing tenants, but these regulations don't apply to vacant apartments, so the protection doesn't extend to newcomers, young people, newly formed households, and those who have been forced to relocate.

There are changes on the horizon that demand our attention. Activists and social movements are drawing attention to the housing crisis and pushing city council to do something. As of 2019, eleven parcels of surplus municipal land are being reconsidered for mixed-income rental housing, rather than simply being sold off to the highest bidder. The city is working on inclusionary zoning, a form of value capture that could require developers to set aside affordable units in higher-density projects. The shift of the Ontario Municipal Board to the Local Planning Appeals Tribunal has raised the bar and lengthened the process for appeals, putting the power to deny or approve development more securely in planners' and councillors' hands. And in response to more ambitious targets in the latest Growth Plan, the city is also reviewing zoning and plans around major transit-station areas, some of which reach into lower-density adjacent neighbourhoods.

We don't yet know what these changes will mean for affordability. It may be that some of these reforms will have adverse or unintended impacts that make affordable development more difficult or exacerbate gentrification. Or it may be that these changes have little impact on the current situation.

But there is almost no political conversation about the overall patterns of exclusionary zoning in neighbourhoods, the effect of the development approvals processes and fiscal policy on the cost and form of new development, and strategies for adding affordable housing in existing residential zones. Public consultation processes and plans tend not to be framed in terms of economics, environmental justice, and affordability. Rather, consultations about new development focus almost exclusively on urban form and local amenities. Nor is public participation in these processes representative of the city's diversity.

I started this essay by questioning the assumption that up-zoning for the missing middle will solve Toronto's housing crisis. Many factors contribute to high housing costs and unaffordability: growth management and the province's greenbelt policy; fiscal and mortgage policies that encourage people to take on excessive debt; lack of incentives for purpose-built rental housing; local and global demand for housing as an investment; income polarization and the gentrification of the older city; and smaller household sizes and inter-generational inequity.

The affordability crisis is also linked to the downloading of responsibility for housing from other orders of government to the municipality and the disinvestment in social-housing agencies like TCHC. Researchers have further pointed to the impact of the financialization of housing, from investors buying apartment buildings in order to raise rents to smaller-scale investors buying and flipping single-family homes.

These problems are also tied to our collective and individual use of home ownership as a nest egg, a retirement fund, a dream, a fetish, and a status symbol. In addition, the city's priorities are increasingly financed not by property or income taxes but through the income generated by real estate transactions (planning fees, development charges, value capture, and land transfer taxes). It is simplistic to think we can fix our housing system by up-zoning across the Yellow-belt, building stacked townhouses on arterial roads or adding laneway housing downtown.

However, it's also magical thinking to suggest that new development can pay for affordable housing at the scale we need it. The city can't continue to grow sustainably without adding new affordable housing in residential areas. This is an issue of equality and fairness, and it is doubly urgent in the face of climate change. Transportation and housing are major sources of carbon emissions, which can be reduced by multi-unit buildings and shorter commutes. Walkable neighbourhoods are also good for people – they promote physical activity and foster the development of social networks within the urban fabric. By maintaining policies and practices that keep people out of neighbourhoods and shifting all development activity to a few places, we have set up a dynamic where sustainability competes with affordability.

If we really want to 'solve' the housing crisis *and* meet our goals for sustainable intensification, we need to both preserve existing affordable housing and add new affordable housing in such a way that these two goals don't compete with each other.

Can we add affordable units in the stable neighbourhoods while maintaining their amenities?

As it happens, these neighbourhood amenities already exist – trees, quiet, schools, parks, transit – and can support many more people. There are a number of ways to add more affordable units. Allowing moderately higher densities by adjusting heights, setbacks, and floor-to-area ratios through zoning and policy is one approach. This could be combined with conditions for a *minimum unit density* (to prevent the construction of very large single-unit houses). Allowing multi-unit buildings as-of-right – that is, without requiring a rezoning application – would significantly ease the way for more of these low-rise buildings in neighbourhoods. This type of up-zoning would be conditional, requiring owners or builders to provide more of the type of housing the city needs.

Public land, in turn, offers opportunities for long-term leases for affordable housing and land trusts. Development charges could be adjusted to incentivize what we want, i.e., reduced for developers proposing purpose-built rental in multi-unit buildings.

Residents could push council to levy higher property taxes, taking the pressure off real estate transactions to fund municipal services, and also ask the provincial and federal governments to assume more responsibility for affordable housing. We could make public planning consultations more inclusive, reframing them in terms of broader economic and social impacts, as well as quality-of-life considerations for existing residents. We can look to zoning, fiscal, and tax policy to promote affordability and explore innovative ways to develop land trusts for publicly owned real estate. Indeed, if public land is leased on a long-term basis to non-profits and land trusts, the city could add significant amounts of affordable rental housing near transit.

With the involvement of under-represented and marginalized communities, such changes could begin to open up possibilities for addressing spatial inequalities and democratizing the housing market. We can change the rules of the game so it works for all instead of against some.

THE THIRD
FLOOR:

HOUSING FUTURE

Previous pages: Spruce Court Cooperative Apartments, 1913.

In high-cost-of-living cities like Toronto and Vancouver, housing markets have created two extremes: increasingly expensive large single-family homes with fewer occupants[1] and increasingly expensive small condominiums with more occupants. In these and other expensive cities, single-family homeownership has become less attainable[2] and notions of what constitutes a house and home are changing.[3]

It's difficult to pinpoint any one culprit – this situation is the result of colonial land 'ownership' and development models; notions of material success that are bound up in the aspiration for a detached single-family house; planning regulations that limit denser low-rise developments to protect the interests of the few; myths of stable neighbourhoods, as if neighbourhoods were static entities impervious to change; and economic and political conditions that have turned local housing markets into international investment vehicles. All this has played out while cities worldwide contend with extreme pressures to provide housing during the largest population migration into cities the world has ever experienced.

Radical Typologies
Annabel Vaughan

We need to re-evaluate how and where housing gets built, and who has the right to it. But Toronto does not need to reinvent the wheel to find answers. There are precedents in other cities that have partnered with planning departments, financial institutions, and communities to create innovative solutions that break with the status quo.

SEATTLE, MINNEAPOLIS, AND PORTLAND: ADJUSTING ZONING TO NEIGHBOURHOOD REALITIES

In 2018, the Seattle Planning Commission (SPC), an independent, sixteen-member body that advises the mayor, city council, and municipal departments on planning goals and policies, released a report called 'Neighbourhoods for All.'[4] Its key recommendation was to advise the city to simply change the Single Family Residential Zone to a category called Neighbourhood Residential and then create guidelines allowing for the outright approval of all of the housing types that already exist to be built in these neighbourhoods. The move recognized that the Single Family designation does not adequately describe the variety of housing configurations and needs that currently exist.

According to the SPC's report, less than 5 percent of all new housing built in Seattle from 2008 to 2018 occurred in the Single Family Residential Zone. With uneven growth across Seattle and a zoning system that fails to promote equitable access to city services, the Single Family zoning regulations had created stagnant and increasingly exclusive neighbourhoods with declining populations that cannot support local amenities like schools, parks, community centres, and libraries – all of which was paid for by previous public investment.

Rather than shuttering these public assets, Seattle has opted to restore the population in these neighbourhoods by creating more density with infill housing. These changes, the SPC report states, 'would allow for the gradual, incremental reintroduction of historic building patterns while helping to preserve them even as we welcome more residents of all incomes, ages, and races.'[5]

Other cities have started to realize that allowing for a more diverse housing stock spreads out the density across postwar neighbourhoods that are not keeping pace with the needs of residents.

The City of Portland is a developing a 'Residential Infill Project' proposal to add more housing options for residents' changing needs in three residential zones, as long as homeowners adhere to limits on the size of new buildings. This move will allow for duplexes, triplexes, and fourplexes while permitting detached houses to have two accessory dwelling units and duplexes to have one.

In 2018, Minneapolis city council voted to allow a comprehensive plan, dubbed Minneapolis 2040, to permit three-family homes (triplexes) in the city's residential neighbourhoods (single-family-home zone), abolish parking minimums for all new construction, and allow high-density buildings along transit corridors. The city enacted the 2040 vision in the hopes of creating diversity and affordability in Minneapolis's housing stock. As journalist Henry Grabar noted in

Slate, the plan represents a sweeping change 'to a policy that has done as much as any to entrench segregation, high housing costs, and sprawl as the American urban paradigm over the past century.'[6]

Time will tell whether these moves deliver on their promise, but they nonetheless represent an overdue acknowledgement that single-family residential zoning is stifling cities' ability to produce a diversity of housing that meets the needs and affordability criteria of their residents.

HAMBURG: MANAGING RISK AND REDUCING SPECULATION IN URBAN REDEVELOPMENT

When the City of Hamburg created a master plan for the redevelopment of its industrial harbour into HafenCity, an inner-city, mixed-use residential, cultural, and commercial quarter, officials set high bars for sustainability, architectural quality, and state-of-the-art infrastructure. As part of the development process, all the housing that gets built in HafenCity is overseen by the Ministry of Urban Development and Housing to ensure the delivery of high-quality development that meets the master plan's ambitions.

As plots of land become available for residential development, the city hosts a competitive tendering process. The winning developer then enters into an exclusive option period during which the planning and design development occur. Architects are brought into the process at this stage through city-held design competitions, ensuring innovative design solutions continue to drive the process. Finally, building approvals are obtained. This entire process is completed in partnership with the city.

Once the planning approvals are in place and a design is finalized, the city and the developer determine a purchase price and financing plan for the project. The order of operations is key. Deferring financial decisions until after the design is approved limits the escalation of land values through speculation.

According to HafenCity officials, this approach reduces risks for both the developer and the municipality while optimizing the quality of the housing, because developers know exactly what they are expected to deliver and can price accordingly.

Instead of the adversarial nature of Toronto development, this process allows all of the partners to collectively deliver on the ambitious vision of the HafenCity master plan. Public investment ensures that close to 30 percent of the projected 7,000 housing units will be subsidized, and the integrated development approvals process ensures that the funding is spread across the quarter as it builds out.

Hamburg's approach underscores the truism that predictability in land development is the kryptonite of the risk-based market we find ourselves in. There are two known impacts about planning regulations: if they are too restrictive, they can grind development to a halt, and if they are too loose, they drive the speculation of what's possible into the stratosphere (anything goes). A curious by-product of the risk-based market conditions of our current system is that land values have soared while the cost of building housing has remained relatively stable.[7] Solutions for affordability will require deep systemic changes in the way cities use and regulate land, how money is loaned, and how we can disengage from the prevailing housing-as-investment model. There are models out there to learn from, but these changes will require all three levels of government and the lending institutions to work together to reinvest in housing as a human right.

VIENNA: AFFORDABLE HOUSING AND THE ELEPHANT IN THE ROOM
The City of Vienna has been proactively involved in the production of affordable (subsidized) housing as a state-backed political program since the 1920s, when a socialist municipal government levied taxes on the wealthy to finance the construction of tens of thousands of apartments on city-owned land in a radical strategy that came to be known as Red Vienna.

In the decades since, Vienna's municipal government has never backed down from using its land to build housing and ensure residents have affordable places to live. According to Vienna's Department for

Housing and Urban Renewal, 62 percent of all housing is subsidized, serving tenants representing all but the wealthiest of income brackets. The city owns 25 percent of all the housing stock, while another 25 percent is owned by limited-profit housing associations. A system of developer competitions creates high construction standards and innovative solutions that continue to improve the architectural quality and meet the ecological and social goals of the housing they build. The national government contributes over $680 million in funding for housing subsidies each year. City-held land is simply never sold off to the highest bidder for short-term cash to fill budget shortfalls.

EDMONTON: THE PORK-CHOP LOT AND LANEWAY HOUSING

Severing a residential lot into two or more smaller properties creates new ownership models and potentially provides access to more affordable residential real estate. Yet homeowners tend to push back against severances, fearing a loss in value of their own properties and a change in the look and feel of their neighbourhood.

In a real estate market with surreal prices, one can ask whether a small house on half a lot behind a typical house would be half the cost. In a bold experiment, the City of Edmonton took up the challenge, testing an approach to severing lots using an idea imported from Denmark, as well as one of the winning entries in the city's 2016 Infill Design Competition.

Many of Edmonton's residential lots have access to a rear lane or are wide enough to allow for street access up front with a driveway. In a pilot project launched in 2017, the city began testing three residential properties with a small lot carved out of each. These so-called 'flag lots' resemble a flag on a pole, notes the city's website. 'It is usually the remnant shape that is left over once a smaller subdivision has taken place to separate a building, in this case a garden suite, from the original parcel.'[8]

According to the *Globe and Mail*, owners Eugene Dening and his partner are hoping to sell their 500-square-foot garden suite for $110,000 to $180,000; it cost them about $70,000 to build it.[9] The

SCENARIO 1	SCENARIO 2
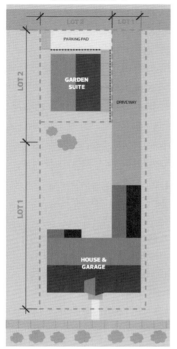	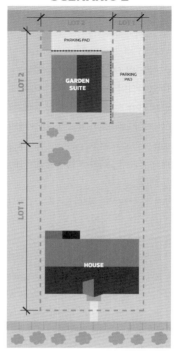

'Pork-chop' lot layout, Edmonton.

latest statistics for Edmonton list average house prices at about $375,000. A quick search reveals just eighty-five houses for sale for under $200,000 in the city, most of them small dwellings in need of work and situated on marginal lots.

Edmonton's experiment differs from most of the laneway housing zones that have been (re)adopted in Calgary (2008), Ottawa (2016), and Toronto and Hamilton (both 2018). None of these allow for lots to be severed, to ensure that this 'new' building stock remains rental accommodation. Vancouver is the only other Canadian city that currently allows for lot severance; since 2017, the city has allowed some lots with laneway houses to be 'strata' titled and sold. (Such titles are also used for condos, as they allow individuals to buy, own and sell dwelling units while sharing common property.)

It turns out that the cost of building these units is not cheap, and bringing services to the rear of a lot can add $50,000 to $100,000 to a project. Owners tend to rent them out at or above market rates.[10] In a very modest concession, Toronto will subsidize twenty projects to try to keep rents affordable on some of the units.[11]

VANCOUVER: SMALL HOUSE/DUPLEX ZONING

When Vancouver rolled out its CityPlan in 1995, municipal officials asked two community-planning groups to come up with visions for their neighbourhoods, including new zoning options to increase housing choice.[12] Residents of Kensington-Cedar Cottage (KCC), a diverse and originally working-class community in East Vancouver, got down to business and spent the next decade creating the innovative 'RT-10/RT-10N' Small House/Duplex Zoning Guidelines, which allow for a variety of housing types on a variety of lot sizes. The objective with this new form of zoning was to keep empty nesters in their neighbourhoods but also attract young families and first-time home buyers.

In the years since RT-10/RT-10N zoning came into effect, small-scale local developers began refurbishing character houses and

Example of residential intensification, Vancouver RT-10 zoning.

introducing smartly designed duplexes, laneway houses, and optimized parking solutions on parcels assembled from two or three lots.

On one street, KCC resident John Buckberrough lives in a tiny 1,100-square-foot cottage, built in 1911, that faces the handsome seven-unit strata built in the neo-Craftsman style. He told the *Vancouver Sun* that the two single-family homes that used to be on that site housed four adults and one child. The site now houses twenty-five people, including eleven children, in five houses. While increased density didn't make Kensington-Cedar Cottage more affordable, the RT-10/RT-10N zoning demonstrated the pay-off of this kind of gentle intensification. 'The neighbourhood was dead or dying,' Buckberrough said. 'The local Safeway was closing. We needed a new library, and the shopping areas along Kingsway were tired-looking. So we had to kick-start the area. And we thought the best way to revitalize the neighbourhood was to get more people in it.'[13]

An abundance of evidence suggests the proportion of Toronto's residents struggling with housing affordability continues to grow. The politics of the day has left it to housing advocates to fight for a solution for the marginalized, the working poor, young people,[14] civil servants (teachers, nurses, police, etc.[15]), and low-income service workers who battle it out for the meager 1.1 percent of available rentals.[16]

In many of Toronto's residential neighbourhoods deemed to be stable or imbued with character, our current zoning regulations make it far easier to build a 5,000-square-foot single-family house than a multi-unit low-rise apartment or a rental suite in a house.

Yet Vienna's long-standing program of developing subsidized housing on publicly owned land serves as an important reminder that the planning reforms discussed elsewhere in this volume, and which are meant to encourage more missing middle housing, will not alone solve the crisis of affordability.

ZONING'S COMPLEX LEGACY

Zoning is the mechanism municipalities use to divide urban land into zones (e.g., residential, industrial), and which therefore determines what uses are permitted or prohibited on any given address. Zoning typically specifies a number of outright and conditional uses and can dictate the size and dimensions of land area and the form and scale of buildings. These guidelines are set by municipalities in order to guide urban growth and development.

Yet zoning is often criticized as a means for promoting social and economic segregation through exclusion. 'Although markets allocate people to housing based on income and price,' noted a 2010 study published in Social Science Quarterly, 'political decisions allocate housing of different prices to different neighbourhoods and thereby turn the market into a mechanism for class segregation.'[17]

Zoning is driven by the sanctity of 'the lot' – a concept embedded in the colonial myth of surveying 'empty land,' which has locked us into an immutable and restrictive paradigm of parcels and transactions. Most of North America was surveyed and divided up in the 1800s, regardless of topography, using the British surveying standard known as Gunter's Chain. A sixty-six-foot-long chain, invented by an English mathematician in the 1600s, it allowed for plots of land to be surveyed for legal and commercial purposes. The chain has left its imperial mark across North America and given us the standard city lot.

Most planning regulations use a standard lot to define land use and density. In Toronto's Residential Detached (RD) zone – what we have defined as the Yellowbelt

in this book – one lot includes one house and one garage (accessory building), the lowest form of density in a city outside of open space. It is an idealized version of growth and a typology that does not reflect the reality of dense and thriving neighbourhoods. But politicians who seek to change these exclusionary and arbitrary zoning categories court great risk.

Like most North American cities, Toronto has a history of incremental development that reflects growth patterns and population shifts. Take a walk through any older neighbourhood and you will see a diversity of housing stock: detached houses, duplexes, triplexes, walk-up apartments, rooming houses, small apartment buildings (fewer than eight to ten storeys), apartments above shops, laneway housing, coach houses, loft apartments in converted warehouses, multi-generational family housing, basement apartments, row houses, and everything in between. It is a perfect mix of housing types that organically grew out of the demands of people moving into the city. Yet the majority of this stock was built before Toronto's zoning regulations came into effect in 1952.[18] Paradoxically, much of what we love about the older parts of Toronto would not be allowed under current regulations.

When changes are proposed to zoning, they are often perceived to be sweeping or rushed. A typical complaint from residents in apparently stable neighbourhoods is that the city has not given them enough time to demonstrate how devastating the proposed zoning changes will be to their communities. They will say they are not opposed to rental housing or to new housing typologies, but specific projects or new zoning allowances will allow too much change and alter a neighbourhood's character for the worse.

The reality is that when the city adopts new zoning regulations in a given area, the actual build-out is slow and steady and may merely formalize practices that have been going on for many years. A perfect example in Toronto is the creation of secondary suites or basement apartments. One 2013 study estimated 75,000 and 125,000 secondary suites;[19] based on the current 2016 Statistics Canada data, those figures mean that about one in ten detached homes have secondary suites, and almost all were built on the down low without city interference, typically by owners trying to defray the cost of a mortgage, provide housing for extended family (parents, adult children, newcomers), or simply creating a rental apartment with surplus space.

In 2000, Toronto city council voted to make secondary suites legal across the city and adopted regulations for their construction (separate entrances, fire-code measures, etc.). While some homeowner groups lobbied strenuously against this change, the city in the intervening years has issued only about 115 permits a year – well under the estimated 10 percent a year growth in such units that predated the bylaw. One reason? A condition in the bylaw meant to ensure the protection of neighbourhood character. The unintended outcome is that the city has slowed the development of a common form of infill rental housing that provides both new supply and other benefits for homeowners.

But with other cases, new gentle-density zoning measures have seen more robust uptake. In 2009, for example, the City of Vancouver capped a laneway housing pilot project at one hundred permits. Yet with the subsequent formalization of the new zoning, Vancouver has seen the construction of about four hundred laneway houses per year, for a total of 3,300 over a decade,[20] but fewer than the 6,600 the city was anticipating. It remains to be seen whether Vancouver's duplex zoning bylaw, which was adopted in 2018 and applies to all single-family residential zones, will see a similar uptake; as of spring 2019, only eleven applications had been submitted.

The conclusion: zoning-policy changes that allow us to incrementally add housing in established neighbourhoods, and that meet residents' needs, should be championed, not shut down.

Annabel Vaughan

Community consultations, an integral part of Toronto's development approvals process, are meant to give local residents an opportunity to provide feedback about a change in their neighbourhood. In 2016, city officials acknowledged the limits of this process, reporting that those who attend these sessions are predominately 'white, male, homeowners, and over the age of 55.'[1]

A Woman's Right to Housing

Cheryll Case

The narrowness of the demographic that participates in these consultations results in policies and decisions that respond to the interests of those most concerned about how new development or lower-income residents could reduce the values of their homes.

What, then, happens when lower-income women participate?

Single women are a particularly vulnerable group. Systemically enforced gendered biases reduce their access to affordable housing. The symptoms of exclusion are most evident during the hunt for a home to rent or purchase. Women typically earn far less than men and, as such, have a higher need for low-cost housing. The 2016 census revealed that in 2015, the average working woman earned $35,461 a year – $12,598 less than the $48,059 in average earnings for men. This wage gap allows the average man to easily outbid the average woman for access to housing.

The impacts of systemic gender bias take effect before the search for affordable housing. Paternalistic ideology shaped the conversations that built Toronto's neighbourhoods. Like other marginalized groups, women were subjects of, rather than participants in, the community planning process. This process and the biases that informed it are the foundations of many of Toronto's neighbourhoods.

A century ago, some women built their lives benefiting from their tenure in apartment homes while wealthier members of society sought to forbid this option. In the early 1900s, some magazines and newspapers warned of the dangers of female independence. Apartment buildings were described as a threat to family values.

According to a 1903 article in *Canadian Architect and Builder*, a Toronto magazine, 'Not only is pride in their families vanishing but pride in their housekeeping as well ... [A]partment life will complete the process.'[2] Apartment buildings, added a 1914 column in the *Globe and Mail*, would produce 'stunted children and unhappy adults.' Women, in other words, were best suited to be mothers in the privacy of single-family homes.

Despite the pushback from pundits and the political establishment, single women found apartment buildings to be an affordable housing option. Between 1905 and 1920, the average apartment was three to four storeys tall – a size that corresponded to the 'missing middle' typology described in this anthology. The typology afforded women additional flexibility: wealthier single women could be independent and rent bachelor apartments, while lower-income women rented multi-bedroom apartment in groups, opting to share one flat instead of boarding in single-family homes. When sharing in the late 1910s, a single woman could pay as little as $2.50 a week.[3] Low rents, in fact, were key to the independence of single women who earned low wages. By the Depression, women accounted for about a quarter of all wage earners, and 84 percent of them were single.[4]

The dominant ideology of the era held that a moral society took care of women by pairing them with men. This belief is exemplified in the treatment of unemployed single women. In 1932, the rent subsidy for an unemployed single woman was two dollars a week. Three years later, the provincial government halved that to one dollar a week. This reduction had negative impacts on the independence and well-being of unemployed single women. Their monthly costs rose dramatically, and they had to eat out because they could no longer afford housing with a kitchen.

Two years after the cut was implemented, Ontario's minister of welfare, David Croll, revealed the role that gender biases played in halving these allowances. In a February 1937 report, he claimed, 'the home placement plan in the case of single women has already demonstrated that we are correct in our attitude.' Policy following the 'home placement plan' for women sought to 'make the single man part of a family group.'[5] Lowering unemployed single women's access to adequate and affordable housing was an early test for the effectiveness of forcing family formation. Women had less political power to oppose such a strategy, and so were an ideal target to test the effectiveness of paternalistic housing policy.

The gender ideologies that influenced the housing policies of the early 1900s still flourished in the mid-century. Unlike the downtown, which permitted single-family and multi-family houses within the same neighbourhood, Toronto's postwar suburbs were developed with separation in mind. Municipalities and developers prioritized wealthier nuclear-family households through planning communities that exclusively permitted detached homes or limited multi-family home development to a tiny minority of land area.

The Etobicoke suburb of Thorncrest Village serves as an excellent example. Built between 1945 and 1960, like many other subdivisions of that era, it contains exclusively detached housing designed for single families. The promoter, Marshall Foss, described Thorncrest's layout as an asset that ensured 'your property values and your living values are secure and stabilized.'[6]

The exclusive design reduced the ability of single women to live in the neighbourhood. In Thorncrest, 27 percent of women were single, 5 percent fewer than the 32 percent average at the Metro Toronto level.[7] More affordable neighbourhoods typically contained a greater number of multi-unit houses (duplexes, walk-up apartments, mid- and high-rise apartments) than more exclusive neighbourhoods. In 1961, for example, 42 percent of women were single in the six Toronto neighbourhoods where 80 to 90 percent of the housing stock consisted of multi-unit homes. This correlation persists to this day. Neighbourhoods like Thorncrest are still zoned exclusively for detached houses, limiting who is able to access housing in those communities. According to the 2016 census, only 38 percent of Thorncrest's resident women are single, whereas the average across the city is 52 percent.[8]

While policy preference for single-family housing was established with the ideal nuclear family in mind, it did not respond to the complexities of the female experience. In a 1979 report entitled *Metro's Suburbs in Transition*, Social Planning Toronto noted that the prioritization of detached housing didn't account for 'the different demographic trends (declining birth rates) and social conditions (e.g. non-family, single parent households, working mothers, ethnic minorities)' observed over the thirty-year period since the 1940s.[9] Because the zoning effectively prioritized the development of single-family housing, as opposed to housing affordability, the social networks of divorced women were often weakened because the neighbourhoods where they lived during their marriages did not offer an adequate supply of housing affordable to them when they became single.

The focus on developing single-family housing led to policies that discriminated against women. The case of 'family' zoning in North York serves as an example. Beginning in 1946, the Township of North York explicitly zoned for 'families.'[10] This bylaw defined 'family' as a household whose residents were related to one another. This was a particularly gendered policy considering that women with lower incomes often had to live in groups with other unrelated, single women.

In 1971, the *Globe and Mail* reported on a high-profile case that ultimately challenged this policy. That year, after five weeks of searching, four women rented a $300-per-month basement apartment in a house on Walwyn Avenue, just north of Weston. Their tenure violated the zoning bylaw, which only permitted families to live in the area.

Within a month, a North York bylaw inspector warned the women that they had to move out or face a court case. The women immediately began to lobby North York to change the bylaw. One of the tenants, a teacher named Barbara Greene,[11] was elected as North York's first female councillor on the heels of her popular fight against the bylaw.[12] In office, she pushed to have the Ontario Municipal Board review the city-wide bylaw. In 1974, Greene celebrated after the discriminatory

Neighbourhood advisory council meeting on Ataratiri, 1991.

bylaw was overturned. OMB records note that the socially restrictive rule did not constitute good planning.[13]

'Council is going to have to become far more liberal,' Barry Swadron, Greene's lawyer, told a reporter. 'It has consistently failed to come to grips with the housing crisis at a time when rents are going out of sight and there is a vacancy rate of less than one percent.'[14] This sentiment is expressed by many who seek to increase access to adequate and affordable housing.

The OMB's ruling was appealed and eventually landed in the Supreme Court, which voted in 1979 to uphold that original ruling against family zoning. Minutes after the verdict was handed down, Greene celebrated with a bottle of champagne. She described the decision as 'an end to people zoning' and was excited that the decision would 'make housing more accessible to a lot of people.'[15]

Despite the victory by Barbara Greene and other women, community-planning consultations continue to under-represent the interests of lower-income women. The City of Toronto has acknowledged that the current design of community consultations is flawed. To address this failing, city officials set up a Planning Review Panel in 2016, consisting of thirty-two residents from across the city who volunteer to provide feedback on a range of high-level community-planning studies. The diversity of the panel broadens engagement for city-wide consultations, but the feedback on local projects remains narrow and most responsive to those concerned about protecting the dollar value of their homes.

Despite the progressive work of leading women, exclusion continues to be on display during the typical community-planning consultation. The Weston area serves as a typical example.

Weston is a special neighbourhood that has much in common with other lower-income communities. Here, the proportion of single-parent households is higher than the city's average; indeed, almost a third of Weston families are led by single women. The neighbourhood's residents are more likely than those in other parts of Toronto to rent and are typically paying more than 30 percent of their income on housing. Yet it is difficult for these residents to get a word in edgewise about their interests when it comes to housing development in their neighbourhood.

In April 2018, the city held a community consultation session to canvass the neighbourhood about a twenty-two-storey condo tower proposed for a location near the Weston UP Express/GO station. The area planner, the local councillor, and the developer were all present, along with about sixty other people, most of them homeowners. After the planner's presentation about local land-use policies, shadow impacts, and traffic projections, the attendees were invited to speak. One after another, the participants stood up to say they opposed the addition of any more affordable housing, even though the developer hadn't proposed any.

'Are there affordable-housing units?' one person said. 'I hope not, because it will lower the value of my home.' Added another: 'There is too much affordable housing in Weston.' About a dozen local homeowners and seniors took to the floor to represent their interests.

They also voiced concerns over the potential damage that would come with affordable housing, increased traffic, and shadows. As homeowners, they seemed to feel entitled to express their views.

But almost no lower-income residents attended or spoke out. One local tenant advocacy group made a statement, and at the end of the session, a young woman interjected to state her views. The meeting's tone, however, had already been set: the majority of those present had loudly opposed any affordable housing.

If the city doesn't make affordable housing a priority at key locations along main streets or adjacent to higher-order transit, how can it be made a priority within the broad reach of neighbourhoods?

To ensure women's rights to affordable housing, we need to redesign the community-planning consultation process. One attempt to rethink the process was Housing in Focus, a series of community-planning workshops I developed, that focused on human rights and the lived experience of residents.[16] From August to November 2018, 140 residents across the City of Toronto participated, exploring how community planning could improve their access to affordable housing. Instead of allowing middle-aged male homeowners to dominate the discussion, the workshops were designed to be accessible to renters, women, and people of various ages. The participants' conclusions differed widely from what is typically produced in traditional consultation sessions.

One of the six workshops was attended solely by women who used shelter services. They reported that access to affordable housing was their priority, as well as amenities such as daycare and transit. The participants developed land-use maps they believed could provide them with adequate affordable housing. The goal was inclusion, not exclusion, as well as the protection of the health and well-being of individuals, not just real estate values.

The Lessons of a Multi-Generational 905 Home

Fatima Syed

My maternal grandfather's house was one of the first to emerge in a new Karachi suburb in post-partition Pakistan. It was a white-walled, two-storey rectangular building flanked by a garden and a large backyard that served as servants' quarters, water source, and playground. To get there, you had to walk down a driveway lined with potted plants, a mini-courtyard elevated by five or so steps, and a chicken coop.

There were three bedrooms inside, each with its own bathroom and one with a separate exit. The property had two major gateways: sturdy, iron-clad ornate gates that required all your strength to open. One was for my grandfather's family downstairs; the other, for whoever was renting the portion upstairs.

Over the years, five generations lived in that house, rarely fewer than three at one time. My mother says she never saw the house empty. Nor was the main door ever locked in the two decades she lived there.

My sister and I were the youngest members of the fourth generation of the family that lived in that house, albeit temporarily. By the 1990s, half the family had become expats, scattered across the Middle East. But somehow, every summer, when we all descended on that unremarkable white house, we would all fit across three bedrooms and a very large living room that had its own exit to the garden – a favoured escape route for the kids who passed through.

Multi-generational living was all we knew growing up. But the progression of time has made that lifestyle less prevalent. My grandparents passed away, leaving behind a house that holds generations of memories, and their kids all started moving away from their childhood neighbourhood – once so affluent and brimming with life, but now, without its founders, slowly rusting into disrepair. Their grandkids moved even farther away, in pursuit of education.

Somewhere, somehow, multi-generational living became a distant, happy memory.

Fatima Syed's grandfather's house in Karachi has been home to five generations. This photo was taken in January 2019, a decade after he died.

My grandfather's multi-generational model is rare to find in North America. Some urban planning experts say the phenomenon first arrived in Toronto in the early to mid-twentieth century with the settlement of Italian, Portuguese, and Greek immigrants who crossed the oceans with big families and built houses with character and grandeur.

The early Southern European immigrants were able to plan for the growth of their families, says Robert Murdie, professor emeritus of geography at York University. They had the space to expand their houses to develop seniors' apartments as they aged and create new living quarters to accommodate new generations.

Then came what Jack Jedwab, the president of the Association for Canadian Studies, calls 'a very individualistic era.' Jedwab's European parents lived with his grandparents before moving to Canada. 'There used to be a sense of responsibility for your parents [among] second-generation kids,' he says.

But that practice has become less common, as he found when he compiled, in 2016, the only statistical data available about multi-generational households in Canada. 'The family unit is more fragmented now,' he adds. Kids move away from their parents, many people increasingly prefer to live on their own, and our capacity to take care of senior members of our families has decreased.

'The Canadian culture is, "You leave home at eighteen and you don't come back,"' says Brea Mann-Lewis, a Toronto-based intern architect who researched architecture that facilitates multi-generational living for her 2014 master's thesis at Carleton University. 'Independence and owning your house is considered so important today, so it's almost taking a step back if you move in with your family and children.'

Mann-Lewis calls this an unfounded 'stigma.' Life in the city has become less affordable, forcing family structures to increasingly evolve to more multi-generational models. Young adults are moving back in with their parents, and the population of senior citizens sixty-five and over – the largest it has ever been in Canadian history – are looking for ways to continue living on their own. 'It seems like a stigma because you're losing your independence. But it's actually extending it,' she says.

While moving 'back home' is seen as regressing, we also don't have the urban planning or house prices to afford either separate homes for each generation or to afford big enough homes for many generations. For seniors, especially, the changing household structure has proven to be 'a big transition,' Mann-Lewis says. 'It can be really scary if you've owned a house for thirty years and you suddenly live by yourself' because everyone has moved out, she explains. Choosing to move in with your kids – or into a retirement home for reasons of health or personal safety – comes with its own challenges. 'I don't think anyone enjoys relying on someone for every single thing,' she observes.

The confluence of increasing isolation, greater distances, and an aging population poses pertinent problems. In the face of rising gentrification and booming condominium culture, the Greater Toronto Area does not yet have the capacity to properly house three or more generations under one roof.

'We don't have the kind of rental accommodation that Southern European populations had,' Murdie says. Today, there's a lack of affordable housing stock within the Toronto area for everyone – whether that is immigrants and refugees who come with more limited financial means, or for families already here looking to move back in together as a cost-saving measure. This lack of suitable housing, Murdie adds, 'is a problem on the horizon.'

According to the 2016 Statistics Canada study conducted by Jedwab, there are more than 400,000 multi-generational households, with 2.2 million people, in Canada. About half of them can be found in Ontario.

While immigration from countries like mine, where similar living arrangements are the norm, has greatly contributed to this rise, the phenomenon of multi-generational housing goes beyond newcomers – 'a reflection of a conflict over the way in which we express our family values,' as Jedwab puts it.

There has been a 37.5 percent increase in these types of households since 2001, linked to 'Canada's changing ethno-cultural composition' and spurred in large part by a wave of immigration from Asian and Middle Eastern countries, according to Jedwab. The subsequent boomerang effect of adult children returning home after living on their own because of the lack of affordable housing in the GTA has increased dramatically: over a third of young adults between the ages of twenty and thirty-four are living with at least one parent, even after forming unions or having children of their own. And for the first time in Canada's census history, there are more seniors than children living in Canada, forcing a conversation about appropriate living arrangements.

In Brampton, a large municipality of 600,000 people northwest of Toronto, one in four residents lives in a multi-generational household. In Markham, another large municipality to Toronto's northeast, 18 percent of the population lives in multi-generational households. Within the City of Toronto, 14 percent of Scarborough residents live in multi-generational households.

In Toronto, nearly half of young adults live with their parents.

The few emerging architects and urban planning or geography experts who have explored this phenomenon have noted that our housing market isn't dynamic enough to accommodate a population that is simultaneously aging and becoming more diverse.

Drive around any Ontario suburb and you can see the rise of mega-sized retirement complexes and blocks of shiny, glass apartments towering over sprawl. If you're a large family, your options are threefold: 1) spend more money to buy a bigger house in the heart of suburban sprawl; 2) either retrofit your home as the makeup of your family changes or buy a lower-cost home you can afford and tear it down; or 3) find innovative living solutions in a two-bedroom-plus-den apartment.

Our society has not worked to create a fluid and adaptable housing stock – one capable of housing every kind of family, including those for whom multi-generational living is a cultural preference, but also for those families who find multi-generational living difficult to escape.

Toronto's multi-generational families have new demands for our urban landscape that are not being met, explains Sandeep Agrawal, an Alberta-based urban and regional planner. 'We're at a stage where we need public amenities that are more to do with senior citizens and kids in their teens or those who are younger,' he says. 'I don't think we have come to terms with that. We haven't planned our communities in that way. We haven't created complete communities. We haven't built a community for all ages.'

Agrawal calls this kind of thinking 'shadow planning' – a city's choice to design urban spaces and infrastructure with the next twenty to thirty years in mind. Households aren't constant, he points out. They change over time as families age and their needs, as well as their ability to pay for housing, evolve.

A more fluid planning approach should be adaptable to changes in household structures, but what would that look like in practice? The only way to create change is through policy and zoning, so that today's single-family home may become a duplex or townhouse tomorrow. But how do governments effect rapid change across housing units that are mostly privately owned?

'We have to figure out how that conversion looks,' Agrawal says. Right now, if multi-generational families want to live together, they will need a larger plot of land to have a larger house, which requires them to move from the urban to the suburban. Does this mean we need more compact development or more urban sprawl? Do we need to create village-type communities or adapt courtyard living from the East here in the West?

'If we addressed it today, maybe designs in the next five to twenty years will change,' Mann-Lewis says. 'But, as of now, we're in a crisis.'

The magic of my maternal grandfather's house in Karachi wasn't just the five generations that grew up within its walls. It was in the village-style neighbourhood, made up of houses equally full of family members as his was. They all met at one another's houses – or in the mosque in the centre of the neighbourhood, or at the park adjacent to it, or inside the market a short distance away – every evening for tea or cricket or parties.

Many of them migrated together – extended relatives and cousins and long-time family friends – and together became a communal family through friendships, marriages, and simply by proximity and daily interaction.

That kind of lifestyle is nearly impossible to replicate in the context of high-rise buildings and sprawling suburbs. Some cities are trying to encourage co-existence with innovative solutions. Courier Place is a multi-generational apartment community built in 2012 in Claremont, California. It consists of three apartment buildings that surround a green courtyard: two dedicated to two- and three-bedroom rental apartments for families, and one building with single bedrooms for lease and marketed to seniors.

In the suburbs of Calgary, too, the idea of co-existence is being put to the test. Three different buildings are under construction, each designed to house different kinds of people, and coupling varying

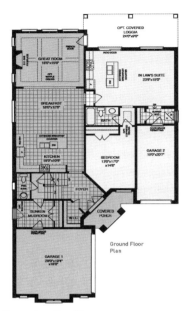

Floor plan: Flex House.

programs. A seniors' home is being combined with an early childcare development centre. The idea is to create a shared space that allows movement within and connection to the community – ideas so natural in my grandfather's neighbourhood but that now need to be fabricated to adjust to change.

Independently, the construction industry is seeing a trend in multi-generational housing that builders are tackling themselves. Ottawa and Toronto changed zoning regulations to allow for laneway homes and secondary suites. In Edmonton, several homebuilders are unveiling a new project on the west side of the city where homes will be built with fully developed, rentable secondary suites.

Craig Marshall has been an Ontario-based builder for almost three decades. He is the creator of Flex House – a dwelling designed with a second 'complete home' inside of the main one. With access to its own garage and a separate private entry, the Flex House allows for what Marshall calls 'a fine balance of proximity and privacy' for large families.

Marshall watches his neighbourhood in Pickering, Ontario, where he has lived for over thirty years, change as his children's friends start returning home. 'Baby boomers made all the money in the housing market,' he says. 'Now, as their kids return to ask for their parents' help, we're seeing people customize their houses.' They are renovating basements, adding stairs and an extra entrance.

But municipalities have only started to adapt their building and planning regulations to accommodate such multi-generational living, says Sneha Sumanth, a Toronto-based intern architect who researched refugee integration in the City of Toronto with her partner, Safira Lakhani, an Edmonton-based intern architect.

'Residential housing and condominiums are being developed in a way that is a barrier to a lot of things,' Sumanth says. 'It doesn't facilitate different groups of people. It's not adapting to different demographics.'

'We aren't doing the best we can right now,' Lakhani adds. The suburban neighbourhood of Meadowvale, in Mississauga, has large houses that are adaptable to bigger families, but that doesn't mean they are functional houses for multi-generational families. 'You can have a house that can house multiple generations, but it's not successful as multi-generational housing because it is still isolated.' Large houses removed from public spaces that cater to all generations – i.e., Agrawal's 'complete community' – are simply large houses. Multi-generational living is the combination of a functional house and an accessible community.

But that idea isn't being discussed at a policy level, where the focus is constantly on density. 'As more people understand and see the need for [complete communities], they will become more prevalent and influence the building code and future design,' Lakhani says. And while 'density is a great thing,' Sumanth adds, 'it's just not always done very well to accommodate all the different kinds of families here.'

My grandfather's Karachi house was home base, and for the generations after him, it maintains its gravitational pull. My grandparents remained rooted within its walls for fifty years.

Living – and growing – in one house for so long is rarely possible in Canada today. The issue isn't just housing affordability but also attainability, says Dr. Raza Mirza of the University of Toronto's National Initiative for the Care of the Elderly. For a long time, housing policy has been centred on the idea that once someone hits retirement age, they will want to downsize and move to a communal home or a smaller house. But that assumption is simply not true anymore – and perhaps never was. Members of the emerging senior population now often want to stay in their house and neighbourhood, but it's becoming ever more expensive to do so.

Minza has noted pockets of multi-generational housing across Toronto, like Chinatown, where families get stuck by circumstance. The younger generation generally can't move into the housing market, and if they do, the older generation often don't want to leave their long-time homes. And if these older adults do sell their large homes, where do they go?

Vacancy rates are at one percent, Mirza says, leaving few options for people to move within the GTA. But there are five million empty bedrooms across Ontario, two million of them owned by senior citizens. 'We can't change policy, but we can look at different models to encourage multi-generational living,' he says.

Mirza pioneered an intergenerational housing exchange with the City of Toronto called the Toronto Home Share Pilot Project, which started in June 2018. It partners students with older adults who have spare bedrooms. The program offers an opportunity for senior citizens to counter isolation, depression, and issues of safety; for students, it allows them to save money in exchange for some chores and companionship.

So far, twelve seniors have been paired with twelve students at Ryerson University, York University, and University of Toronto. These unlikely roommates are matched by a social worker and bound by a rental agreement from September to January. 'Multi-generational housing is not necessarily about families living together,' Mirza notes. 'It's just different generations living in the same home and having similar needs and supporting each other in ways we haven't thought of.'

It is time, Mirza suggests, to embrace such possibilities. With the region's housing market and demographics, 'we're not heading toward a crisis,' he says. 'We are in one. And the crisis isn't going to be solved very shortly.'

The consensus is that, over the next two decades, Ontario will have an oversupply of condos and townhouses – neither of which are suitable for an era of bigger families of various kinds.

Immigrants and Canadians of past decades could once find a house and grow and age with it. That housing narrative is just not possible anymore. 'We have to make housing appropriate,' Mirza says. 'We have to look at where we're building and how we're building, and who we're missing.'

To restore neighbourhoods to their historic populations, the City of Toronto should consider establishing 'density transition zones' between arterial streets and the abutting residential areas. This area could extend from the centre line of those main streets designated as 'Avenues' or 'Major Streets' to a specified distance (100 to 200 metres, for example) inside adjacent neighbourhoods. Within these zones, the city could promote intensification using

The Affordability Case for Transition Zones

Blair Scorgie and Sean Hertel

missing middle housing forms. Such a policy change would maintain the stability of neighbourhoods while encouraging the development of ground-related housing along their edges, areas with good proximity to commercial main streets, frequent and reliable public transit, parks, and other amenities.

As with older missing middle housing types, there are a handful of areas around Toronto, especially in the older city, where we can see such transition zones, such as along the Danforth and elsewhere in the former Borough of East York. These corridors may also have smaller industrial or commercial buildings as well as low-rise apartments – evidence of the more permissive zoning that existed in the pre–World War II city.

Around Yonge and Lawrence, a major intersection within a few minutes' walk of Toronto's most exclusive real estate, some nearby residential streets feature duplexes, triplexes, fourplexes, and walk-up apartment buildings developed between the 1920s and the 1950s. More recently, a small number of townhouse clusters developed between the 1990s and 2000s. The area is an example of a transitional zone featuring the kind of gentle-density housing forms that serve as a buffer between the commercial high street and neighbourhoods with single-family homes.

But in the years after the war, Metropolitan Toronto's newer suburban boroughs – North York, Etobicoke, and Scarborough – relied on more rigid zoning, with discrete categories of land designations for commercial, residential, and industrial development. None of the postwar zoning bylaws reflected the flexibility of pre-war zoning, and consequently those transitional zones did not develop.

As we think about how to add gentle density around the city, transition zones offer the potential to diversify the existing housing stock. But they would also make communities more vibrant and resilient by increasing residential populations, thereby improving the use of existing physical and social infrastructure (everything from sewer mains to local libraries and transit).

They might also ease the development pressures facing mid-rise apartments on main streets. Under the Official Plan, mid-rise projects are encouraged, but the side facing back onto low-rise neighbourhoods must be tapered down, a configuration specified by the city's mid-rise design guidelines. These design requirements are meant to protect adjacent homeowners from feeling overwhelmed by a large neighbouring structure, but they impose a cost on the developer in terms of the loss of marketable space on often fairly shallow building sites. A transition zone would have the effect of allowing that stepping down to occur across a range of structures instead of placing the entire aesthetic burden on a single multi-storey block with mixed-use buildings.

Within the broader context of other more dramatic policy interventions – such as eliminating all zones that only permit detached single-family dwellings – density-transition zones have the potential to serve as a palatable solution to addressing the city's housing-affordability crisis.

More generally, they would dovetail with other existing land-use planning policies and could represent, if adopted, the next logical step forward in an already well-defined, accepted, and rational approach to city-building. After all, one of Jane Jacobs's most important insights about cities is that strictly enforced separation of land uses creates sterile and car-dependent urban environments. Great cities are all about interwoven spaces and districts that blend together in interesting and occasionally unexpected ways.

Where should the city allow transition zones?

While Toronto planners have identified 324 kilometres of Avenues as well as other major streets, transition zones won't be appropriate everywhere. To reintroduce missing middle housing forms, in fact, city officials need to pinpoint potentially viable areas and conduct planning studies to determine whether they would be suitable for this kind of intensification.

To answer that question, Toronto's planning officials should develop evaluation criteria as well as gain an understanding of perceived market demand and growth potential. Planners would be looking for factors such as these:

- the proximity of urban centres and/or major transit hubs;
- the proximity and capacity of existing transit infrastructure;
- the proximity and capacity of services such as schools, libraries, community centres, childcare facilities, parks, and open spaces;
- the capacity of existing hard infrastructure (roads, sewers, and watermains); and
- the potential for low-rise intensification within a 100- to 200-metre distance of the adjacent Avenues and/or Major Streets.

These assessments, which city planners routinely undertake when they consider changing policies and regulations, would eventually identify specific areas adjacent to major streets, with geographic limits based on typical lot, street, and block conditions, that could be redesignated as density transition zones.

As with any zoning and land-use change, the creation of density transition zones would require a series of further steps – perhaps a classification system (some areas may have more potential than others); policies governing the desirable form, type, and extent of intensification; and ultimately amendments to the Official Plan and the city's Zoning By-law. Our view is that Toronto should create a new Urban Structure designation – 'Density Transition Zones' – to complement others that are already part of the Official Plan (Downtown and Central Waterfront, Centres, Avenues, and Employment Areas).

The city's Neighbourhood land-use policies will require changes to allow for the introduction of transition zone building heights and mass, densities, and building types that would differ from those within the interior of neighbourhoods. Amendments would also be required to encourage more intense forms of development along Major Streets.

Ultimately, all the land within these new density transition zones should be subject to area-specific Zoning By-law amendments. The reason? To properly align local zoning regulations with the Urban Structure and Land Use policy objectives laid out in the Official Plan. This is where political will comes in, because these new zones shouldn't be limited to single-family dwellings. They are, by definition, areas where we want more density than low-rise neighbourhoods, but perhaps less than might be found on Avenues and Major Streets that increasingly feature mid-rise or high-rise, mixed-use buildings.

While the concept of formally designated Density Transition Zones may be new to Toronto, several other North American municipalities have implemented this kind of land-use planning policy. These include Davis (a suburb of Sacramento), Seattle, and Minneapolis. The approach is also being considered in Austin, Portland, and Vancouver.

The prospect of encouraging missing middle housing in Vancouver inspired Urbanarium, a non-profit aimed at fostering discussion about the future of cities, to host a design competition centred on finding new solutions to address housing affordability issues. As it happened, the winning entry came from Haeccity Studio Architecture for a proposal to introduce three-block deep 'Buffer Zones' between mixed-use commercial corridors and adjacent single-family residential neighbourhoods. According to Haeccity's submission, such zones would be suitable for missing middle/low-rise housing. More broadly, this idea signals a form of renewal meant to counter land speculation, improve housing affordability, and increase density.

In the end, the case for density transition zones is grounded in the recognition that rigid land-use planning policies and zoning regulations have contributed to Toronto's housing affordability crisis. Yet our municipal land-use policy framework can become part of the solution, too. As Toronto's designated growth areas intensify beyond their carrying capacity, its neighbourhoods decline. Transition zones can direct small-scale investment and moderate population growth into residential areas with falling populations while acknowledging and responding to the complexity of the resulting political challenges.

Just as important, they promote the principles of social, economic, and environmental sustainability. These zones on their own won't solve the housing affordability crisis that afflicts the city, but if permitted to take root in our planning frameworks, they can create – or, more precisely, recreate – a more nuanced built form capable of providing more housing choices to more households across a broader swath of the city.

D ensity, in the form of a cube. This idea drives a series of four-storey apartment buildings designed to fit into in a postwar apartment neighbourhood in the German city of Bremen. The architects, Lin, won a design competition in 2011 with their concept for these buildings, dubbed Bremer Punkt. Two have now been built.

In 2019, SvN Architects + Planners included the Bremer Punkt buildings in a report commissioned by the Ontario Association of Architects, *Housing Affordability in Growing Urban Areas* (see Appendix 2).

The High Cost of Building a Box

Alex Bozikovic

They're smallish and elegant: boxes 14 metres (45 feet) on a side, packing up to eleven apartments per building onto less land than a single suburban house in Toronto would occupy. Their external stairs, while unconventional, make them efficient in their use of space. They include accessible units and potentially a wide range of suite configurations, all well-lit and close to the ground, all with outdoor space. They make good neighbours. So why not build them in Toronto? Why does Toronto not see development projects like this?

As it turns out, there are many reasons, and they have to do with regulation and taxation.

Let's take a logical site in a Scarborough neighbourhood ripe for development: a single-family house at 1 Trophy Drive. It's a bungalow on a corner lot, facing a group of four-storey apartment buildings across the street. And the property is less than a 200-metre walk from a new Crosstown LRT station at Sloane Avenue and Eglinton Avenue East.

The neighbourhood has an aging population and a middling population density, despite the presence of apartment and condo buildings nearby. It has lots of green space, parks, public schools, and a library within walking distance. This community could take more people.

While the actual examples in Bremen are built with prefabricated mass timber structure, you could do a simpler version out of conventional wood framing. Technically and logistically, such a project would be simple; the contractor could buy everything at Home Depot. In urban design terms, it would be defensible; if you built a Bremer Punkt building here, it would have a comparable footprint to the house that's here now. It would be no taller than the neighbouring apartment buildings. To a casual observer, it wouldn't look dramatically different in scale from the existing houses.

But the difference, in planning terms, is enormous. This lot falls within an 'RD' zone on the city's Official Plan. A Bremer Punkt would break rules with its form (too tall, at four storeys), as well as its 'setbacks,' or distance, from the street and lot line, which would probably be slightly too small. The Punkt's lack of parking spaces would also violate rules.

But first and most importantly, as an apartment building, it would be explicitly forbidden. In an RD zone, the only type of dwelling permitted is a detached house, with a small secondary unit.

To put an apartment building here – even a four-storey one – a builder or owner would require a zoning bylaw amendment and probably an Official Plan amendment, each of them an expensive,

Bremer Punkt by LIN Architects Urbanists.

Bremer Punkt interior.

complex, and contentious legal process. In this location, the developer would be almost certain to lose.

Let's imagine, however, that such a change was possible. Say the city wanted modest apartment buildings on sites like this. In that case, a zoning bylaw amendment would still be required. The developer would need to hire a planner and lawyer to start this process, incurring considerable cost.

Then the fees would start stacking up: about $43,000 for an application for rezoning and plan amendment and $23,000 for a Site Plan Approval application, another step in the process. If the developer somehow won permission to build, the building-permit fees would come in around $15,000. That's $81,000 in city fees.

But by approving development permits, the city could expect to receive big cheques. Under the new development charges in effect as of 2020, this theoretical building of six two-bedroom units would have to pay $289,320 in development charges, as well as another 'parkland dedication,' which would be in the six-figure range, as much as $200,000. The fees to the city could easily reach $600,000.

That enormous number demands a commercial justification. So look at the business model, making generous assumptions. Construction costs, using typical methods, would total about $2.5 million, and a developer could sell eight large two-bedroom units for perhaps $700,000 each, or $5.5 million total. Allowing $1 million for land costs, the builder could expect $2 million to cover 'soft costs' (including design and planning and city fees), contingency, and profit. After city fees, that's as much as a $1.4 million return on a $3.5 million investment, over roughly four years.

Such a development could make sense, if it were allowed – which, again, it absolutely is not.

Instead, what is permitted here is a new single-family house. As a developer, you could plausibly tear down the existing bungalow and get permission to build a much larger two-and-a-half-storey house. That dwelling, of about 3,000 square feet for a single family, would be cheaper to build and easy to sell. It would generate a similar profit margin with much less risk and much less time. And such a project would face almost no city fees and charges.

This second scenario, the sprouting of McMansions, is exactly what's happening across the city; right now, in more desirable affluent neighbourhoods, but increasingly in less posh ones, too. If current policies continue, the mansions will come to Trophy Drive, as well – brought here by business logic, retrograde ideas about what a 'neighbourhood' should look like, and public policy that taxes dense, small-scale development to death.

Sheppard Avenue, for many years, has played a starring role in Toronto's planning debates. Its intersection with Yonge Street is a hub for rapid transit and high-rise office and residential development. Local politicians argue about extending the Sheppard subway east to Scarborough and west to Downsview. North York City Centre, which extends north of Sheppard, is one of Toronto's fast-growing urban-growth nodes.

Sheppard Avenue and the Red Ribbon Problem

Sean Galbraith

Yet if you travel east or west of Yonge on Sheppard for even a block, all that urban intensity abruptly vanishes, leaving in its wake a strip of postwar bungalows, many of them converted into small offices.

There's an old saying that you get the city you plan for, which begs the question: how did Toronto plan to have shabby single-storey houses within a stone's throw of a downtown served by rapid transit?

The answer has everything to do with the thin red ribbons that criss-cross Toronto's planning maps, representing what planners refer to as 'mixed-use corridors.' In this part of the city, a mixed-use corridor runs along Yonge Street, encompassing an eclectic blend of office and condo towers, cultural buildings, a civic centre precinct, and low-rise retail strips.

But west of Yonge, another red ribbon on Sheppard delineates only a thin corridor of land – essentially, the lots that hold those old bungalows. Almost everything north and south of that red stripe is a so-called Residential Detached (RD) zone, the sort of 'stable' area where only detached single-family homes are allowed.

These planning abstractions have very specific implications for the way development has evolved in Willowdale. To create a new building fronting on Sheppard West, such as a mid-rise apartment with shops on the main floor, you must be able to shoehorn the entire structure within a shallow parcel.

Such constraints pose serious design challenges. These zoning regulations, in fact, explain why this stretch of Sheppard remains significantly underdeveloped, despite its proximity to North York City Centre.

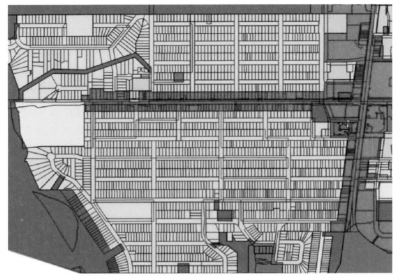
Existing zoning, Sheppard Ave. West and surrounding neighbourhoods.

Toronto's Official Plan has been very clear in directing new residential growth to certain areas, and that is exactly where we see so much high-rise development. Besides downtown, these patterns are most evident in two of the city's 'Urban Growth Centres': Yonge/Eglinton and North York Centre.

The Official Plan has also succeeded in restricting residential growth everywhere else. In many neighbourhoods, populations have stagnated or declined while detached residences are replaced at a rapid pace with larger homes.

It's time to revisit these core precepts of the Official Plan. But to do that, we need to understand just how tightly current planning policies lock down much of the city to new development.

Consider the Mixed Use Areas in the Official Plan, designated as ribbons of red primarily along major east-west roads and portions of some north-south roads. As the name suggests, these zones allow all sorts of development: offices, stores, multi-unit residential buildings, and so on. But with few exceptions, the mixed-use corridors include only the lots that immediately front on the main street. The

Proposed transitional zoning, same corridor.

surrounding areas are meant to remain unchanged.

Outside of the Urban Growth Centres, the city intends that most of these mixed-use corridors will see mid-rise development. The rule of thumb is that mid-rise buildings should be about as high as the adjacent street is wide – about twenty metres in the old City of Toronto, and thirty-six to forty-five metres in suburban areas. A twenty-metre height limit will yield a six-storey building, while thirty-six to forty-six metres is equivalent to ten to twelve storeys. Of course, virtually none of the land on those red ribbons is vacant, so development of these areas means the redevelopment of existing structures; large sites such as car dealerships, gas stations, and strip plazas are obvious targets.

The rest of the city, meanwhile, is more or less off limits to intensification. These areas include parks and open spaces, employment lands, utility lands, institutions, and, of course, the neighbourhoods. In these areas, the land-use policies can be easily summed up: if it isn't already there, you can't build it. Such restrictions create impediments to adding gentle density within those zones.

But the strong protections for Yellowbelt neighbourhoods not only halt most new development; they also affect the form of new development on these adjoining mixed-use corridors. City planners are concerned that building shadows and sightlines – so-called 'overlook' – can affect privacy for homeowners living near apartment buildings.

In many older parts of the city, apartment buildings have sat next to detached single-family homes for decades. But in recent years, the city has sought to mitigate these shadow and privacy concerns with design policies such as the Mid-Rise Building Guidelines (MBG), which influence the shape of new mid-rise buildings. These are more than guidelines, however – they are rules. Through the MBG, the city expects developers to limit shadow and overlook impacts. These requirements, combined with narrow lot widths and shallow lot depths in the older parts of the city, have made it challenging to develop mid-rise buildings in areas where such projects would be most desirable, and where they could take advantage of existing public transportation infrastructure and public services.

The guidelines require mid-rise buildings to step back as they rise, so that upper-floor units keep their distance from low-rise neighbourhoods. This produces inefficient designs, although such configurations do a decent job of protecting the detached or semi-detached homes behind the project. In my view, this approach represents a waste of limited land resources.

When the planning department published the MBG in 2010, officials also proposed the idea of Enhancement Zones that would allow mixed-use properties with shallow depths to achieve their potential for mid-rise development, mainly by assembling larger parcels through the acquisition of land behind the properties fronting the main streets.

Planning staff initially considered testing Enhancement Zones along St. Clair Avenue West, but the idea was met with stiff resistance from local homeowners. When the report reached council, a city councillor moved that the Enhancement Zone idea be struck from the guidelines, and city council backed the motion. While the idea of Enhancement Zones was not ideal, it was at least an acknowledgement that the relationship between the mixed-use areas and adjacent neigh-bourhoods needed to be rethought to make mid-rise buildings work.

Almost a decade later, it's time to revisit the prospect of creating transitional zones between the mixed-use corridors on main streets and Toronto's protected neighbourhoods. Ultimately, I think Toronto would be best served by rezoning all residential areas out-side of the Residential Apartment–zoned areas to the Residential 'R' zone, which permits all residential forms, from detached houses to small apartments. But that isn't going to happen any time soon, and there is a model for compromise: transitional zoning, or what American urban planner Donald Shoup calls 'graduated density.' Essentially, council should revise its Official Plan policies, zoning rules, and design guidelines to allow more intense development near mixed-use corridors.

What could transitional zoning look like along Sheppard Avenue West? I propose several new types of land-use designations and zoning:

Apartment zoning. Within at least 500 metres of the subway interchange (excluding the high-density lands next to Yonge Street), the land would be zoned for apartments. This could encourage land assembly to create parcels large enough to develop some density, generally at mid-rise scale. Because these lands are not on major roads, they wouldn't need to have commercial units at grade. These areas would form a transition from the high-density Yonge corridor to the low-rise areas to the west.

A wider mixed-use zone. The red ribbon of mixed-use lands along Sheppard should be expanded so it is at least two lots deep. The city could encourage or even require lot assembly to allow for more sub-stantial developments and appropriately sized commercial units at the ground level. Access to the properties could be via the existing road to the rear instead of from Sheppard itself.

Missing middle zone. North and south of the mixed-use area along Sheppard should be rezoned to allow for much of what can be found in the old City of Toronto's Residential (R) zone. The zoning in this area would allow for everything from single detached dwellings all the way to four-storey walk-up apartment buildings, as well as assembling or splitting lots.

This zone would produce a downward transition in scale and unit density from the Sheppard mid-rise heights while opening up the possibility for a wide variety of residential built forms. It becomes a 'missing middle' or 'gentle density' zone – and absorbs the shadows and overlooks from development on Sheppard, making those sites easier to develop. Ideally, over time, these transitional areas north and south of Sheppard might evolve into neighbourhoods more like the Annex or Parkdale: an eclectic mix of houses next to apartments next to triplexes next to semis next to sixplexes. Let's allow for experimentation and see what happens.

Triplex zoning. The larger areas on the map would be largely unchanged from the current detached house forms, with one notable shift: they would all permit duplexes and triplexes, maybe even fourplexes, housing forms that are illegal under the area's current zoning. To facilitate these new housing types, the city would permit dwelling heights up to three storeys.

Along Sheppard West, and almost certainly elsewhere in Toronto, a transitional zoning scheme would significantly increase the area's density compared to what currently exists. Increased density can also allow for more parks or open spaces and provide the population growth needed to support new retail along Sheppard. While the three blocks north and south of Sheppard could see fairly dramatic changes, most of the neighbourhood beyond those blocks will retain the same look and feel they've had for decades, with one important difference: more kids attending local schools, new people out walking their dogs, and a greater sense of community.

If we want to allow Toronto's neighbourhoods to evolve, the city must provide enough flexibility so these areas can adapt to the changes in family sizes and composition. If we can't remove detached-house-only zoning entirely, transitional zoning can provide more equitable access to Toronto's neighbourhoods and help create complete communities.

When Torontonians talk about development – in public meetings or on neighbourhood Facebook pages – they often focus on the same few questions. What does the new building look like? Does it match the context? Does it fit in?

Often, the perceived answer is no. A new development doesn't fit. It isn't the right kind of housing for the neighbourhood. But what *would* the right kind of housing be? If you flipped this rhetoric around to articulate a vision for the city, what kind of buildings would that suggest, and what kind of housing would it produce?

Context with a Twist:
Batay-Csorba Architects' Triple Duplex
Alex Bozikovic

This is the question I put to the emerging design firm Batay-Csorba Architects. Writing for the *Globe and Mail*, I asked them to rethink a site on Clinton Street in Seaton Village, now filled with two skinny semi-detached houses from about 1910. How would they create housing that responded to typical neighbourhood demands, but was as dense as possible?

'We relish this opportunity to challenge people's assumptions right off the bat,' said Andrew Batay-Csorba, who runs the office with his partner and wife, Jodi Batay-Csorba. 'We want to challenge what it means to be contextual, to think about how people actually live now.'

Their scheme, which they've dubbed 'Triple Duplex,' has a friendly aspect from the street. Its front face is made of red brick, a mix of solid wall and a permeable screen of bricks. It also has a sloped roof. 'People acknowledge context as being a pitched roof,' said Jodi Batay-Csorba. 'If it has brick, and a porch, it's contextual.'

Behind that facade is a radical – for Toronto – vision. Their plan allows for three spacious houses, of about 2,500 square feet each, stacked one in front of the other. They have front doors facing the front, backyard, and side yard. Each has a two-bedroom apartment that opens onto the courtyard. This arrangement would allow for rental income or, with a few easy changes, an even bigger house that could accommodate different family or collective living arrangements.

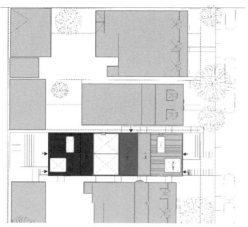

Three houses, back to back, punctuated by courtyards (shown in white).

The houses themselves have comfortable room sizes and good floor plans. They are, in many ways, superior to the traditional configuration of houses in pre-automotive Toronto neighbourhoods. Instead of long and skinny, they are square, which makes for more flexibility and less wasted space. And they each gain an outdoor area – a tall square courtyard – that is partially sheltered and semi-private. It's a great place for barbecuing or hanging out with the kids – more useful, in fact, than the nearby front porches and tiny front lawns.

So what would be lost with this kind of development? A backyard and a garage. The first isn't necessarily a great loss. When old Toronto houses are divided into apartments – which is still common – the backyard is often a no man's land. As for the garage, any resident of an old Toronto neighbourhood knows that such structures are used for many purposes, and often simply for storing junk. Why not housing?

Of course, such a development would be impossible under Toronto's current planning rules. For one thing, the combined building would be bigger and denser than the zoning on this site currently allows. The fact that one of the houses is entered only from the back lane could also pose a problem. The technicalities would stack up against their concept.

Yet we should ask why such a project has become so difficult to develop. From the street, its two-and-a-half-storey mass, its form, and its materials are just as 'contextual' as anything else on this mixed-up block. And the density of the building (basically, its total above-grade

The view from the street: brick, and a sloped roof.

floor space) is not much higher than some of the monster homes that are currently being approved and built in such neighbourhoods. But the Batay-Csorba design houses three, or four, or five families. All this without the bulk of a walk-up apartment building.

There are a few lessons here. One, that 'gentle density' involves trade-offs; two, that those trade-offs are often smaller than we think; and three, that different approaches are not only possible, but bring their own benefits. 'The building has to connect to its context,' said Andrew Batay-Csorba, 'but it doesn't have to do that in the way that certain people hope it will.'

A new building can give everything neighbours say they want, and still change the city.

In 2018, our studio, Workshop Architecture, entered the Missing Middle Competition, run by Urbanarium, a Vancouver-based non-profit. The organization's goal was to generate discussion about how middle-density dwellings could contribute to affordable housing in the Greater Vancouver region.

Extra Special Housing
Helena Grdadolnik

Our proposal built on the success of the 'Vancouver Special' housing type – a low-cost house design prevalent in the region since the 1970s, whose form was developed as a direct expression of the maximization of existing zoning bylaws. These houses are reasonably big – about 2,400 square feet over two levels – with the main living areas on the second floor and often a secondary unit on the main floor.

Our design proposal is a mash-up of the Vancouver Special with Brooklyn brownstones and Chinese courtyard houses, resulting in a typology we call 'Extra Special.' This form provides options for living in a residential neighbourhood – a missing middle between the single-family house and a condo or apartment home.

THE TORONTO CONTEXT

In the mid-twentieth century, Toronto didn't develop a housing type equivalent to the Vancouver Special, a design that maximized its zoning envelope and was intended for multiple families. The Victorian and Edwardian semi-detached house was joined, in the inner suburbs, by low-density, single-family houses.

Although our design proposal doesn't fit perfectly on Toronto sites, the general approach, if allowed, through zoning regulations, would increase housing options and introduce flexibility in living arrangements in the city by combining two or three single-family residential lots, with a resulting increase in dwelling units and building area.

ZONING

In our Vancouver submission, we proposed the creation of a new zoning category for corner sites called 'Residential Extra.' It would apply when two lots adjacent to a street corner are combined to create a lot at least fifty feet wide. In many areas in Toronto, three lots would be required to achieve the same minimum width.

On such a site, we proposed an increase in the number of dwelling units allowed from two to nine, and permission for larger buildings that covered more of the lot. In this way, we added more flexibility in dwelling types, sizes, and ownership options: condos, co-operatives, co-housing, or rentals.

The courtyard would serve as a meeting place.

With streets on two sides and a laneway, the corner sites allow for easier access to multiple dwellings. And as there is only one immediate neighbour, Extra Specials would have very little privacy impact on the existing or new dwellings.

CONNECTIONS

The Extra Special dwelling encourages sociability in the form of a stoop and shared courtyard, but careful positioning of windows also lends privacy, while each unit has its own dedicated outdoor space.

The Extra Special design was developed from the inside out to ensure livable spaces with outdoor connections. A garden-level pass-through and courtyard brings more sunlight from the south into the homes and makes the garden-level units accessible. The composition of the exterior facade hints at the potential for linking units, both vertically and horizontally.

Many front doors, but a low and compact building.

The living spaces in the Extra Special design are more generous than typical condominiums or even town homes, providing family-sized spaces that also can support different cultural traditions and living arrangements.

The Extra Special building form also unlocks multiple ownership combinations that range from one multi-generational household living on-site to six owners and three secondary suites. Unit combinations range from nine separate households, in one- to three-bedroom homes, to three households with three to eight bedrooms each.

The range of unit sizes and the ability to combine them in multiple ways in the Extra Special design provides market choice, tenure options, and the flexibility to meet the changing needs of a multi-generational or 'found' family, and for co-living between seniors or single people. This flexibility provides social benefits, but also economic benefits: elder care and child care are significant costs in urban areas, and sharing meal prep can help with busy schedules. None of this is new; these ideas reflect how the Vancouver Special, the brownstone, and siheyuan, a Chinese residential compound form, have been used over many generations.

DESIGN DETAILS

First-floor overhangs and second-floor patio spaces were successful elements that we borrowed from the Vancouver Special. We also kept the front door and stair configuration, which allows the two top floors to be connected into one larger home, or for individual access to two separate homes.

The Brooklyn brownstone has also been successful in adapting over time to changing needs, from larger dwelling units to apartments and back. For the Extra Special design, we borrowed the brownstone's stoop – the tall front stairs that serve as a gathering place – and how it tucked the front entrance to the garden level under the stairs. The

EXTRA SPECIAL **EXTRA SPECIAL**

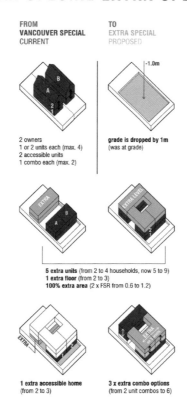

FROM
VANCOUVER SPECIAL
CURRENT

TO
EXTRA SPECIAL
PROPOSED

|-1.0m

2 owners
1 or 2 units each (max. 4)
2 accessible units
1 combo each (max. 2)

grade is dropped by 1m
(was at grade)

5 extra units (from 2 to 4 households, now 5 to 9)
1 extra floor (from 2 to 3)
100% extra area (2 x FSR from 0.6 to 1.2)

1 extra accessible home
(from 2 to 3)

3 x extra combo options
(from 2 unit combos to 6)

back entrance of the Extra Special is a walkout at the same level as the back courtyard, just like in the brownstone. A drop-off in ground level at the front of the building defines a private patio space near the street and keeps neighbours away from the front windows. This patio does not block sunlight from entering the lower-level windows because grating is used instead of a solid deck surface.

BUILDING FORM IS NOT ENOUGH

In Urbanarium's Missing Middle Competition, an important goal was housing affordability. We developed a building form and new zoning rules to answer the competition challenge, but affordability is relative. In Vancouver's inflated market, Extra Special units would not be low-cost, but they could be within reach for families who are able to co-develop a site together. In Toronto and Vancouver, the goal should be to maintain a home's affordability in the longer term; new 'missing middle' zoning categories could increase speculation and land costs, so they should be available only for co-operative or non-profit developments, to incentivize affordable housing and shared ownership models.

It's time to encourage innovation in design forms that are the middle ground between a house and a tower. But, to achieve lasting affordability, we also need to implement policies that break the cycle of land speculation in home ownership.

Extra Special Housing was designed by Workshop Architecture. Project led by Helena Grdadolnik and Kellie Chin, with support from David Colussi, Thomas Petch, and Elaine Chau.

'It's always life that's right – and architecture that's wrong.'

– Le Corbusier[1]

In a working-class Hamilton neighbourhood, a developer is building a new mid-rise project that combines old insights about the way low-income families acquire real estate with an approach to construction rooted in the vernacular of slab-and-column commercial buildings.

Vertical Subdivisions:
An interview with John van Nostrand and Drew Sinclair

John Lorinc

The structure, 468 James Street North – by Parcel Developments (formerly John van Nostrand Developments) with Sinclair van Nostrand Architects & Planners and Office Architecture, a long-time collaborator with both Parcel and SvN – will be an eight-storey mid-rise that canl accommodate up to ninety residential units. It is situated in an older, predominantly residential neighbourhood with single-family houses, low-rise apartment buildings, and street-level retail.

Its internal organization will be unlike traditional condo projects, which typically involve fixed apartment layouts of varying sizes. By contrast, 468 James North provides owners with the option of purchasing multiple 'lots' to create varying floor areas ranging from 250 to 1,000 square feet in order to fashion studio, one-, two-, or three-bedroom units of their choice. Owners who purchase more than two lots can rent out their additional ones. Owners can also customize the internal configuration of their units and alter them in the future as their household sizes evolve. The lots, in effect, are like building blocks.

The embedded flexibility comes from the project's internal design.

Pro-Home Options from 800 to 2,000 sq.-ft, as well as 400 sq.-ft on the split-level roof accessed from upper floors (see page 208) of 466-468 James St., Hamilton.

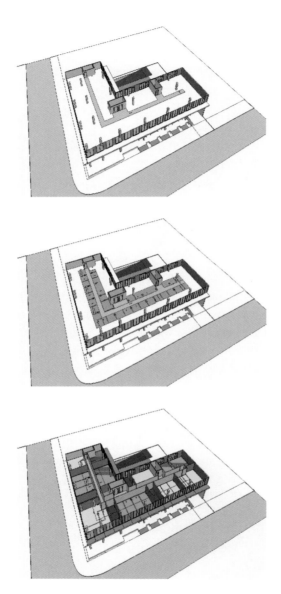

Typical floor plates at 468 James in Hamilton, Ont. (Parcel Developments). Top: elevator, fire exit stairs, corridor, structural columns and exterior walls which can be configured by owners. Middle: wet zones for bathroom and kitchens; Bottom: Possible build-out and subdivision showing variety of unit sizes and layouts.

In most mid- and high-rise apartments, units are separated from one another by so-called shear walls – poured concrete, load-bearing party walls. At 468, however, the building is supported using the sorts of columns and floors found in older warehouse structures. That means the partition walls don't bear weight, and can be added, moved, or taken away as necessary. The building's internal systems – pipes, air ducts, etc. – are routed through service walls located on every second lot line, along the hallways.

With this approach, the owner of a three-bedroom apartment who no longer needs all that space can subdivide the unit and sell the unneeded space to someone who is looking for a smaller dwelling. Conversely, owners who need more space – for a growing family, for example – may be able to add a lot to their apartment if a neighbour in an adjacent apartment decides to sell. (Older co-op apartment buildings in Manhattan have functioned like this for decades.)

The insight behind this project (which, as of mid-2019, was still in the development approvals process) traces back to the way the lower-income 'working class' created real estate for itself in many cities, including Toronto, in the nineteenth and early twentieth centuries.

As of 1950, most residents in nineteenth- and early-twentieth-century Canadian cities had purchased land and built their own homes. The agency they exercised was the single most important

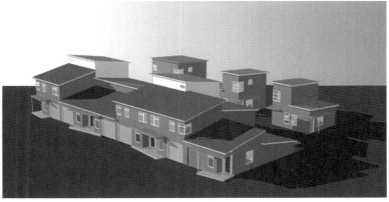

Rendering of variations in Pro-Home build-out by owners over time.

factor in defining the character of emerging neighbourhoods. Although these landowners likely didn't see themselves as city builders – they were taking advantage of demand for housing for personal financial betterment – their investment resulted in diversity and opportunity. Municipalities only needed to deliver basic infrastructure, and the landowners would do the rest, depending on their needs.

That all changed with post–World War II planning. The 1943 *Plan for Metropolitan Toronto*, by Eugene Faludi, sought to 'get away from the grow-as-you-go city – where the lot next door to you might become a gas station overnight' – and replace it with a 'fully planned' approach that sought to fortify newer suburbs from change. But this philosophy produced neighbourhoods affordable only to those in the top 35 percent of the income range – not the workers who were hired to staff new suburban factories.

In response, land developers and Toronto planners drew on European examples to begin creating new 'labour housing centres' to accommodate the other 65 percent of the population. The first of these was Thorncliffe Park, modelled closely on Vällingby, Sweden – one of several new labour housing centres developed around Stockholm. Like Vällingby, Thorncliffe Park consisted of mid-rise slabs and high-rise towers. Since then, Toronto's growth has been dominated by two housing forms – low-rise bungalows, detatched homes, and townhouses, owned by the top 35 percent, and mid-rise slabs and high-rise towers rented by the rest – a division that has driven the growing income and racial divides across the city.

As a young Toronto architecture student in the early 1970s, van Nostrand travelled through Latin America, where he discovered the informal settlements growing on the fringes of cities like Lima, Peru. 'We soon came to realize that the entire community was being built out by its inhabitants who organized themselves around existing infrastructure – in houses that were initially built out of reed-mats, and then gradually replaced by mud-brick walls,' he says.

Van Nostrand wasn't the only foreign architect to notice the extraordinary growth of Lima. John Turner, a British architect who became an outspoken proponent of 'self-building,' lived in Peru from 1957 until 1965, working mainly for Peruvian government agencies to promote self-help housing programs in villages and urban squatter communities. In 1976 he published *Housing by People: Towards Autonomy in Building Environments*, based on his experiences. In his preface, affordable-housing advocate and anarchist writer Colin Ward noted:

> John Turner absorbed in Peru the lessons offered by illegal squatter settlements: that far from being the threatening symptoms of social malaise, they were a triumph of self-help which, overcoming the culture of poverty, evolved over time into fully-serviced suburbs, giving their occupants a foothold in the urban economy.

'I was excited by what I saw in Lima and throughout Latin America – and fascinated by the idea that people themselves could be so engaged in the planning, design and construction of their own communities,' says van Nostrand.

After early stints with architect George Baird and the Ontario government, he ended up working on a Canadian International Development Agency (CIDA) project with squatter communities in Botswana. He learned first-hand how the residents of these makeshift settler communities co-created their homes and neighbourhoods, using only their own labour and ingenuity. 'The settlers had a profound sense of pride in their accomplishments, and where they had come from – something they sought to reflect in the "look" – the architecture – of their housing,' observes van Nostrand, whose CIDA team assisted by creating legal land tenure and designing the infrastructure necessary for such emerging settlements. 'Upgrading their community was a way for them to participate in a new economy,' he adds. 'Renting out rooms was key to financing initial ownership. The first building most squatters erected was a rental unit – to create an initial economy that they can leverage to finally build their own room – and then others – but rarely relinquishing the ability to continue to sublet.'

Inspired by these examples, Planning Alliance, van Nostrand's firm, in 2000 developed the so-called Pro-Home concept (see pages 206-207), with pro as shorthand for progressive. The idea was to find ways for low-income families to gain a foothold in the housing market by providing opportunities to build inexpensive prefab dwellings that can be expanded over time, permitting households with modest means an entry point into the economy of home ownership.[2]

In a 2018 interview, John van Nostrand and Drew Sinclair discussed their vision.

Q: *The Pro-Home concept, developed partly with funding from Canadian Mortgage and Housing Corporation in 2000, explored a 'variable' approach to affordable 'owner-built' housing. Could you describe the concept?*

John van Nostrand: Canada developed a very interesting approach to housing veterans returning from World War II when the federal government introduced a 'Build Your Own Home' program in the late 1940s. This approach drew together ten to twelve vets who were taught how to build a very basic 600-square-foot starter home on lots in small subdivisions located on the edges of larger cities. They would then work together to build their new houses and draw straws to select who would get first choice. Where good soils existed, the program would offer the vets the option to occupy two lots. They could start growing their own food and move on to building their starter homes. Eventually, they could sever off and sell the second lot to finance the expansion of their initial house.

Our Pro-Home approach focused on lower-density housing allowable under the Ontario Building Code, for dwellings up to three-and-a-half storeys. We proposed that these structures could be erected in planned neighbourhoods where both infrastructure and housing could be upgraded or expanded over time as residents' social and economic conditions evolved. It also built in the potential for owners to create one or more rental units to finance their mortgages and, by following conventional wood-frame construction sizes and techniques, offered them an opportunity to build all or part of the house themselves – or not!

Q: *The firm was involved with planning and designing the Athletes' Village for the Toronto 2008 Olympic bid and the Toronto 2015 Pan American Games. You have also identified the wider affordable-housing potential for the configurations of these facilities – i.e., unit floor plans that can be configured to provide for a variety of different forms of occupancy by a changing number of occupants. What are the opportunities and challenges with this approach?*

JvN: The requirements for athletes' villages are really interesting in that they require short-term accommodation for a large number of competitors in buildings that are then converted as a long-term legacy. With the 2015 Pan Am Games village, we worked on buildings that were designed as long-term, mixed-use residential condominium housing, including market and affordable housing types – what is now known as the Canary District. The project anticipated the long-term legacy by including adaptable units that would be re-appropriated into long-term condominiums and residential amenity spaces.

There were some real lessons from this experience. For the Games, we had to work out the interim partitioning of the longer-term units – say a two- or three-bedroom unit – to accommodate as many athletes as possible and permitted under local occupancy codes. We discovered these units could legally accommodate significantly more occupants than we thought possible – for example, up to six or seven people in a two-bedroom condo, or eight to nine in a three-bedroom. These units could, in fact, be designed for ongoing variability, which would allow household size to fluctuate over time – a pattern of occupancy that characterizes large, sometimes multi-family, immigrant households.

Q: *SvN's City of Hamilton West Harbour Investment Guide is a tool that allows landowners to understand the unbuilt potential of their properties. Do you see the 'owner-built' or 'owner-developed' solution for adding gentle neighbourhood density as an alternative to the conventional large-format development projects?*

Drew Sinclair: There was a time when the number of agents impacting 'city form' was directly proportional to the number of landowners. That fruitful relationship between city building and land or home ownership has somewhat stagnated. The development process has ceded home building, duplexing, and even subdivision development to a limited number of professional players. This evolution in the way we build neighbourhoods has exacerbated the crisis of affordability because fewer and fewer people are able to use 'real property' to improve their financial well-being and develop multi-generational economic stability.

Economies need robust consumers in every part of the socioeconomic spectrum to flourish. The *affordability* space is still an enormous, but often overlooked, portion of the urban housing economy. Consumers living in affordable spaces who lack equity have limited opportunity to exercise their agency as consumers. Land, or real property, creates opportunity by providing collateral. Through debt tools such as second mortgages or subsidized down-payment support, moderate-income households can build up equity and thus gain entry to the wider spectrum of the consumer economy.

Q: If historic patterns of community planning, or even historic methods of building high-rise structures (column and slab), yielded more options for owners, what are the fundamental changes in the design of modern apartment towers that now prevent this kind of adaptability?

JvN: The great majority of high-rise building forms built since 1960, and right up to today, are based on shear-wall construction. Load-bearing party walls are incorporated into the structure to reduce cost. As a result, those walls define the apartment units from the outset. It is also in the interest of the developer to build as many units as possible in order to maximize profits. Therefore, most high-rise buildings now consist of a large percentage of one- and one-and-a half-bedroom units (i.e., approximately 70 percent) and a smaller percentage of two-bedrooms. Very few blocks or towers have three- or four-bedroom apartments, the sizes required by many families.

Practically, many of these buildings have been initially marketed to singles and young professionals. In other words, they're targeted to upwardly mobile households, and the owners moved on within six to ten years, once they have families and needed larger homes in suburbs. When they left, lower-income – often immigrant – households moved in and were prepared to live in much more crowded conditions. Early developments, such as St. James Town, Thorncliffe Park, and other early public housing towers, emerged as large immigrant reception centres where occupancy was, and remains, largely uncontrolled. In turn, these high-rises became hubs of poverty and inequity with low-density neighbourhoods nearby.

Based on this analysis, the 468 James project and others in JvNd's pipeline, use the more open, column-and-slab form of construction often used in large-format retail. That means these flexible new buildings can adapt to a mix of uses, combining residential retail, commercial, and office. The floor plates are subdivided into 'lots' (separate legal parcels) served by central corridors, as well as water, wastewater, and energy lines, if they are required. Potential buyers can elect to purchase one, two, three, four, or more lots, depending on their needs and ability to pay. This approach works in much the same way as the traditional forms of ground-related sub-division that characterized the growth and change of Canadian cities before 1950. These new buildings provide a 'three-dimensional' infrastructure that supports ongoing growth and change in much the same way that larger urban and regional infrastructure do in larger metropolitan areas.

Q: *How will the built-in flexibility work in the 468 James building?*

DS: Individual apartments can be purchased in two forms. The 'basic' unit can be legally occupied and will provide owners with a sink, toilet, shower, and basic kitchen. The 'turnkey' unit is completely built-out, as in a conventional condominium. The basic units may be completed by their owners over time, with or without the assistance of the developer. In units of two parcels or more, owners can create additional rental units with street access.

This approach, we believe, offers the most direct means for owners to create value with sweat equity – an approach far more typical of ground-related housing. Economically, the building provides opportunities for not only the developer and the contractor, but also the owners themselves, and freelance trades located in the adjacent neighbourhood.

In Toronto, it's clear the unplanned older city remains economically strong, socially diverse, and dynamic, while the planned newer city has come to be characterized by poverty, polarization, and social inequality.

The twenty-first century's challenge is to learn from both older and newer Toronto – how to combine their best aspects to create a more equitable balance between rich and poor, unplanned and planned.

In *Housing by People*, John Turner, working in Peru in the 1970s, introduced us to his three 'Laws of Housing.' The first states:

> When dwellers control the major decisions and are free to make their own contribution to the design, construction and management of their housing, both the process and the environment produced stimulate individual and social well-being. When people have no control over, nor responsibility for, key decisions in the housing process, dwelling environments may instead become a barrier to personal fulfillment and a burden on the economy.[3]

That's why our housing and planning work is built on a few maxims:

Planning and designing for land development and housing need to focus on providing what people cannot already provide for themselves.

The housing we deliver in our country, towns, and cities must have the built-in ability to change over time, as people's needs and aspirations change. No matter what their income may be, the ability of any individual or household to gain access to the ownership of property or housing constitutes a fundamental ingredient of a stable urban economy; a stable personal economy; and ultimately the alleviation and/or avoidance of poverty.

Housing affordability is not simply a question of design, policy (including law), or market (construction) costs; rather, solutions must address all three simultaneously.

As a result, we focus on growth and the infrastructures required to support it at the provincial, regional, local, and household levels. The objective is to provide frameworks within which cities, neighbourhoods, and families can create and recreate themselves. We need to plan and design cities, neighbourhoods, and buildings that are stable, but also capable of adaptation, mutation, and change, and, in so doing, strike a new balance.

In an era of fiscal austerity, can public-private partnerships be leveraged to finance and deliver much-needed urban social service facilities such as homeless shelters?

A New Approach to Developing Homeless Shelters:
The Case of the Red Door Family Shelter

Matti Siemiatycki

Over the years, urban-development public-private partnerships have been widely critiqued as a form of neoliberal governance that prioritizes private profit ahead of the public interest, contributing to gentrification, affluent enclaves, greater inequality, and social polarization. Yet we are also seeing new forms of partnerships that more meaningfully attempt to deliver public benefits through the development of creative mixed-use buildings that combine private-market condominiums, grocery stores, and offices with public schools, recreation centres, and cultural facilities.

Another salient example involves an upscale condominium project that incorporates South Riverdale's Red Door Shelter, which serves women and their families. This project – the first of its kind in Toronto and possibly Canada – reveals how inter-institutional partnerships make it possible to develop multiple-use residential buildings that none of the partners could have realized on their own.

The Red Door story also illustrates how long-term collaborative relationships can be forged between public, private, and non-profit stakeholders with different interests and levels of development expertise, and seemingly incompatible needs.

The Red Door redevelopment poses a critical question: can a purpose-built emergency homeless shelter be a feasible partner within a mixed-use market condominium building? The answer can inform future attempts to integrate necessary human or social services into market-driven building projects.

Homeless shelters take a variety of forms and serve different purposes and populations. Emergency shelters provide drop-in overnight housing or housing for short-term stays. Large-scale dormitory-style emergency shelters can be located in customized facilities or within religious institutions. But there are also smaller emergency shelters that serve specific homeless populations, such as families, youth, new immigrants, or women leaving situations of domestic violence. The length of stay in such facilities may be anywhere from a few days to a year, and they tend to include supportive services on-site to assist with transitioning into more permanent housing. In addition to emergency shelter services, there are a variety of affordable and supportive housing formats meant to provide long-term residence to people on low incomes. These include social housing in buildings that are owned publicly or by non-profits, housing cooperatives, publicly subsidized apartment units within private market rental buildings, and single-room-occupancy hotels.

Homeless shelters – and affordable-housing buildings more broadly – are widely identified as 'difficult to locate' facilities and often characterized as locally unwanted land uses. Homeless people are commonly stigmatized by prejudice and bigotry, and plans for new shelters spur fears of criminal activity, diminished neighbourhood property values, traffic, and loitering. However, a facility's physical appearance is also influential – an attractive building or one that blends into its surroundings can lower public opposition. But community resistance to homeless shelters is also influenced by the perceived degree of culpability in the clients' situation and the dangerousness of the homeless population being served.

Overall, an unmistakable hierarchy of acceptable shelters has emerged. Strong community opposition is most likely to be mobilized against large-scale dormitory-style drop-in shelters providing services to single men or unaccompanied youth. By comparison, shelters serving families, children, or women escaping domestic violence tend to be viewed by communities as a less threatening and more deserving homeless population to serve locally, especially in smaller-scale facilities with separate rooms where tenancy may be longer.

Rendering: 875 Queen East (Harhay Developments). Red Door Family Shelter, lower right.

As is the case with many major cities, including Vancouver, New York, San Francisco, and London, Toronto is experiencing an acute shortage of affordable housing caused by population growth, an influx of refugees, dramatically rising property prices and rents, a luxury condominium construction boom, low vacancy rates, and limited construction of new public housing or affordable rental units. While the city's extensive network of shelters can accommodate about 4,000 homeless people per night, the system operates virtually at capacity, with 96 percent nightly occupancy rates. But efforts to develop new homeless shelters to keep up with demand and extend the coverage of such facilities outside of the downtown core have met with strong local opposition, and most ultimately have not been built.

The Red Door shelter redevelopment took place against this backdrop. One of the first emergency shelter services specifically for women and families in Toronto, the Red Door had operated out of a United Church building in the city's east end since 1982. (The shelter's name goes back to the Great Depression, when an east-end minister began helping poor and homeless families, painting the entranceway a bright red to indicate where they could find relief.)

Red Door's 106 beds represented 17 percent of the city's permanent family shelter spaces and served over five hundred families each year. It is run by a non-profit that leases space within the church building, operates through a City of Toronto contract, and has an annual operating budget of $5.2 million. Approximately half comes from the City of Toronto, with the remainder from the provincial government and fundraising. Given its location in an aging converted church building, the original facility was less than ideal as a shelter space for vulnerable populations. It included a mix of private and semi-private rooms and shared washroom facilities in a dark, unwelcoming space that's been described on Red Door's website as 'institutional, inadequate and depressing.' Nevertheless, Red Door provided high-quality service and developed a strong relationship with the surrounding community.

In 2010, the United Church decided to sell the building, located in South Riverdale, once a working-class neighbourhood. Historically, the area had a significant concentration of low-income residents, was speckled with disused industrial properties, and had a record of electing progressive politicians. It also had a small but socially mobilized community of homeless people and illegal-drug users who had deep roots within the neighbourhood and made use of local social services.

Yet South Riverdale was in a period of rapid transformation. Affluent residents and trendy shops were moving in, property prices soared, and tensions had arisen over the uncertain future of local social services. As the City of Toronto planner responsible for the South Riverdale explained in an interview, community consultations found that residents in the area would 'not allow gentrification to wash it all clean of anything else other than people who can afford new land value.'

When the church building was put up for sale, the Red Door agreed to buy the structure and maintain it as a shelter. However, the city declined to provide Red Door with a $4 million grant or a loan guarantee, nor could its board access a private loan to close the transaction. Instead, Red Door assigned its purchase agreement to a development company called Rose and Thistle, hoping the developer would include a $6 million shelter in a new market condominium to be built on the site.

But in 2013, some of the firm's investors accused Rose and Thistle's owner of financial wrongdoing, prompting a judge to put the church property into the hands of a receiver. Harhay Developments, the builder that eventually purchased the property out of receivership, had little familiarity with the Red Door shelter. The firm initially intended to develop a conventional upscale condominium on the site. 'When we came into this project,' said the developer in an interview, 'because of the receivership situation, we really didn't know about it.'

The shelter's managers and local residents feared the new owners would evict the Red Door. Indeed, the shelter had no entitlement to be on the site once its lease expired. Moreover, finding a new site for a large-format shelter in the same neighbourhood would be difficult and prohibitively expensive.

In response, local councillor Paula Fletcher and the Red Door's management mobilized a community drive to save the shelter, eventually gathering 50,000 signatures on a petition, as well as considerable financial donations to the shelter. In 2014, Toronto city council confirmed its support for the shelter by passing a motion directing staff to find an arrangement to retain the shelter in the community. Over the next eight months, city staff and Fletcher worked with Harhay, as well as Red Door's management, to find a suitable arrangement.

The result of these negotiations was a unique development proposal – a seven-storey condominium apartment building with ground-floor retail facing Queen Street East. Integrated into the side and rear of the building is a 20,000-square-foot purpose-built shelter with ninety-four beds, each in separate family rooms with private washrooms. The new building is designed to provide natural light and customized spaces, including meeting rooms, a food bank, on-site social programs, a preschool, a computer room, and outdoor play

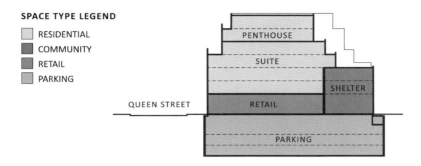

SPACE TYPE LEGEND

- RESIDENTIAL
- COMMUNITY
- RETAIL
- PARKING

PENTHOUSE

SUITE

SHELTER

QUEEN STREET

RETAIL

PARKING

space. So, while the new shelter will have twelve fewer beds than the old facility, the private rooms and improved amenity spaces will provide greater comfort and functionality.

The project was made financially possible through a variety of arrangements. Council allowed the developer to add one additional floor, valued at up to $250,000. The city, in turn, owns the shelter portion of the building and funded the capital construction costs of the facility through a reserve fund. Red Door raised money to furnish and equip the building, and collaborated with the Bank of Montreal and other philanthropists on a $3 million fundraising campaign.

Initially, a mixed-use, joint development building was not the preferred model for any of the key stakeholders. Indeed, at various points in the redevelopment process, each stakeholder – the developer, the city, and the shelter – articulated a desire to proceed on their own in a direction that best met their respective interests and needs. But as it transpired, the mixed-use joint development model provided an opportunity for each stakeholder to resolve financial, land access, planning, or community opposition constraints that would have delayed or derailed the project.

Harhay gained access to a valuable site, a density bonus, municipal funding to build the shelter, and sufficient reputational boost to build an upscale condominium in a location where it otherwise would have faced strong public resistance. The city, in turn, reduced its financial risk by retaining ownership of the new shelter building.

The local councillor and community, for its part, retained a valued social service.

Indeed, finding a collaborative advantage was central to the way the key stakeholders envisioned the project. As the chair of the Red Door's board of directors explained in an interview: 'It's a very complex solution that speaks to the excellence that each party can deliver. So each party gets to do what they do really well.'

For all those synergies, the deal emerged from a complex, unpredictable, and contentious process that took place publicly. The parties did not simply arrive at this solution through routine discussions. Rather, the eventual partnership required the catalyst of a high-profile 'Save the Red Door Shelter' campaign, initiated by Fletcher, volunteers, and a public relations firm. As the head of the PR firm explained, the goal was to make the loss of the shelter 'go from a quiet little problem to a very public discussion with action items, and a call to action.'

The resulting public awareness and pressure empowered Fletcher to obtain a motion from council tasking city staff to find a way of saving the shelter. From then on, there was strong collaboration between the three partners – the developer, the multi-department team of city staff, and the shelter operator – to find a design and financial structure that would make the project feasible.

But integrating a shelter into a luxury condominium building pushed the boundaries of complementary land uses within a single building. Across Toronto, proposals to develop homeless shelters have faced widespread NIMBY opposition from local residents, as is common across the country.

The exemplary reputation of the Red Door as a responsible service provider with a long-standing presence in the community was critical in making a mixed-use building a viable option for the various stakeholders. The shelter was actively embraced as a key part of the community fabric. Aesthetically and programmatically, the Red Door fit the profile of a good neighbour. It had been well maintained for many years, and didn't have large numbers of people congregating around it who were perceived by neighbours as dangerous or threatening. The shelter had also maintained close connections with local businesses and non-profit service providers, with the children integrating into the surrounding community by attending neighbourhood schools.

For the developer, the compatibility of land uses was predicated on the ability to sell the upscale residential units. The private development aspect of the project was made feasible because there was support for the shelter within the surrounding community as well as a market for the units. 'In terms of the condo sales, we believe that [the shelter] is not going to have any adverse impact,' the developer said. 'People are accepting of it.'

While it became apparent that there was a fit between Harhay's objectives and those of the shelter and the community, individual personalities played an important role in advancing the project. For example, the receiver originally appointed by a court to manage the sale of the church property had himself served as a volunteer board member of a Toronto social service agency, making him especially sensitive to finding a financial deal to preserve the shelter.

Fletcher's advocacy, in turn, played a central role in raising Harhay's awareness about the risk to the shelter and the need to find a resolution. As this mid-sized family-run firm became aware of the shelter's circumstances, Harhay's managers opened their minds to the possibility of incorporating the Red Door in the new development. The company recognized it could make money from this project, though at a lower rate of return and with more risk than a conventional mid-rise. But Harhay also saw the project as a chance to assist families in need, burnish its reputation as a socially conscious developer, and leave a legacy of effective city building.

Finally, the city appointed a single staff person to coordinate the project across the multiple internal departments. This official was specifically selected because he had extensive experience as a senior political staffer and a senior bureaucrat, with long-standing relationships in both camps. He saw his role as 'being the liaison between the bureaucracy and the political face,' providing the strategic management 'that is across clusters and across divisions and is more entrepreneurial and business in its approach.'

The experience of the Red Door shelter illustrates the political spaces and planning possibilities that can be opened up through deep, meaningful partnerships between public, private, and non-governmental sectors. By working toward a collaborative advantage, partnerships have the potential to spur the realization of more equitable outcomes than any of the partners could have realized on their own under the circumstances. The Red Door redevelopment sets out a model whereby partnerships with the private sector can be used to provide hard-to-site social services with a place to call home, delivering a site-specific approach to enable development to occur without necessarily spurring displacement.

The case study points to three key insights:

• First, there is a need for a strong political champion with the capacity to bring people together from diverse organizations and promote the mutual benefits of a collaborative undertaking.
• Second, complex municipal bureaucracies require a single senior staff person to take responsibility for innovative partnership projects. This point person can lead the coordination of policy implementation across various departments and have the stature to quickly resolve problems at a high organizational level.
• Third, in addition to providing high-quality social services, service providers benefit from being deeply rooted in their local community. Building strong external relationships with facility neighbours, local businesses, and institutions has the potential to challenge unwarranted stigmas about service users where they exist, and creates community allies that will advocate on behalf of the service provider to make them part of any urban redevelopment plans.

The partnership approach, of course, is not a panacea for providing critical social services. Though unique, this arrangement will not generate sufficient new private or philanthropic money for critical social infrastructure, nor does it redress structural income, gender, or racial inequalities within society. Moreover, such joint development buildings won't reverse the broader patterns and impacts of neighbourhood gentrification, and they are unlikely to be viable for the most difficult-to-locate social services. The redeveloped Red Door shelter will provide a residence space for low-income, vulnerable women and families to remain on an emergency basis in a community that is growing more expensive. Yet the influx of new upscale shops and services creates a community environment where low-income residents may not feel truly at home, without local services such as an affordable grocery store or other shops to fulfill their daily needs.

Indeed, planners cannot overlook the broader urban context surrounding these innovative, mixed-use facilities that blend social services and luxury condominiums. The Red Door project demonstrates that public-private partnerships can create site-specific spaces for some important but hard-to-locate social services to be provided. Development without displacement requires that equity and inclusiveness be viewed at a broader scale, so all residents of a neighbourhood can have their daily needs met locally and feel welcome within their surrounding community.

Why build the missing middle? Why should a city, and Toronto specifically, welcome more people into established neighbourhoods?

This book sets out a number of reasons to question our current system, which has transformed house neighbourhoods into gated communities. It is clear what's wrong with that status quo: many of Toronto's most pleasant places to live are now off-limits to everyone but the affluent. Planning policies that restrict certain housing types also restrict certain kinds of people. Such rules are inherently unjust.

Conclusion
Alex Bozikovic

In Toronto today, these land-use rules often fail to make good places. Where our current system allows new development, it favours bigness: big plans, big sites, big buildings, big capital, and big billings for planners and lawyers who know how to navigate the maze of regulation and consultation that governments have put in place. The city – government and entrepreneurs alike – should be able to build new housing at every scale in every area. Right now, we cannot.

That's a problem. More multi-family housing means more affordable market housing – at least in the sense that it provides lower-priced options than single-family houses. Broad intensification means a more inclusive city, a better quality of life for more people, and improved social cohesion. This approach uses public infrastructure more efficiently. Density means genuinely walkable neighbourhoods that can be effectively served by mass transit and rely less on the car. More to the point, denser living, in smaller homes and with shorter commutes, produces a low-carbon city.

In today's political discourse, those final two points about sustainability often seem incidental. But – likely very soon – these goals will become all-consuming. The imperative of a low-carbon society could and should provide the catalyst to rethink how our cities grow and where people live.

In the next generation, the fact of climate change caused by human behaviour will become a dominant theme, if not *the* dominant theme, in our politics. Climate scientists are already telling us that humanity faces a global emergency. According to a 2018 United Nations report, the most likely increase in average temperature – of 2.7 degrees above pre-industrial levels by 2040 – will have disastrous consequences and displace tens of millions of people.[1] Mainstream scientists believe the opportunity to avoid serious change has now passed; the question is how much ecological destruction and human suffering climate change will wreak. We have an obligation to mitigate that change.

That means changing how we live and where we live. These are local questions. The only ethical imperative for urban planning in the twenty-first century will be to mitigate the effects of climate change. If we want to substantially reduce our society's carbon emissions, we need to end sprawl and put more people's homes within walking distance of their workplaces, schools, and amenities. We need to get as many people as possible out of cars and onto mass transit.

Buildings, transportation, and electricity use are major sources of carbon emissions in Canada, adding up to about half of the total in 2016. Transportation is the second-largest source of carbon, closely linked to the output of the largest emitter: oil and gas production.

Transportation, according to most North American estimates, generates more carbon emissions than buildings. The American journal *Building Green*, in a 2018 paper, examined new office buildings in the U.S. The authors found that car commuting by office workers accounts for 11 percent more energy than is used by the buildings where they work, even when those buildings are new and follow regulations for energy efficiency.

This is true in Toronto as it is elsewhere, and the details have a lot to do with land use.

In a 2007 academic paper,[2] Jared R. VandeWeghe and Christopher Kennedy estimated the per capita greenhouse-gas emissions for 'residential activities' (essentially, housing and transportation) for census districts across Greater Toronto. They concluded that car use generated significantly more carbon emissions than buildings did.

They also found dramatic variances within the city. Most of the neighbourhoods in the downtown and nearby – i.e., the pre–World

War II walkable city – had average emissions ranging between three and five tonnes per capita per year. Other areas, including parts of East York and a large swath centred on the Bridle Path (along with almost all of the 905 region), had average emissions ranging between eight and thirteen tonnes per year. In places where the car dominates, our carbon footprints are double or even triple.

Buildings have their own sizable emissions footprints. The larger our homes and workplaces, the more energy they consume. Much of this energy is drawn directly or indirectly from fossil fuels. The construction of new buildings and the production of building materials also generate significant carbon emissions. It is possible to build homes that are more energy-efficient, but the math is difficult. An average single-family house, of around 2,000 square feet, will never be able to compete with a 1,000-square-foot unit within a multi-family building.

The development industry's reliance on concrete – an extremely high-carbon material – in apartment and condo construction does hurt the case for multi-family housing. But increasingly, there is a green alternative: wood, including new assembly techniques known as mass timber. These are now being used to construct mid-rise buildings in Toronto.

More to the point, regular wood-frame construction is both cheap and common for buildings up to four storeys. The missing middle can and should be made largely of wood. The current pattern of concentrating density into high-rise towers – which have structures and underground garages made of concrete – substantially increases the carbon footprint of Toronto housing.

This quick analysis leads to a clear conclusion. If we wish to reduce our carbon footprint, then the single most powerful tool at our disposal is middle-density intensification in established, walkable neighbourhoods.

But how will the climate imperative shape local land-use policy? It's easy to imagine that federal and provincial policy will require cities to plan for lower-carbon development.

There is precedent. In the Toronto region, the Greenbelt Plan imposed by the province more than a decade ago did important work in curbing sprawl. In this moment, we need to go much further.

Progressive American politicians are making an urgent and explicit case for zoning reform. In California, Governor Gavin Newsom has called for dramatically increasing the construction of housing in zones served by transit, building on the energy of young progressives who see YIMBY – Yes In My Backyard – as serving the interests of affordability and sustainability.

In short, some American progressives now clearly understand the connection between land use and the climate, and such thinking is taken for granted in transportation and land-use planning across most of Europe. Many Canadian progressives have been slow to follow, and the reasons are complex. But, essentially, this blind spot is the legacy of Jane Jacobs.

In Canada outside of Quebec, and certainly in Toronto, opposing new development of all kinds is a political default for many on the left. In the early 1970s, the Reform movement in Toronto politics rolled back the pro-development agenda of the 1960s. Young progressives argued to save the old neighbourhoods of the city, then socially and economically mixed, from aggressive development.

Jane Jacobs herself was a friend and a mentor to the Reform movement's politicians and planners. They shared her love for the small scale, fine grain, variety, and diversity of the old Toronto neighbourhoods: the 'sidewalk ballet' that she identified in the working-class streets of the West Village in Manhattan and found, too, after relocating to Toronto.

But much has changed since the anti-blockbusting fights of the 1960s and 1970s. House owners in Toronto are now affluent. Their dwellings are worth much more, on the whole, than the 'luxury condos' that many people like to decry. And as they fight new developments, many neighbourhood groups demonstrate their political power.

However knee-jerk their dislike of change, however frank their opposition to 'double density,' Toronto homeowners can justify their

NIMBYism by wrapping it in Jane Jacobs's values. But let's be clear: they are no longer the underdogs, protecting inner-city immigrant enclaves from the wrecking balls. Today, the mainstream Torontonian opposition to denser housing, captured in the Yellowbelt and associated policies, is in fact locking down much of the city to new residents of all stripes.

But thus far, there have been few calls for zoning reform in Toronto or the region. This is where the climate crisis must alter the discussion: we now have an urgent reason to reconsider our outdated assumptions about the social importance of 'stable' neighbourhoods. Anti-growth sentiment is hollowing out too much of the old Toronto, and it's stopping postwar Toronto neighbourhoods from evolving into more urban and walkable places.

More neighbourhoods that are dense with people, dense with different kinds of activity, rich in amenities, and served with transit. This is what Toronto needs now, and it is what the planet now demands from Toronto.

In a time of housing crunch, characterized by rising costs and low availability, Toronto's housing supply is not keeping up with demand. Increasing stock is essential to meeting the needs of residents and newcomers. But a large portion of the city is blocked off to development due to zoning restrictions. Even though the city is growing, in the last fifteen years over half of Toronto's residential neighbourhoods have seen population decline, meaning growth is unevenly distributed throughout the city.

Appendix 1

A Citizen's Guide to Gentle Density

Proposed changes and development in neighbourhoods can be unwelcome. Residents may feel as though they are losing their neighbourhood or that its character will be significantly altered. This concern may manifest as opposition to new proposals, and can also be based on the perception that development will negatively affect current residents. However, research has shown that the negative impacts feared by community members never actually come to pass. This guide addresses community concerns about gentle density in their area.

WHAT IS GENTLE DENSITY?

Gentle density is defined as attached, ground-oriented housing that is denser than a detached house but of a similar scale and low-rise character. Unlike medium or high-density projects, gentle density is 'gentle' because of the comparatively minimal impact it has on established communities. It's a modest, often invisible way to add residential density and revitalize existing neighbourhoods while retaining the qualities that make them desirable.

HOW WILL DEVELOPMENT AFFECT YOUR NEIGHBOURHOOD?

Myth: My property will lose value if my neighbourhood intensifies. **Fact:** A 2004 study by Harvard's Joint Centre for Housing Studies showed that neighbourhoods with more diverse types of housing have higher property values than neighbourhoods where multi-unit

'The Missing Middle.'

homes do not exist. Another study conducted in 2001 by the National Association of Home Builders found that homes with multi-unit dwellings nearby appreciated in value faster than in areas with only one type of housing.

Myth: Infrastructure, services, and amenities in my neighbourhood will be overextended if more people have to share them.
Fact: Gentle density requires less extensive infrastructure than brand-new development. Services like sewers, electricity, roads, and schools already exist. Increased usage can lead to reinvestment and improvements of these services. A 2012 study from Washington also showed that the quality of neighbourhoods, measured by features such as walkability, increases with density.

Myth: Traffic will increase on my street if more units are added.
Fact: Multi-family units located near reliable transit are likely to attract new residents with lower rates of car ownership. This could include low-income families, seniors, or people with disabilities who do not own cars. A 2003 study by the Institute of Transportation Engineers revealed that on a weekday, the number of automobile trips per household in apartment neighbourhoods was 42 percent less than in single-detached household areas. On the weekend, apartment households take 50 to 60 percent fewer automobile trips than single-detached households.

Myth: Renovations, additions, and redevelopment on my block will change the character of the neighbourhood.

Fact: Some residents see multi-dwelling homes as disruptive to stable neighbourhood character. However, higher-density homes must still comply with the same building restrictions and design standards as other houses in the neighbourhood. These restrictions are set out in the zoning bylaw, the official plan, neighbourhood design guidelines, the building code, and any other policies associated with the neighbourhood.

FIVE BENEFITS OF NEIGHBOURHOOD DENSITY

1. Utilize Existing Services: A major benefit of neighbourhood density is that introducing gentle density in the right areas makes use of existing public amenities such as parks, libraries, schools, and public transportation services. Increased usage from a growing population can lead to reinvestment in these services without having to fund capital expenditure to build new facilities.

2. Boost the Local Economy: Density is good for local businesses and may provide residents with a better quantity and quality of shops and services.

3. Healthy Neighbourhoods: Denser neighbourhoods may promote healthy activities such as walking, cycling, gardening, and, for children, outdoor play.

4. Increase Housing Stock: Gentle density contributes to an increased supply of housing and, potentially, a higher vacancy rate.

5. Retain Neighbourhood Feel: The nature of gentle density is that new units are added gradually, so neighbourhoods are revitalized at a suitable pace and scale. The pre-existing low-rise character of the established neighbourhood is preserved, retaining the familiar neighbourhood feel, while adding diversity of housing design, as well as residents and family types.

In its Official Plan, the City of Toronto defines Neighbourhoods as 'physically stable areas made up of residential uses in lower scale buildings such as detached houses, semi-detached houses, duplexes, triplexes and townhouses, as well as interspersed walk-up apartments that are no higher than four storeys. Parks, low-scale local institutions, home occupations, cultural and recreational facilities and small-scale retail, service and office uses are also provided for in Neighbourhoods.'

Currently, the city reinforces the notion of physical character through the protection and promotion of 'Prevailing Building Types,' as laid out in Official Plan Amendment 320. This means that if a neighbourhood is currently zoned for single-detached houses, only single-detached houses are permitted in the future.

However, building typology is not the only way to understand the unique identity and character of residential neighbourhoods. It's important to consider which specific elements make neighbourhoods great. For example, the City of San Francisco has identified eight other elements:

• Walk to Shops	• Gathering Places
• Safe Streets	• City Services
• Get Around Easily	• Special Character
• Housing Choices	• Part of a Whole

These features determine how the broader neighbourhood can look and feel without focusing on the physical built form of individual buildings. They also highlight how tangible and intangible elements work together to create great places to live.

NEIGHBOURHOOD CHARACTER

HOW TO ADD DENSITY TO YOUR NEIGHBOURHOOD

To make changes to houses in existing stable neighbourhoods, there are three options available to property owners:

1. Stay within as-of-right permission.
2. Obtain a minor variance to the zoning bylaw from the Committee of Adjustment.
3. Apply for a rezoning.

As-of-Right

Working within the as-of-right land uses is the easiest and least expensive option, as it avoids any delays or cost burdens associated with seeking variances or rezoning. Homeowners must ensure that the zoning is adhered to and obtain a building permit. The risk and uncertainty factors are low, but the degree of change is also low. Key considerations to remember are height, density, setback from the edges of the property, distance between surrounding buildings, lot coverage, secondary suites, and massing.

Minor Variance

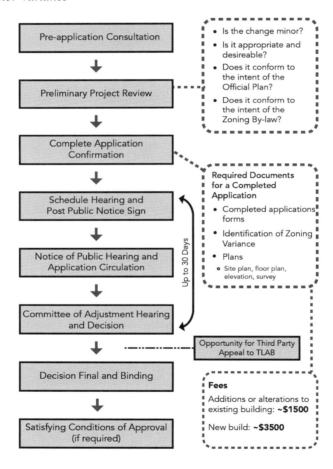

Official Plan and Zoning Bylaw Amendments

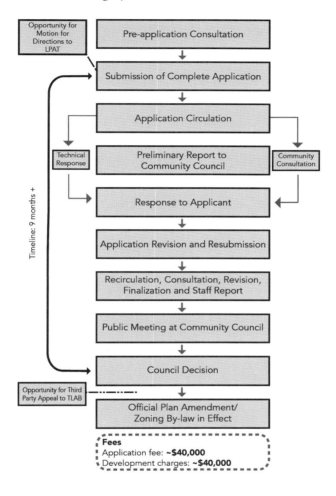

Prepared by Charlotte Balluch, Alexis Beale, Jessica Brodeur, Tessa Chapman, Davin McCully, Michael Niezgoda, Candace Safonovs, and Vickey Simovic as part of a master's studio project for Ryerson University Urban and Regional Planning program. Supervisor: Randolph Hodges.

The Ontario Association of Architects' Housing Affordability Task Group is exploring design and regulatory opportunities that address housing affordability in growing communities across Ontario and beyond.

Why? This is a significant issue impacting millions of current and future citizens in Ontario.

Appendix 2
Excerpt from *Housing Affordability in Growing Urban Areas*
Ontario Association of Architects

Affordable Housing is typically used to define lower-income housing needs that are eligible for Federal or Provincial Subsidies. *Housing Affordability* refers to the lack of affordability across not only lower- but also middle- and even higher-income households – be they rented or owned – subsidized or not. This is the real issue.

GOAL A: INCREASE SUPPLY

Actions
Increase Density + Free Up Land
• Promote low-rise infill and intensification within Neighbourhoods through renovations, additions, redevelopments;
• Expand permissions for semis, duplexes, triplexes, four-plexes, townhouses, walk-up apartments and secondary suites (i.e., basement suites, garden suites, and laneway suites);
• Promote low- to mid-rise intensification along Corridors, particularly those with frequent and reliable public transit; and
• Promote mid- to high-rise intensification within Centres.

Optimize Existing Zoning Potential
• In some urban areas, a significant proportion of development potential, based on existing Zoning permissions, remains unrealized; and
• Landowners should be encouraged and incentivized to develop their properties to full capacity in order to maximize the provision of additional residential units.

Increase Zoning Potential
- In other urban areas, opportunities exist to increase Zoning permissions in order to allow for increased densities and a greater range of building types;
- Municipalities should be encouraged to update existing Zoning permissions to promote the diversification of the housing stock.

Update Municipal Density Targets to Match Those Set Out in the Growth Plan (2017)
- Municipalities throughout the Greater Golden Horseshoe (GGH) do not set densities for existing Neighbourhoods which match those required for new Neighbourhoods under the Provincial Growth Plan (2017); and
- Municipalities need to ensure that their specified densities conform with those outlined in The Growth Plan (2017).

Results

Taking these actions has the potential to increase supply to meet housing demand of one and a half million persons in Ontario's cities over the next twenty-five years.

GOAL B: MAKING HOUSING FINANCIALLY ATTAINABLE

Actions

Reduce Construction Costs
- Increase Zoning permissions in Neighbourhoods and Corridors;
  - Reduce development charges and application fees;
  - Promote modular and prefabricated housing.

Changes to the Ontario Building Code (OBC)
- In addition to revising current municipal land use regulations and Zoning permissions, the Ontario Building Code should be revised to remove regulatory hurdles in order to reduce construction costs. Example: Create an alternative means of achieving Ontario Building Code compliance to permit a four-storey building with a single exit. This would require oversight by a Licensed Architect

Financial Model Opportunities
- The OAA should support the exploration and development of new Financial Models that are supportive of housing affordability.

Results
Taking these actions has the potential to make housing available to citizens with incomes ranging from $25,000 to $120,000.

GOAL C: ADDRESS THE URGENCY

Actions
Speed Up Delivery
- Streamline and simplify the development approvals process;
- Expedite development review, evaluation, and approval timelines;
- Incentivize construction methods (i.e., modular, prefabricated, and wood-frame construction) with quick turnaround; and
- Make public land available through Development RFPs.

Results
Taking these actions has the potential to meet municipal and federal targets to deliver affordable housing.

The report was prepared by SvN Architects + Planners Inc. (John van Nostrand, Liana Bresler, and Blair Scorgie, with the support of Eric Pitre and Jorge Quesada Davies), with the direction and assistance of the OAA Housing Affordability Task Group. The complete version is available here: www.oaa.on.ca/oaamedia/documents/OAA%20 HATG%20-%20Feb%2011% 20-%20Low%20Res.pdf

Notes

'Introduction,' John Lorinc

1. In Greater Toronto, 78 percent of low-income and 33 percent of middle-income households pay over 30 percent for their housing; for those earning above $120,000, the figure shrinks to 3 percent. Ontario Association of Architects. Housing Affordability in Growing Urban Areas. February 2019. www. oaa.on.ca/news %20&%20events/news/detail/Housing-Affordability-in-Growing-Urban-Areas:-Now-Available/2455.

2. In 2018, the average condo sold for $521,239 and the average non-condo (i.e., house) went for $887,025. Source: *The Big Picture (It's not just about housing).* Presentation by political scientist Zack Taylor, University of Western Ontario.

3. Ibid., Taylor. The income required to carry typical mortgages for average-priced condos and houses is $93,000 and $160,000 respectively. As of 2015, Toronto's median total household income was just under $66,000 (www.toronto.ca/wp-content/uploads/ 2017/10/8f41-2016-Census-Backgrounder-Income.pdf).

4. As a company official told Dow Jones in 2015, 'The ambition is to continue to grow by cherry picking suitable properties … We will invest C$5 million over the next three years, including over $1 million in common areas improvements. We do this in order to provide a Better Living for current and future tenants.' According to a Postmedia story published on 19 October 2018, Montreal officials issued a stop-work order on one of Ake-lius's newly acquired Montreal properties after tenants complained that the heating had been turned off for two weeks. 'Akelius, which owns 50,000 apartments worldwide, has faced similar complaints in Toronto,' the story noted.

5. Jill Mahoney and Matthew McClearn, 'Inside the Flipping Frenzy at Toronto's X2 Condo.' Globe and Mail, 6 May 2017. www.theglobeandmail.com/news/investigations/investigation-x2-condo-toronto/article34906278/.

6. Richard Harris, *Unplanned Suburbs: Toronto's American Tragedy, 1900–1950* (Baltimore: Johns Hopkins University Press, 1999), 92.

7. Richard Dennis, 'Toronto's First Apartment-House Boom: An Historical Geography, 1900–1920,' research paper (Centre for Urban and Community Studies, University of Toronto, October 1989). citiescentre.webservices. utoronto.ca/Assets/Cities+Centre+2013+Digital+Assets/Cities+Centre/Cities+Centre/Digital+Assets/pdfs/publications/Research+Papers/177+Dennis+1989+Torontos+First+Apartment+House+Boom.pdf.

8. Eve Blau, *The Architecture of Red Vienna, 1919–1934* (Cambridge: MIT Press, 1999), 45.

9. Hope Daley, 'Vienna Leads Globally in Affordable Housing and Quality of Life,' *Archinect*, 25 July 2018. archinect.com/news/article/150074889/vienna-leads-globally-in-affordable-housing-and-quality-of-life.

10. David Hanna and Francois Dufaux, *Montreal: A Rich Tradition in Medium Density Housing* (CMHC, 2002), 43.

11. Ibid., 44.

12. David Hulchanski, Neighbourhood Change. (www.neighbourhoodchange.ca)

13. Henry Grabar, 'Minneapolis Confronts its History of Housing Segregation,' Slate, 7 December 2018.

14. Ibid.

15. Graham Haines and Brianna Aird, 'Finding the Missing Middle in the GTHA,' Ryerson City Building Institute, October 2018. www.citybuildinginstitute.ca/portfolio/missing-middle/.

16. Some pundits have also advocated 'filtering,' the practice of encouraging the development of high-end dwellings, on the assumption that they'll encourage residents further down the housing food chain to trade up, thereby creating more availability all the way through the market. It's true that some luxury homes may eventually be carved up into apartments over long periods of time as they become too costly to maintain, but these sorts of inter-generational churn cycles hardly qualify as an intentional housing-affordability plan.

17. Richard Florida, 'Does Upzoning Boost Housing Supply and Lower Prices? Maybe Not,' CityLab, 31 January 2019.

18. In his paper, published in early 2019 in Urban Affairs Review, Freemark reviewed the prior research on the relationship between zoning and supply. Among the findings: that regulations limiting density lead to higher land and housing costs, although the relationship isn't strictly causal; that market forces are stronger than zoning rules in determining housing prices; and that up-zoning would increase the development potential of properties and therefore fuel speculation. From 'Upzoning Chicago: Impacts of a Zoning Reform on Property Values and Housing Construction,' Urban Affairs Review, 29 January 2019.

19. Kenneth Chan, 'Rental Rates Falling in Seattle Due to Flood of New Supply from Building Boom,' Daily Hive, 31 January 2019.

20. Alex Baca and Hannah Lebovitz, 'No, Zoning Reform Isn't Magic. But It's Crucial,' CityLab, 5 February 2019. www.citylab.com/perspective/2019/02/zoning-reform-house-costs-yonah-freemark-research/582034/.

21. Housing New York 2.0 (2017). nyc.gov/assets/hpd/downloads/pdf/about/

hny-2.pdf. Accessed February 22, 2019.

22. Henry Goldman, 'NYC Comptroller Says Bill de Blasio Housing Plan Fails Needy Families,' Bloomberg, 29 November 2018. www.bloomberg.com/news/articles/2018-11-29/nyc-comptroller-says-de-blasio-housing-plan-fails-needy-families.

The Yellowbelt Index

1. See p. 105.
2. www.mapto.ca/maps/2017/3/4/the-yellow-belt.
3. What is the Missing Middle, Evergreen and Canadian Urban Institute, 8. https://www.evergreen.ca/downloads/pdfs/2018/What_is_the_Missing_Middle_Evergreen_CUI_s2.pdf.
4. Ibid., 10.
5. Ibid., 15.
6. Graham Haines and Brianna Aird, 'Finding the Missing Middle in the GTHA,' Ryerson City Building Institute, October 2018. www.citybuildinginstitute.ca/portfolio/missing-middle/.
7. Planning project.
8. Toronto Region Board of Trade. Better Housing Policy Playbook. 2018. www.bot.com/Portals/0/BOARD_AFG_Municipal01_housing_playbook_FINAL.pdf.
9. City of Toronto research request.
10. Zack Taylor, The Big Picture (It's not just about housing), N.D.
11. Ibid.
12. Ibid. Finding the Missing Middle in the GTHA.
13. Housing Affordability in Growing Urban Areas, Ontario Architects Association, 2019. https://www.oaa.on.ca/oaamedia/documents/OAA%20HATG%20-%20Feb%2011%20-%20Low%20Res.pdf.
14. http://spacing.ca/toronto/2018/04/25/airbnb-torontos-rental-apartment-market/.

'The Spadina Gardens,' Emma Abramowicz

1. 'Houses Are Very Scarce: Fully Two Thousand Families Are Homeless in Toronto: Buying Is Heavy: Fifteen Hundred More Residences Needed,' *Globe*, 12 October 1901, 30.

2. 'A "Long Felt Want" Filled: A [sic] Idea of Montreal's That Should Be Copied Here,' *Globe*, 2 August 1890, 9.

3. 'The Yellow Danger: Chinese as Chambermaids in Toronto Houses: Taking the Place of Female Domestic Help – Canadian Girls Attracted to the Pan-American by Promises of High Wages. *Globe*, 23 April 1901, 12.

4. 'How Toronto Is Growing: Building Operations in the City for the Year Show a Marked Increase: The First Apartment House,' Globe, 30 December 1899, 21.

5. 'Solution of Some Domestic Problems: Apartment Houses Strongly Advocated for People of Toronto: Company to Build Them: Correspondent of The Star Tells Why They Are Needed – Estate Men's Views,' *Toronto Daily Star*, 26 July 1901, 1.

6. 'Will Relieve the Situation,' *Globe*, 31 October 1903, 23.

7. Library and Archives Canada, Ottawa, Series RG 76-C, Roll T-480.

8. The Toronto City Directory (Might Directories Ltd., 1903).

9. 'Residential Apartments,' *Globe*, 19 September 1903, 28.

10. 'The Growth of the Apartment Idea in Toronto,' *Globe*, 9 April 1904, 4.

11. The Toronto City Directory (Might Directories Ltd., 1904).

12. 'Real Estate Review,' *Globe*, 11 February 1905, 4.

13. City of Toronto Fire Insurance Plans, Plate 32, 1884–1903, City of Toronto Archives.

14. The Toronto City Directory (Might Directories Ltd., 1906–08).

15. 'Simplicity Marks Rites for Col. Harry McGee,' *Globe and Mail*, 14 April 1939, 17.

16. The Toronto City Directory (Might Directories Ltd., 1906).

17. 'Oppose Apartment House: Lowther Avenue Residents Resent an Intrusion: Declare That Family Hotel Will Depreciate Real Estate Values in That District,' *Globe*, 18 March 1905, 24.

18. 'Preparing to Build Apartment House,' *Toronto Daily Star*, 1 May 1905, 1.

19. 'Sharp Work in This Real Estate Deal: And the City Will Help the Property Owners in Fight Against an Apartment House, *Toronto Daily Star*, 31 March, 1905, 1.

20. 'Suit over Grocer's Bill,' *Toronto Daily Star*, 22 August 1905, 1.

21. 'Preparing to Build Apartment House,' *Toronto Daily Star*.

22. Hill, Robert G., and Robert McCallum, *Biographical Dictionary of Architects in Canada, 1800–1950*. Retrieved from dictionaryofarchitectsincanada.org.

23. 'A Tale of Two Houses of Flats: Controllers Allow One on Queen Street But Object to Another at Huron and Cecil Streets,' *Toronto Daily Star*, 29 March 1905, 5.

24. 'Preparing to Build Apartment House,' *Toronto Daily Star*.

25. 'Apartment House Scheme,' *Globe*, 19 May 1905, 8; 'He Has No Permit: And City Will Prosecute Alfred Howes [sic] for Putting Up an Apartment House,' *Toronto Daily Star*, 19 May 1905, 5.

26. 'An Apartment House Builder Goes to Law,' *Toronto Daily Star*, 1 June 1905, 6.

27. 'Apartment House Permit Has Been Issued,' *Globe*, 28 June 1905, 10.

28. The Society Blue Book, Toronto (Dau's Blue Books, Inc., 1910 & 1913).

29. The Toronto City Directory (Might Directories Ltd., 1911 & 1912)

30. The Toronto City Directory (Might Directories Ltd., 1912); Census of Canada, 1911, Ward Four, Toronto North, Ontario, Library and Archives Canada, Ottawa.

31. Miscellaneous Directory, City of Toronto (Might Directories Ltd., 1925).

32. 1950 Toronto City Directory (Might Directories Ltd., 1950).

33. Library and Archives Canada, various censuses and voters lists, 1911–35.

34. City of Toronto Aerial Photographs, 1947–70, City of Toronto Archives.

35. 'A Tale of Two Houses of Flats,' *Toronto Daily Star*.

36. 'Garage at Oriole and St. Clair Avenue: Because Owner of Corner Was Prevented from Building Apartment House: Residents Are Indignant,' *Toronto Daily Star*, 4 March 1912, 4.

37. 'Noise Disturbed Him: Mr. L. H. Bowerman Erected a Sound-Proof Fence: His Residence Adjoins Large Apartment House – Now City Officials Say It Threatens the Fire Protection and Want It Down,' *Globe*, 29 July 1909, 14.

38. 'A Tale of Two Houses of Flats,' *Toronto Daily Star*; 'Preparing to Build Apartment House,' *Toronto Daily Star*; 'Garage at Oriole and St. Clair Avenue,' Toronto Daily Star.

39. 'Said That Attack Will Be Made on Apartment By-Law: Act Contemplates That Each Street Is to Be Dealt with on Its Merits: Whole Districts Are Included: Cannot Hope to Do Away with Such Houses as Conditions Are To-day: Are Already Restricted: Long List of the Places Where They Are Forbidden under the New Law,' *Toronto Daily Star*, 14 May 1912, 1.

40. 'Urges Small Apartments: Board of Control Wants the Residential Restrictions to Be Relaxed: M'Bride Has Scheme,' *Globe*, 12 December 1918, 7.

'The Genesis of the Yellowbelt,' Richard White

1. Richard Dennis, 'Interpreting the Apartment House: Modernity and Metropolitanism in Toronto, 1900-1930,' *Journal of Historical Geography*, 20, 3 (1944), p.306

2. Statues of Ontario, 4 Edward VII (1904), Chapter 22, Section 19; and 3 George V (1912), Chapter 40, Section 10

3. City of Toronto, Council Minutes, various years

4. City of Toronto Planning Board, 'The Changing City,' 1959

5. 'Towards a New Plan for Toronto,' 1965, p.21

6. Don Vale Working Committee, 'Don Vale Urban Renewal Scheme,' 1969, p.92

'The War of the Rosedales,' Ed Jackson

Centre for Urban and Community Studies, University of Toronto, 1989.

City of Toronto Planning Board. Rosedale Planning District: Appraisal. Toronto, 1960.

Crawford, Bess Hillery. *Rosedale*. Erin: Boston Mills Press, 2000.

Dennis, Richard. *Toronto's First Apartment-Home Boom: An Historical Geography, 1900–1920*.

LeBlanc, Dave. 'When Modernism and Yellow Brick Invaded Old Rosedale.' *Globe and Mail*, 15 October 2015.

Lorinc, John. 'Rosedale Apartment Proposal Sparks War between Residents and Developer.' *Globe and Mail*, 3 May 2018.

White, Richard. *Planning Toronto: The Planners, The Plans, Their Legacy*. Vancouver: UBC Press, 2016.

'Why Density Makes Great Places,' Alex Bozikovic

1. 'Are There Enough Playgrounds for Children?' *Toronto Daily Star*, 21 April 1952, 6.

'The Urban Legend,' Ana Teresa Portillo and Mercedes Sharpe Zayas

Baiocchi, G. 'Communities over Commodities: People-Driven Alternatives to an Unjust Housing System. Right to the City Alliance,' 2018. homesforall.org/wpcontent/uploads/2018/03/Communities-OverCommodities_Full-Report.pdf.

Dear, M., and J. Wolch. *Landscapes of Despair: From Deinstitutionalization to Homelessness.* Princeton: Princeton University Press, 1987.

Kipfer, S., and R. Keil. 'Toronto Inc? Planning the Competitive City in the New Toronto.' *Antipode* 34(2), 2002: 227–64.

Lost Rivers. N.D. 'The Town of Parkdale and the Village of Brockton.' www.lostrivers.ca/content/points/parkdale.html.

Parkdale Intercultural Association. N.D. 'Our History.' www.piaparkdale.com/about-us/our-history/.

Parkdale Village Business Improvement Association. N.D. 'History.' parkdalevillagebia.com/history/.

Samson, C. 'The Rule of Terra Nullius and the Importance of International Human Rights for Indigenous Peoples.' *Essex Human Rights Review* 5(1), July 2008.

Slater, T. 'Toronto's South Parkdale Neighbourhood: A Brief History of Development, Disinvestment, and Gentrification.' Centre for Urban and Community Studies 28, 2005: 1–7.

Slater, T. 'Municipally Managed Gentrification in South Parkdale, Toronto.' *Canadian Geographer* 48 (3), 2004: 303–25.

Suttor, Greg. 'Taking Stock of Supportive Housing for Mental Health and Addictions in Ontario.' Wellesley Institute, 2016. www.wellesleyinstitute.com/wpcontent/uploads/2016/11/Taking-Stock-of-Supportive-Housing.pdf.

Whitzman, C., and T. Slater. 'Village Ghetto Land: Myth, Social Conditions, and Housing Policy in Parkdale, Toronto, 1879–2000.' *Urban Affairs Review* 41(5), 2006: 673–96.

'A City of Houses,' Gil Meslin

1. 'Is the Apartment House Home,' *Toronto Daily Star*, Saturday September 7, 1907. Page 18.

2. Housing Problem Being Discussed. *Toronto Daily Star.* March 8, 1907: 7.

3. 'Proposals for a New Plan for Toronto,' Toronto Planning Board, 1966.

'Defining "Affordable,"' Katrya Bolger

1. See: www.toronto.ca/ wp-content/uploads/2017/10/8f41-2016-Census-Backgrounder-Income.pdf.

'Two Million Empty Bedrooms,' Joy Connelly

1. Shane Dingman, 'Toronto's Low-Rise Neighbourhoods Losing Sensity as "Overhousing" Spreads,' *Globe and Mail*, 15 March 2018. www.theglobeandmail.com/real-estate/toronto/torontos-low-rise-neighbourhoods-losing-density-as-overhousing-spreads/article38285466/.

2. Statistics Canada, 'The Shift to Smaller Households over the Past Century,' last modified 17 May 2017. www150.statcan.gc.ca/n1/pub/11-630-x/11-630-x2015008-eng.htm.

3. Statistics Canada, 2016 Census, Ontario and Canada.

4. Statistics Canada, Fertility: Overview, 2012 to 2016, released 5 June 2018. www150.statcan.gc.ca/n1/pub/91-209-x/2018001/article/54956-eng.htm.

5. Lisa Freeman, 'Toronto's Suburban Rooming Houses: Just a Spin on a Downtown "Problem"?' Wellesley Institute, October 2014, 12.

6. Immigration, Refugees and Citizenship Canada, 'The Housing Experience of New Canadians: Insights from the

Longitudinal Survey of Immigrants to Canada,' last updated 1 August 2012. www.canada.ca/en/immigration-refugees-citizenship/corporate/reports-statistics/research/housing-experiences-new-canadians-insights-longitudinal-survey-immigrants-canada-lsic/owner.html.

7. Jennifer Yang, 'Census Shows Big Changes in Scarborough's Little China,' *Toronto Star*, 28 October 2017. www.thestar.com/news/gta/2017/10/25/census-shows-big-changes-in-scarboroughs-little-china.html.

8. The full report is available here: cpplanning.ca/project-work.

9. Statistics Canada, 'Young Adults Living with Their Parents in Canada, 2016,' released 2 August 2017. www12.statcan.gc.ca/census-recensement/2016/as-sa/98t8-200-x/2016008/98-200-x2016008-eng.cfm.

10. Laura J. Miller, 'Family Togetherness and the Suburban Ideal,' Sociological Forum 10:3 (September 1995), 393–418. www.jstor.org/stable/684782?seq=1#page_scan_tab_contents.

11. City of Toronto, Backgrounder, 2016 Census: Income, 14 September 2017. www.toronto.ca/wp-content/uploads/2017/10/8f41-2016-Census-Backgrounder-Income.pdf.

12. CMHC, Rental Market Report, Greater Toronto Area, October 2017.

13. Ibid.

14. Freeman, 12

'Dissecting Official Plan Amendment 320,'
Blair Scorgie

1. As the ruling noted, 'The prevailing building type and physical character of a geographic neighbourhood will be determined by the most frequently occurring form of development in that neighbourhood. Some Neighbourhoods will have more than one prevailing building type or physical character. The prevailing building type or physical character in one geographic neighbourhood will not be considered when determining the prevailing building type or physical character in another geographic neighbourhood. While prevailing will mean most frequently occurring for purposes of this policy, this Plan recognizes that some geographic neighbourhoods contain a mix of physical characters. In such cases, the direction to respect and reinforce the prevailing physical character will not preclude development whose physical characteristics are not the most frequently occurring but do exist in substantial numbers within the geographic neighbourhood, provided that the physical characteristics of the proposed development are materially consistent with the physical character of the geographic neighbourhood and already have a significant presence on properties located in the immediate context or abutting the same street in the immediately adjacent block(s) within the geographic neighbourhood.'

2. For example, the story of a proposed triplex intended to replace a postwar bungalow on Westhampton Drive, an Etobicoke residential street just south of the interchange between highways 401 and 427. In that case, the zoning in the area actually allowed for a triplex, but city-planning officials, in February 2019, opposed the minor variances requested for this application, saying the project didn't adhere to the prevailing character and building types on the street.

'Radical Typologies,' Annabel Vaughan

1. Shane Dingman. 'Toronto's Low-Rise Neighbourhoods Losing Density as "Overhousing" Spreads.' *Globe and Mail*, 15 March 2018.

2. Statistics Canada. 'Housing in Canada: Key Results from the 2016 Census.' 25 October 2017.

3. Ann-Marie Nasr, Andrea Oppedisano, and Annely Zonena. Growing Up: Planning for Children in New Vertical Communities. Draft Urban Design Guidelines. Toronto: Strategic Initiatives, Policy & Analysis, May 2017.

4. Seattle Planning Commission, Neighborhoods for All: Expanding Housing Opportunity in Seattle's Single-Family Zones. 2018.

5. Ibid.

6. Henry Grabar. 'Minneapolis Confronts Its History of Housing Segregation.' Slate, 7 December 2018.

7. Josh Ryan-Collins, Toby Lloyd, and Laurie Macfarlane. Rethinking the Economics of Land and Housing (London: Zed Books, 2017): 8.

8. City of Edmonton. 'Flag-Shaped Lot Pilot Project.' www.edmonton.ca/city_government/urban_planning_and_design/flag-shaped-lot-pilot-project.aspx.

9. Tim Querengesser. 'Coming to Edmonton's Housing Market: The "Pork Chop" Lot.' Globe and Mail, 21 September 2018.

10. City of Vancouver. Amendments to the Zoning and Development By-law – Laneway Home Regulations. Policy Report, Planning, Urban Design and Sustainability, 2018.

11. Lynda H. Macdonald. Changing Lanes: The City of Toronto's Review of Laneway Suites. Final Report, Community Planning, Toronto and East York District, City-Initiated Official Plan Amendment and Zoning Amendment, 2018.

12. Ann McAfee. 'Tools for Change: CityPlan Vancouver's Strategic Planning Process.' Built Environment 2013: 438–53.

13. Pete McMartin. 'Kensington-Cedar Cottage: Where Dense Doesn't Mean Stupid.' Vancouver Sun, 21 October 2014.

14. Statistics Canada. 'Housing in Canada: Key Results from the 2016 Census.' 25 October 2017.

15. Molly Hayes. 'Data Analysis Reveals Three-Quarters of Toronto Cops Reside Outside the City.' Globe and Mail, 8 January 2019.

16. Canada Mortgage and Housing Corporation. 'National Vacancy Rate Down for Second Year.' Media Release. 28 November 2018.

17. D. S. Massey and J. T. Rothwell. 'The Effect of Density Zoning on Racial Segregation in U.S. Urban Areas.' Social Science Quarterly 91(5), 2010: 1123–43. www.ncbi.nlm.nih.gov/pmc/articles/PMC3632084/.

18. Toronto Public Library. 'A Brief History of Zoning Bylaws in Toronto.' Toronto Reference Library Blog, 14 December 2015.

19. Jeremy Kloet. 'Secondary Suites: A Methodological Approach to Estimate Their Prevalence within the City of Toronto.' Master's Research Paper, School of Urban and Regional Planning, Ryerson University, 2013. digital.library.ryerson.ca/islandora/object/RULA:3024.

20. City of Vancouver. Amendments to the Zoning and Development By-law.

'A Woman's Right to Housing,' Cheryll Case

1. 'Introducing the Inaugural Toronto Planning Review Panel,' City of Toronto, 2016. web.archive.org/web/20170329192620/http://www1.toronto.ca/City%20Of%20Toronto/City%20Planning/Planning%20Review%20Panel/Downloads/TPRP_Guiding%20Values_Web.pdf.

2. Richard Dennis, Toronto's First Apartment House Boom: An Historical Geography (1900–1920), research paper, Centre for Urban and Community Studies, University of Toronto, October 1989.

citiescentre.webservices.utoronto.ca/Asset
s/Cities+Centre+2013+Digital+Assets/Citi
es+Centre/Cities+Centre+Digital+Assets/
pdfs/publications/Research+Papers/177+
Dennis+1989+Torontos+First+Apart-
ment+House+Boom.pdf.

3. Richard Dennis, '"Zoning" Before
Zoning: The Regulation of Apartment
Housing in Early Twentieth Century Winnipeg and Toronto,' *Planning Perspectives*
15:3, 2000, 267–99.

4. Bryan D. Palmer and Gaéten
Héroux, *Toronto's Poor: A Rebellious History* (Toronto: Between the Lines, 2016).

5. Ibid.

6. Patrick Vitale, 'A Model Suburb for
Modern Suburbanites,' *Urban History
Review* 40:1, Fall 2011, 41–55.

7. 1961 census.

8. 2016 Canadian census.

9. Metro's Suburbs in Transition, Social
Planning Council of Metro Toronto, April
1979. 3cities.neighbourhoodchange.ca/
files/2011/05/1979-Metro-Suburbs-in-Tran-
sition-Overview-Part1-up-to-Chap-6.pdf.

10. 'Career Girls Controversy: Planner
against Communal Living,' *Globe and
Mail*, 26 August 1971.

11. 'JP Convicts Career Girls' Leader
under North York Families-Only Law,'
Globe and Mail, November, 17, 1971.
search-proquest-com.ezproxy.lib.ryer-
son.ca/docview/1241751723?pq-origsite=
summon.

12. 'North York Still Simmers over Bias
Probe,' *Globe and Mail*, March, 28, 1974.
ezproxy.lib.ryerson.ca/login?url=https://se
arch-proquest-com.ezproxy.lib.ryerson.
ca/docview/1239681065?accountid=13631.

13. 'OMB Rejects North York Family
Zoning Changes,' *Globe and Mail*, December, 21, 1974. search-proquest-com.
ezproxy.lib.ryerson.ca/docview/128745987
0?pq-origsite=summon.

14. Ibid.

15. 'Bylaw Limiting Home to Family Is
Struck Down, *Globe and Mail*, April 25,
1979. ezproxy.lib.ryerson.ca/login?url=
https://search-proquest-com.ezproxy.
lib.ryerson.ca/docview/1239254544?accou
ntid=13631.

16. Housing in Focus received funding
support from the Laidlaw Foundation, the
McConnell Foundation, Innoweave, and
Evergreen.

'Vertical Subdivisions,' John Lorinc

1. Philippe Boudon. *Lived-In Architecture: Pessac Revisited.* Cambridge: MIT
Press, 1979.

2. The Pro-Home study is available at
publications.gc.ca/collections/collection_2
011/schl-cmhc/nh18-1-2/NH18-1-2-26-
2000-eng.pdf.

3. John Turner. *Housing by People.*
London: Marion Boyars Publishers Ltd.,
1976.

**'A New Approach to Developing Home-
less Shelters,' Matti Siemiatycki**

Angotti, T. New York for Sale: Community Planning Confronts Global Real
Estate. Cambridge: MIT Press, 2008.

Banister, D. 'The Sustainable Mobility
Paradigm.' Transport Policy 15 (2), 2008:
73–80.

Beauregard, Robert. 1998. 'Public-Pri-
vate Partnerships as Historical
Chameleons: The Case of the United
States.' In *Partnerships in Urban Governance:
European and American Experiences*, ed. Jon
Pierre. New York: Palgrave, 1998.

City of Toronto. Daily Shelter Census,
2016. www1.toronto.ca.

City of Toronto. 'Staff Report: Secur-
ing a Future for the Red Door Shelter.'
2015.

City of Toronto. 'Toronto Social Housing
by the Numbers.' 2013. www1.toronto.ca.

Dear, M. 'Understanding and Overcoming the NIMBY Syndrome.' *Journal of the American Planning Association* 58(3), 1992: 288–300.

Diller, M. 'Form and Substance in the Privatization of Poverty Programs.' *UCLA Law Review* 49, 2002: 1739–56.

Fainstein, S. *The Just City*. Ithaca: Cornell University Press, 2010.

Goetz, E. G., and M. Sidney. 'Revenge of the Property Owners: Community Development and the Politics of Property.' *Journal of Urban Affairs* 16(4), 1994: 319–34.

Graham, S., and S. Marvin. *Splintering Urbanism*. New York: Routledge, 2001.

Grant, J. 'Mixed Use in Theory and Practice: Canadian Experience with Implementing a Planning Principle.' *Journal of the American Planning Association* 68 (1), 2002: 71–84.

Harvey, D. 'From Managerialism to Entrepreneurialism: The Transformation in Urban Governance in Late Capitalism.' *Geografiska Annaler*. Series B, Human Geography 71 (1), 1989: 3.

Hodge, G., and C. Greve. 'Public-Private Partnerships: Governance Scheme or Language Game?' *Australian Journal of Public Administration* 69 (Suppl. 1), 2010: S8–S22.

Hourani, N. B. 'Urbanism and Neoliberal Order: The Development and Redevelopment of Amman.' *Journal of Urban Affairs* 36(S2), 2014: 634–49.

Huxham, C., and S. Vangen. 'What Makes Partnerships Work.' In *Public-Private Partnerships: Theory and Practice in International Perspective*, ed. S. P. Osborne,. London: Routledge, 2000. 293–310.

Jabareen, Y. R. 'Sustainable Urban Forms: Their Typologies, Models, and Concepts.' *Journal of Planning Education and Research* 26 (1), 2006: 38–52.

Klodawsky, F. 'Home Spaces and Rights to the City: Thinking Social Justice for Chronically Homeless Women. *Urban Geography* 30(6), 2009: 591–610.

Kort, M., and E-K. Klijn. 'Public–Private Partnerships in Urban Regeneration Projects: Organizational Form or Managerial Capacity?' *Public Administration Review* 71(4), 2011: 618–26.

Lau, S. S. Y., R. Giridharan, and S. Ganesan. 'Multiple and Intensive Land Use: Case Studies in Hong Kong.' *Habitat International* 29 (3), 2005: 527–46.

Lehrer, U., R. Keil, and S. Kipfer. 'Reurbanization in Toronto: Condominium Boom and Social Housing Revitalization.' *disP – The Planning Review* 46 (180), 2010: 81–90.

Leitner, H., and M. Garner. 'The Limits of Local Initiatives: A Reassessment of Urban Entrepreneurialism for Urban Development.' *Urban Geography* 14(1), 1993: 57–77.

Leyden, K. M. 'Social Capital and the Built Environment: The Importance of Walkable Neighborhoods.' *American Journal of Public Health* 93 (9), 2003: 1546–51.

Louw, E., and F. Bruinsma. 'From Mixed to Multiple Land Use.' *Journal of Housing and the Built Environment* 21(1), 2006: 1–13.

Lyon-Callo, V. 'Making Sense of Nimby: Poverty, Power and Community Opposition to Homeless Shelters.' *City & Society* 13(2), 2001: 183–209.

Majoor, S. 'Conditions for Multiple Land Use in Large-Scale Urban Projects.' *Journal of Housing and the Built Environment* 21 (1), 2006: 15–32.

Miraftab, F. 'Public-Private Partnerships: The Trojan Horse of Neoliberal Development?' *Journal of Planning Education and Research* 24 (1), 2004: 89–101.

Nijkamp, P., M. van der Burch, and G. Vindigni. 'A Comparative Institutional Evaluation of Public-Private Partnerships in Dutch Urban Land-Use and Revitalisation Projects.' *Urban Studies* 39(10), 2002: 1865–80.

Rabianski, J. S., et al. 'Mixed-Use Development and Financial Feasibility: Part II.' *Real Estate Issues* 34 (2), 2009: 17–21.

Red Door Shelter. About Us. 2016. www.reddoorshelter.ca/about-us.

Red Door Shelter. Red Door Family Shelter: Building a Community of Hope Capital Campaign. 2016. www.reddoorshelter.ca.

Reynaers, A-M, and G. De Graaf. Public Values in Public–Private Partnerships. *International Journal of Public Administration* 37, 2014: 120–28.

Rosen, G., and A. Walks. 'Castles in Toronto's Sky: Condo-Ism as Urban Transformation.' *Journal of Urban Affairs* 37(3), 2015: 289–310.

Rowley, A. 'Mixed-use Development: Ambiguous Concept, Simplistic Analysis and Wishful Thinking?' *Planning Practice and Research* 1(1), 1996: 85–98.

Sagalyn, L. B. 'Public/Private Development.' *Journal of the American Planning Association* 73 (1), 2007: 7–22.

Scheller, D. S. Neighborhood Hierarchy of Needs. *Journal of Urban Affairs* 38(3), 2016: 429–49.

Schwartz, A. 2006. 'The "Poor Door" and the Glossy Reconfiguration of City Life.' *New Yorker*, 22 January 2016.

Shaw, K., and I. Hagemans. '"Gentrification without Displacement" and the Consequent Loss of Place: The Effects of Class Transition on Low-income Residents of Secure Housing in Gentrifying Areas.' *International Journal of Urban and Regional Research* 39(2), 2015: 323–41.

Siemiatycki, M. 'Reflections on Twenty Years of Public-Private Partnerships in Canada.' Canadian Public Administration 58(3), 2015: 343–62.

Takahashi, L. *Homelessness, AIDS, and Stigmatization.* Oxford: Clarendon Press, 1998.

Vale, L. J., and S. Shamsuddin. 'All Mixed Up: Making Sense of Mixed-Income Housing Developments.' *Journal of the American Planning Association* 83 (1), 2017: 56–67.

Veness, A. R. 'Designer Shelters as Models and Makers of Home: New Responses to Homelessness in Urban America.' *Urban Geography* 15(2), 1994: 150–67.

Weighe, G. 'Public-Private Partnerships and Public-Private Value Trade-Offs.' *Public Money and Management*, June 2008: 153–58.

Wynne-Edwards, J. Overcoming Community Opposition to Homelessness Sheltering Projects under the National Homelessness Initiative. Ottawa: Government of Canada, 2003.

Yin, R. *Case Study Research: Design and Methods.* London: Sage Publications, 1984.

'Conclusion,' Alex Bozikovic

1. International Panel on Climate Change. 'Special Report: Global Warming of 1.5° C.' www.ipcc.ch/sr15/.

2. Jared R. VandeWeghe and Christopher Kennedy, 'Spatial Analysis of Residential GHGs in Toronto Area,' *Journal of Industrial Ecology*, Vol. 11 No. 2, 2007.

Image Credits

p. 17. City of Toronto Archives, Fonds 200, Series 372, Subseries 33, Item 836; p. 18. Library and Archives Canada/Canadian Courier/Vol. xv, issue 9, Jan. 31, 1914; p. 21. Archives de la Ville de Montréal, P132-2_076-010; pp. 30–31. City of Toronto Archives, Fonds 1244, Item 2489; p. 35. City of Toronto Archives, Fonds 1257, Series 372, Subseries 33, Item 1891; p. 39. City of Toronto Archives, Fonds 1257, Series 1057, Item 8469; p. 43. City of Toronto Archives, Fonds 220, Series 65, File 77, Item 2; p. 44. City of Toronto Archives, Fonds, 1653, Series 975, File 2233, 32715-2; p. 45. City of Toronto Archives, Fonds 1653, Series 975, File 2233, 32715-9; p. 51, 52. Courtesy of John Kettle; p. 55. From South Riverdale Conservation District Study, 2002; p. 57. Courtesy of the Canadian Architectural Archives, Panda Associates fonds, 141A/82.26, PAN 58099-A6; p. 60. Courtesy of the Canadian Architectural Archives, Panda Associates fonds, 131A/82.16, PAN 571563-1; p. 65. Toronto Public Library Archives, Toronto Star Public Archives, tspa_0111696f; p. 69. City of Toronto Archives, Series 382, Subseries 58, Item 1899; p. 77. City of Toronto Archives, Series 1465, File 98, Item 24; p. 81. 1893 fire insurance maps, Goad's Atlas of the City of Toronto, www.goadstoronto. blogspot.ca; p. 84. Courtesy of Tatum Taylor Chaubal; pp. 88–89. City of Toronto Archives, Fonds 1266, Item 127312; p. 95. Courtesy of Gil Meslin; pp. 100–106. Courtesy of Daniel Rotsztain; p. 107. Courtesy of Cheryll Case; p. 117. City of Toronto Archives, Fonds 1244, Item 8211; p. 120. City of Toronto Archives, Fonds 1244, 1964; p. 123. 1931 to 1971: S. Wargon. 1979. Canadian Households and Families. Statistics Canada, Catalogue no. 99-753. 1981 to 2011: censuses of population, 1981 to 2011; p. 135. City of Toronto Archives, Fonds 1128, Series 380, Item 86; p. 144. Courtesy of Anna Kramer; pp. 154–155. City of Toronto Archives, Fonds 1244, 3106; p. 162. City of Edmonton, 'Flag Lot Pilot,' 2017; p. 163. City of Vancouver, 'RT-10 and RT-10N Small House/Duplex Guidelines,' November 2005; p. 171. City of Toronto Archives, Series 1465, File 653, Item 8; p. 175. Courtesy of Fatima Syed; p. 180. Courtesy of Craig Marshall; p. 190, 191. Copyright Nikolai Wolff, Fotoetage; pp. 194, 195. Courtesy of Sean Galbraith; p. 200. Courtesy of Norm Li/Batay-Csorba Architects; p. 201. Courtesy of Batay-Csorba Architects; pp. 203, 204, 205. Courtesy of Workshop Architecture; p. 207, p. 208, p. 209. Courtesy of SvN Architects + Planners (formerly planningAlliance) from 'Pro-Home: A Planned, Progressive Approach to Affordable Homeownership,' 1999; p. 220 Courtesy of Harhay Developments; p. 223. Courtesy of Matti Siemiatycki; pp. 236, 239, 240, 241. Courtesy of the Ryerson Master of Planning students, Fall 2018, from "Gentle Density: A How-To Guide"; p. 269. Courtesy of John Lorinc.

The Contributors

Emma Abramowicz is a planner at ERA Architects.
She holds a Master of Planning in Urban Development from Ryerson University. Her understanding of evolving housing typologies is informed in part by her previous planning work at the Town of Banff, where she experienced a microcosm of a zero percent vacancy housing market, and the gentle densification policies and strategies designed to address it.

Charlotte Balluch graduated from the Master of Planning program at Ryerson University in 2019. She is interested in finding innovative housing solutions for Toronto's growing population, mixed-use development, and sustainable urban growth.

Alexis Beale graduated from the Master of Planning program at Ryerson University in 2019. Prior to completing her master's, she gained experience and knowledge working as an environmental planner for a consulting firm. Alexis focuses her interests on green infrastructure, city parks, and publicly accessible spaces. She is motivated by the important relationship between green spaces and human well-being.

Cherise Burda, executive director of Ryerson University's City Building Institute, leads research, education, and communications strategies to advance urban solutions. Her previous roles include Pembina Institute's Ontario director and program director with the David Suzuki Foundation in Vancouver. She holds an MA in environmental legislation and policy, a BSc in environmental science, and a BEd. Cherise has authored dozens of publications and is a frequent spokesperson and presenter.

Katrya Bolger is a Master in Journalism student at Ryerson University. She has worked at the *Globe and Mail*'s Live News Desk. Previously, she worked as a sub-editor at the *Bangkok Post* in Thailand.

Jessica Brodeur is an urban planner motivated by climate action, community-building, and beautiful, accessible public spaces. Her background is in geography and communications. She's built her career on facilitating cities' transition to a post-carbon world and facilitating sustainable, equitable lifestyles for citizens.

Tessa Chapman is an assistant planner at the Ministry of Municipal Affairs and Housing and a recent graduate of the Master of Planning in Urban Development at Ryerson University. As comfortable crafting high-level policy as she is with hands-on city-building initiatives, Tessa has extensive experience working on projects supporting the rental and affordable-housing sectors in both urban and Northern Ontario.

John Clapp was adopted by a Mennonite family at fourteen months and grew up on a farm until the age of fifteen. He worked in various labour trades and performed as a professional musician until his early twenties. John attended the University of Toronto but dropped out at thirty-one when he struggled to finance his post-graduate studies. In 2009, at forty-four, John went on ODSP.

Joy Connelly has worked in affordable housing her entire adult life as a street outreach worker, co-op housing manager and developer, and, for the past eighteen years, a consultant to government and non-profit organizations. She writes an occasional blog called openingthewindow.com.

Diane Dyson is a non-profit leader and researcher interested in issues of neighbourhoods, schooling, and poverty. She moved onto her street in Toronto's east end as a young, single-income mother, and has lived there for more than a quarter century. In 2018, she ran for municipal council.

Sean Galbraith is a professional urban planner in Toronto and the owner of Galbraith & Associates, Inc., a planning consultancy focusing on small projects in the GTA and telecommunication towers across Canada. In his spare time, he argues about arcane things relating to zoning on Twitter.

Helena Grdadolnik is a director of Workshop Architecture, an architecture and urban design studio based in Toronto that delivers creative solutions to complex design problems for buildings and public spaces. Helena leads the studio's urban design work and cultural projects and is a member of the Metrolinx Design Review Panel.

Sean Hertel leads a small Toronto-based urban-planning practice specializing in transit, transit-oriented development, and housing policy. He also serves as a contract lecturer at Ryerson University's School of Urban and Regional Planning, as well as the University of Waterloo's School of Planning. Sean is a Registered Professional Planner and a member of both the Ontario Professional Planners Institute and the Canadian Institute of Planners.

Randy Hodge is a partnership strategy consultant whose practice includes affordable and social housing, long-term care and seniors housing, land development, economic development, developing public and private partnerships, public decision making, mediation and negotiation, and strategic advice. Prior to setting up his own consulting practice, Randy worked for the Ontario government. He also teaches in Ryerson University's School of Urban and Regional Planning.

Ed Jackson, in earlier incarnations an activist, journalist, and community health educator, now focuses his attention on the social history of Toronto's urban and queer past. He is a co-editor of the anthology *Any Other Way: How Toronto Got Queer* (Coach House Books, 2017).

Anna Kramer teaches urban planning at the University of Toronto. She is currently immersed in a research project on zoning, residential density, and housing affordability funded by an Insight Development Grant from the Social Sciences and Humanities Research Council.

Michael McClelland is a registered architect and founding principal of ERA Architects. He has specialized in heritage conservation, heritage planning, and urban design for over twenty-five years. Having begun his career in municipal government, most notably for the Toronto Historical Board, Michael works with a wide range of public and private stakeholders to build culture through values-based heritage planning and design. He has co-edited several Coach House anthologies, including *Concrete Toronto* (2007), *The Ward* (2015), and *The Ward Uncovered* (2018).

Davin McCully is a graduate of Ryerson University's Master of Planning program (2019). He believes that urban sustainability can be achieved by employing efficient neighbourhood design and maximizing active and public transportation opportunities. Besides his work on the Yellowbelt, Davin's research centres on analyzing the effect of light-rail transit on the regeneration of urban brownfields.

Gil Meslin is a Toronto-based urban planner, educated at Ryerson University and the London School of Economics. He has practised as a consultant in cities across Canada, and with a non-profit developer. Gil believes planning should advance inclusivity, and that to remain relevant, codes must be regularly examined and reinterpreted.

Michael Niezgoda graduated from the Master of Planning program at Ryerson University in 2019. He has a background in politics and governance and has worked in planning roles in both the public and private sector. Michael is interested in development planning and real estate, and the role that industry can play in delivering complete communities.

Andrea Oppedisano is an urban planner who started her career in 2007 with the City of Toronto. She has worked on several important projects, including the Avenue & Mid-Rise Buildings Study, Eglinton Connects, and Growing Up: Planning for Children in Vertical Communities. In 2018, she began working as development manager for Streetcar Developments.

Ana Teresa Portillo works for Parkdale Activity-Recreation Centre as a rooming house tenant organizer and for Parkdale People's Economy as a community benefits organizer. She is a PhD candidate at York University in Social and Political Thought with a background in anti-racist theory, anti-colonial theory, and Indigenous theory and practice. She currently sits on the board of the Neighbourhood Land Trust in Parkdale.

Daniel Rotsztain is the Urban Geographer, an artist, writer, and cartographer whose work examines our relationship to the places we inhabit. An admirer of libraries, malls, and strip malls, Daniel explores the diverse settings of the city's public life. The author of *All the Libraries Toronto*, Daniel has had work featured in the *Globe and Mail*, *Spacing Magazine*, and *Now Magazine.*

Candace Safonovs graduated from the Master of Planning program at Ryerson University in 2019. She also holds a certificate in GIS and is interested in evidence-based policy, open data, affordable housing, smart cities, and social equity.

Blair Scorgie is the business development director, as well as a senior planner and urban designer, at SvN Architects + Planners Inc. Over the course of his career, much of Blair's work has focused on issues associated with neighbourhood character, infill development, and intensification. He also serves as a contract lecturer at Ryerson University's School of Urban and Regional Planning. Blair is a Registered Professional Planner and a member of both the Ontario Professional Planners Institute and the Canadian Institute of Planners.

Mercedes Sharpe Zayas is the workforce planning coordinator for the Parkdale People's Economy, a network of over thirty community-based organizations and hundreds of residents organizing toward decent work, shared wealth, and equitable development. She holds a Master of Science in Urban Planning from the University of Toronto and a Bachelor of Arts in Honours Anthropology from McGill University.

Matti Siemiatycki is Canada Research Chair in Infrastructure Planning and Finance and interim director of the University of Toronto School of Cities. His work focuses on delivering large-scale infrastructure projects, public-private partnerships, and the effective integration of infrastructure into the fabric of cities.

Vickey Simovic graduated from the Master of Planning program at Ryerson University in 2019. She has a background in public administration and worked as an FOI coordinator for the TTC and Metrolinx. Vickey is interested in equitable transit-oriented development, affordable housing, smart city technology, and urban resiliency planning.

Drew Sinclair is an architect and the current managing principal at SvN Architects + Planners. He is a past recipient of the Canada Council Prix de Rome for Emerging Practitioners and frequent sessional faculty at Toronto-area schools of architecture. Drew's work prior to joining SvN focused on the relationship between legal ownership structures and land tenure in municipalities and rural areas in Canada and Latin America, a focus he's extended into his work with John van Nostrand at SvN.

Fatima Syed is the investigative reporter for *National Observer* in Toronto, with an eye for environment, urban affairs, and politics issues. She was previously with the *Toronto Star* and the *Walrus*, and is the author of a chapter in *Subdivided: City Building in an Age of Hyper-Diversity* (Coach House, 2016).

Tatum Taylor Chaubal is a writer, heritage planner, and Texan transplant currently based in Toronto. She holds a Master of Science degree in historic preservation from Columbia University and works as a project manager for Timmins Martelle Heritage Consultants. She has co-edited three anthologies about marginalized heritage in Toronto for Coach House Books: *The Ward* (2015), *Any Other Way* (2017), and *The Ward Uncovered* (2018).

John van Nostrand is an architect and planner, and founder of a forty-year-old consulting practice (currently named SvN Architects + Planners) that has pioneered new approaches to land development and housing in areas of rapid growth, throughout the Greater Toronto Area, across Canada, and in developing cities across Africa, Latin America, and the Middle East.

Richard White is an author and university lecturer specializing in the history of urban planning. He holds a PhD in history from the University of Toronto. His most recent book is *Planning Toronto* (UBC Press, 2016), a comprehensive history of Toronto postwar planning.

The Editors

Alex Bozikovic is the *Globe and Mail*'s architecture critic, covering architecture and urbanism. He has won a National Magazine Award and has also written for *Architectural Record*, *Azure*, *Dwell*, and *Toronto Life*. Alex is an author of *Toronto Architecture: A City Guide* (2017). In 2019, he served as a jury member for the City of Edmonton's Missing Middle Design Competition.

Cheryll Case is the founding principal of cp Planning, a groundbreaking urban planning firm that digs deep into addressing the urban conditions that affect access to housing, work, and play. She specializes in designing inclusive conversations that build relationships between various stakeholders within the non-profit, private, and public sectors. To facilitate conversation, Cheryll uses research, data analysis, and storytelling to describe community relationships with land. Since graduating from Ryerson University's Bachelor of Urban and Regional Planning program in 2017, Cheryll has been a driving force in public discourse about community planning and belonging.

John Lorinc is a Toronto journalist and editor. He reports on urban affairs, politics, business, technology, and local history for a range of media, including the *Globe and Mail*, the *Toronto Star*, *Walrus*, *Maclean's*, and *Spacing*, where he is senior editor. John is the author of three books, including *The New City* (Penguin, 2006), and has co-edited four other anthologies for Coach House Books: *The Ward* (2015), *Subdivided* (2016), *Any Other Way* (2017), and *The Ward Uncovered* (2018). John is the recipient of the 2019/2020 Atkinson Fellowship in Public Policy.

Annabel Vaughan is an Architect and Project Manager at ERA Architects Inc. Her recent interest lies in the intersection between architecture as a spatial practice reflected in a single built work and the broader role of architecture as an agent for cultural production in the city. She writes, teaches and participates regularly in discussions concerning the role that architecture and public art can play as agents of political change in the city. Her professional work includes small-scale landscape architecture insertions, civic and residential building design, urban design and research, performance art lectures, and curatorial projects.

Entrance, 1 Rosedale Rd.

Acknowledgments

It took a neighbourhood to create this anthology. The co-editors would like to thank some of the people who played a direct or indirect role in a project that we came to see as both a wake-up call and a provocation: Kevin Vuong, Michelle German, Michael Paz, Liv Mendelsohn, Ken Greenberg, Mark Sterling, Nigel Terpstra, Paul Bedford, George Dark, Andrew Blum, Jens von Bergmann, Michael Wright, Ellen Leesti, David Hulchanski, Richard Joy, Pamela Robinson, Richard Harris, Gord Perks, Danny Roth, and Catherine Riddell. An early inspiration for this book came from *The Vienna Model: Housing for the Twenty-First-Century City*, a traveling exhibit and monograph focused on the Austrian capital's innovative policies, curated by Sabine Bitter and Helmut Weber. ERA Architects always has a spare and welcoming boardroom for editorial meetings, some of which included cheese, crackers, and scotch.

We are also grateful to the hard-working journalists who cover housing, real estate, and affordability, and provide Canadians with so much important information about the issues we have sought to explore in these pages. They include Tess Kalinowski, Shane Dingman, D'Arcy McGovern, Janet McFarland, David Rider, Jeff Gray, Emily Mathieu, Vincent Donovan, Matt Blackett, Frances Bula, and Dave LeBlanc.

The Coach House Books family is, as ever, a true pleasure to collaborate with, and includes Crystal Sikma, Ricky Lima, James Lindsay, Rick/Simon, Romanne Walker, Yasmin Emery, Tali Voron, John De Jesus, Ingrid Paulson, and Stuart Ross. We are guests in the wonderful house that Stan Bevington built. Alana Wilcox makes it all possible.

Typeset in Aragon and Aragon Sans.

Printed at the Coach House on bpNichol Lane in Toronto, Ontario, on Husky Opaque Offset White paper, which was manufactured, acid-free, in Saint-Jérôme, Quebec, from second-growth forests. This book was printed with vegetable-based ink on a 1973 Heidelberg KORD offset litho press. Its pages were folded on a Baumfolder, gathered by hand, bound on a Sulby Auto-Minabinda and trimmed on a Polar single-knife cutter.

Edited by Alex Bozikovic, Cheryll Case, John Lorinc, and Annabel Vaughan
Designed by Alana Wilcox
Cover design by Ingrid Paulson
Cover image by Daniel Rotsztain

Coach House Books
80 bpNichol Lane
Toronto ON M5S 3J4
Canada

416 979 2217
800 367 6360

mail@chbooks.com
www.chbooks.com